Forever Feminine

Women's Magazines and the Cult of Femininity

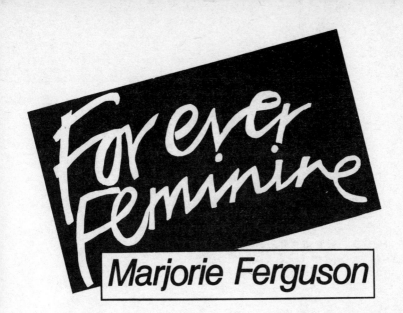

For ever Feminine

Marjorie Ferguson

Women's
Magazines
and the
Cult of Femininity

Heinemann · London, Exeter (NH)

Heinemann Educational Books Ltd
22 Bedford Square, London WC1 3HH
4 Front Street, Exeter,
New Hampshire 03833

© Marjorie Ferguson 1983
First published 1983

British Library Cataloguing in Publication Data

Ferguson, Marjorie
　　Forever feminine
　　1. Women's periodicals, English—History
　　2. Women—Great Britain—Social conditions
　　I. Title
　　741.65　　　　PN5130

　　ISBN 0–435–82301–9
　　ISBN 0–435–82302–7 Pbk

Library of Congress Cataloging in Publication Data

Ferguson, Marjorie.
　　Forever Feminine.
　　Bibliography: P.
　　Includes Index.
　　1. Women's periodicals, English. 2. Women's periodicals,
American. 3. Women in the press—Great Britain. 4. Women in
the press—United States.
　　I. Title.
　　PN5124.W6F47　　　1982　　　052'.088042　　　83–149
　　ISBN 0–435–82301–9

Typeset by Inforum Ltd, Portsmouth
Printed in Great Britain by Biddles Ltd, Guildford, Surrey

Contents

Preface

This book is the result of two very different types of experience – ten years in women's magazine journalism followed by undergraduate, and then postgraduate, study in the Department of Sociology at the London School of Economics and Political Science. Given my work in both fields, I continued by acquiring new insights and methods, and then applying them to the problem of understanding the wider social role of women's magazines.

My academic interest in the subject of women's magazines developed out of more than my practical experience, however. It also developed out of the feeling that too little was known about the cultural significance of this medium. Two questions arose from all this, questions which alternately drove me on, and drove me to despair, in my search for their answers. These were: 'what is the role of women's magazines in society?', and – more pragmatically – 'why are fewer women buying them today than formerly?'.

The ensuing research into these questions extended over a period of seven years: the first stage, from 1974 to 1978, was undertaken for my doctoral thesis; the second stage, from 1979 to 1981, for this book. Throughout, my prior experience in women's magazines conferred both benefits and costs. It invested me with a combination of credibility and curiosity in the eyes of those I sought to interview ('don't you miss the excitement – and the money?'); it also helped me to formulate the questions most relevant to my quest in that I knew the 'language' which the participants spoke. Prior experience also imposed constraints. In particular it required me to be ever vigilant of the possibility of over-empathising with interviewees, over-intuiting meaning in what they said, or over-interpreting findings and events. To re-enter and further explore a world that one formerly inhabited – through a different door and following a different route map – proved to be a continuously challenging experience. This book represents the response to those challenges, and the result of that experience.

This study is concerned with those messages which women's magazines have been transmitting to women over the post-war period, principally in Britain, but where relevant in the United States. It looks at how those messages have responded to the impact of social, cultural and economic change upon their female audiences. It also looks at how those messages come about: the interaction between editors, their teams, their organisations and their audiences. I have drawn upon a combination of methods and sources: content analysis, interviews, observation, documentation, statistical data and my prior experience. In interpreting the findings from these various sources I was determined to work with categories of analysis that emerged from the findings rather than to approach the sources with preconceived categories in my mind. Similarly, with the theoretical perspective that I have drawn upon for this book – this, too, emerged at a later stage in the analysis, after various other explanatory models had been tried and found wanting.

This study and this book owe much to people as well as research methods. Without the encouragement and cooperation of many individuals inside the academic and publishing worlds there would have been no study at all. My first thanks must be to those publishers who gave me access to people and to sources of data: E.G. 'Teddy' Court, and Ron Chilton, past and present Chairmen and Chief Executives of IPC Magazines Ltd; Marcus Morris, Deputy Chairman of National Magazine Company Ltd; and, at the very beginning, Gordon Brunton, Managing Director of The Thomson Organisation Ltd. Next I wish to thank *all* the editors who were interviewed and who gave so generously of themselves and their time. In particular I wish to thank for her valued help and encouragement, Mary Grieve, editor of *Woman*, 1940–62, to whom I owe a special debt of gratitude. Not only did she employ me as a trainee writer in the first place, but also at the later stage of this study she opened her personal archives to me which illuminated the role of the British women's press during the Second World War and the immediate post-war period.

Many other women's magazine editors and journalists were helpful in many large and small ways. I hope those who are not named here will allow me to acknowledge the special help which has been given by the following: Mary Dilnot, former editor of *Woman's Weekly*; Deirdre McSharry, editor of *Cosmopolitan*; Jane Reed, editor-in-chief of *Woman*, and former editor of *Woman's Own*; and Audrey Slaughter, former editor of *Honey* and *Over 21*, in Britain. Those whose help was particularly appreciated with the American fieldwork were: Helen Gurley Brown, editor of *Cosmopolitan*; Patricia Carbine, publisher of *Ms.* magazine; Sey Chassler, former editor-in-chief, *Redbook*; and Pat Miller, Director of Cosmopolitan International.

To everyone else who contributed by giving of their knowledge and expertise – and they will know who they are – my thanks for the wealth of 'fact', rumour, 'inside stories' – printable and unprintable – and all the other data that they provided which kept me at my quest. Throughout, I was tracking a moving target: the changing world of women's magazines. For this reason, I especially wish to thank those who produced the readership and market data over the years, in particular Michael Bird of Thomson Publications Ltd and Alan Smith of IPC. Others who helped with this important aspect were: Brian Braithwaite and Martin Celmins of National Magazine Co. Ltd and Andy Collyer, Derek Davies, David Hardill, Roger Horslen and Shibu Mukherjee of IPC.

My thanks equally are due to those within the academic world who encouraged me that the study was worthwhile and feasible. I wish particularly to thank Professor J.D.Y. Peel for treating this subject as one worthy of academic endeavour, and for his helpful comments on chapters of the book. My appreciation is also due to Professor David Martin who supervised my Ph.D. thesis, to Dr A.N. Oppenheim for critical guidance on the problems of content analysis, and to my colleagues in the Department of Social Science and Administration who generously applied their expertise (and their pencils) to various chapters: Martin Bulmer, David Downes, Peter Levin, Jane Lewis and David Piachaud.

Finally, I owe a special acknowledgement to Charlotte Lewis for her valued research assistance with the early content analysis, and to those who later turned illegible typescript into readable manuscript: Bridget Atkinson and Anne de Sayrah.

Marjorie Ferguson
July 1982

1

Introduction

This book is about women's magazines, one of the most significant yet least studied social institutions of our time. Alongside other social institutions such as the family, the school, the church and other media, they contribute to the wider cultural processes which define the position of women in a given society at a given point in time. In this exchange with the wider social structure, with processes of social change and social continuity, these journals help to shape both a woman's view of herself, and society's view of her.

For these periodicals are about more than women and womanly things, they are about femininity itself – as a state, a condition, a craft, and an art form which comprise a set of practices and beliefs. In this they present a paradox, for they are specialist periodicals yet concern themselves with a general audience: everyone born female is a candidate for their services and sacraments. This points to a hidden message behind their presence on the bookstalls. The fact that they exist at all makes a statement about the position of women in society as one which requires separate consideration and distinctive treatment.

In making this statement, women's magazines use their front covers as their advertisements for themselves. Their titles and photographs proclaim these journals are for women only, as titles such as these communicate: *Hers, She, Woman's World* (Britain); *Ladies' Home Journal, Ms., Good Housekeeping* (USA); *Elle* (France); *Brigitte* (Germany); *Damernas Värld* (Sweden); *Margriet* (Holland); *Grazia* (Italy); *Fair Lady* (South Africa).

The scale of their audience, women, and the breadth of their specialism, femininity, also sets these journals apart, and serves to differentiate this genre of periodicals from the majority of the mass media in industrial societies. Radio, records, television, cassettes, books, newspapers, the stage or the pulpit – in the main these concern themselves with general audiences of both sexes. A second difference concerns the longevity of this medium. For example, magazines published periodically and specifically for women have existed since the late seventeenth century in Britain, preceding the post-war trend to increased specialisation within consumer periodicals by almost three centuries. Many writers (e.g. Maisel, 1973; Van Zuilen, 1977) have commented on this trend, citing the disappearance of more general audience magazines such as *Saturday Evening Post* in America (or *Picture Post* in Britain).[1] Against this background women's magazines stand out as all the more remarkable in being simultaneously specialist and generalist: specialist in that they are for a single sex, women, yet generalist in that most extend their content appeal across a wide spectrum of feminine concerns.

In these respects such journals are operating very differently from specialist magazines for men. There is no men's periodical press in the same generic sense that there is for women. Men's magazines are aimed at particular groups of males and cater for parts of a man's life – his business, hobby or sporting interests – not for the totality of his masculinity, nor his male role as such. This difference in audience approaches seems to rest on an implicit assumption shared between editors and publishers that a female sex which is at best unconfident, and at worst incompetent, 'needs' or 'wants' to be instructed, rehearsed or brought up to date on the arts and skills of femininity, while a more powerful and confident male sex already 'knows' everything there is to know about the business of being masculine.

Women's magazines also are pervasive in the extent to which they act as agents of socialisation, and the remarkable degree to which they deal in and promulgate values and attitudes. What makes women's magazines particularly interesting in this sense is that their instructional and directional nostrums are concerned with more than the technology of knitting or contraception or cooking. They tell women what to think and do about themselves, their lovers, husbands, parents, children, colleagues, neighbours or bosses. It is this, the scope of their normative direction, rather than the fact of its existence, which is truly remarkable. Add to this the power of the advertising which is directed at women through their pages and the conclusion follows: here is a very potent formula indeed for steering female attitudes, behaviour and buying along a particular path of femininity, and a particular female world view of the desirable, the possible and the purchasable.

As a genre of specialist periodical production, women's magazines are notable also for the size of the audience they command. In the UK, for example, they are directed at the 22.9 million females aged 15 and over. This potential audience is one whose attention, money and brand loyalty publishers and editors strive to grasp and to hold, the better to woo the advertisers whose revenue spells the difference between profit and loss. In 1981 458.1 million copies of British women's magazines were sold. Thirty-two of these had weekly or monthly circulations of over 100,000 each, while four weeklies, *Woman*, *Woman's Own*, *Woman's Weekly* and *Woman's Realm* between them sold a total of 5.5 million copies and were read by 16 million women every week. Some 49 per cent of the female population aged 15 and over saw a women's weekly, and 45 per cent a women's monthly during that year.*†

This scale of production and consumption is noteworthy, yet it represents a considerable decline from the post-war circulation peaks of the 1950s and 1960s, a phenomenon which is analysed in greater detail in Chapter 2. Yet sales figures alone do not indicate the extent of the women's magazine audience. Readership data show the degree to which a single copy is read by several people. A copy of *Woman's Own*, for example, has 3.9 readers, a copy of *Good Housekeeping*, 7.0, and a copy of *Vogue*, 16.0. They are also read by men: 13 per cent of the 20.5 million males in the United Kingdom aged 15 and over see a women's weekly, and 18 per cent a women's monthly magazine.*† This extensive secondary readership contributes an additional dimension in their potential social influence. To the extent that their female readers accept their messages, the influence of those messages can be multiplied many times through a mother's influence on her children, a wife's influence on her husband, a lover's influence on her partner, and women's influence on one another.[2]

The approach and field of this study

Little has been written by sociologists on the subject of women's magazines.[3] This meant that this study was necessarily exploratory, which meant that it took the form of a quest. Initially, some general questions were asked to find a 'way in' to the subject material. As more was learned, it became possible to formulate more specific questions and make a more structured analysis. This process began by asking: 'Over the post-war period what have women's magazines been telling women about the sorts of women they are, or ought to be?', 'What do women's magazines "do" for women?', 'Why are fewer women buying these periodicals today?' and 'What is the role of the editor in all this?' The field of study to which these questions were

---

* Readership: National Readership Survey (NRS), Jan.–Dec. 1981.

† Sales: Audit Bureau of Circulation (ABC); publishers' statements. Jan.–Dec. 1981.

addressed focused on 'adult women's' magazines in Britain, whilst drawing on American and 'young women's' titles for comparative purposes.

Collection of the material extended over a period of seven years. Formal methods of social investigation were used alongside less formal methods, which involved taking advantage of opportunities and documents presented to me in cars, pubs, cloakrooms and kitchens. Such unobtrusive measures provided insights which usefully complemented material gathered in a more systematic way.

The method employed to discover the meaning of women's magazine messages was that of content analysis. Content analysis involves selecting specific categories of subject matter and counting the number of times there is a reference to a topic or category of topics in a particular issue of a particular year. The set of categories devised for this analysis emerged from a pilot study, and was used to identify and quantify dominant themes, values, goals and roles, for example, the roles of wife, mother and 'waiting to wed'. The three largest selling women's magazines in Britain *Woman, Woman's Own* and *Woman's Weekly* were analysed in this way. Two studies were made: the first took a random sample of issues for the period 1949–74; the second, follow-up study used a random sample for the 1979–80 period and applied the same analytical framework.

The investigation of the editorial processes of women's magazines focused on the role of the editor, and involved both interviews and observation. Some thirty-four women's magazine editors in Britain and the United States were interviewed concerning their role, beliefs and professional practices and how they perceived the impact of social change upon their magazines and audiences (full methodological details are given in Appendix II p. 199). A further ninety-seven journalists, artists, publishers and managers were interviewed about their perceptions of the editorial processes, publishing organisations and market context of women's periodical production.

Women's magazines and the cult of femininity

From this array of materials came seven more specific questions concerning the role of women's magazines as a social institution – all dealing with aspects of their relationship with their female readers.

- How do women's magazines distinguish and define their target/ client group?
- In what ways do their messages denote a selective filtering and interpretation of aspects of 'the world'?
- What beliefs and values are incorporated in those messages and in what forms are they transmitted?

- What individual behaviour patterns and attitudes do they foster among readers?
- Who decides the content of messages, and how?
- What social behaviour and collective attributes do women's magazines foster among readers?
- How might the answers to the above questions have changed over time?

The early results which gave rise to these questions suggested that there were elements of the 'sacred' both in the professional beliefs and practices of editors and in the womanly ones which they presented to their audience. This suggested that it might be profitable to look at women's magazines from a more general sociological and anthropological perspective. The writings of Durkheim (1976) on the sociology of religion suggested that there were interesting parallels between the feminine observances promulgated by women's magazines and the social purposes of the cult.[4]

Through further analysis it became apparent that the questions formulated above could be applied to the formation of any religious cult in that they corresponded with many of the elements treated by Durkheim. For this reason, some *prima facie* answers to these questions are given below which point to the creation and maintenance of a 'cult of femininity' as the principal explanation advanced by this study as to the role of women's magazines in society.

There were several parallels between the characteristic elements of the religious cult as delineated by Durkheim (1976), and the relationships celebrated by women's magazines and their audiences. For example, cults have regular festivals and ceremonies and their adherents reaffirm their communal existence through these periodical observances of the group's sacred rites and rituals. Cults also have totems who are worshipped, and 'sacred beings' who act as channels for that worship. In addition, Durkheim allowed for the existence of sex-segregated totems: 'this new sort of totem [sexual totemism] resembles that of the clan particularly in that it, too, is collective; it belongs to all the people of one sex' (1976: 165).

All these elements were relevant to what this study terms the 'cult of femininity' which is promulgated by women's magazines. The direct parallels are these: the oracles that carry the messages sacred to the cult of femininity are women's magazines; the high priestesses who select and shape the cult's interdictions and benedictions are women's magazine editors; the rites, rituals, sacrifices and oblations that they exhort are to be performed periodically by the cult's adherents. All pay homage to the cult's totem – the totem of Woman herself.

*How do women's magazines distinguish and define their client/
target group?*

By means of their titles, cover photographs, subject matter and advertisements women's magazines define themselves as a distinctive form
of specialist periodical: their primary distinction is a biological one,
based upon female sex. This has implications for how the gender
characteristics of females are acquired, and how the position of
women in society is defined. As a social institution, women's magazines play a part in shaping the characteristics of femininity, because
they themselves are part of, and contribute to, the culture of society as
a whole. Precisely what part is open to investigation and debate.

Observation, participation and interviews confirmed the extent to
which editors' professional and intuitive judgements about what subjects interest women qua women, guide their decisions as to what will
appear in their pages. They also confirmed the extent to which their
ultimate editorial credo is that femininity and womanliness are so
wholly different from masculinity and maleness that they require a
separate vocabulary, dialogue and tone of voice. The identification of
the client group to which these specialist periodicals are appealing,
and the distinguishing of their target audience, are made apparent
through such cover lines as: 'Working Mums: help, advice and
phone-in' (*Woman's Own*, 5 April 1980); 'Wrap up Christmas: count
down for cool cooks, gifts for girls' (*Woman*, 6 December 1980);
'*Marriage*: an expert proves it's great for husbands, lousy for wives'
(*Cosmopolitan*, February 1980); 'You deserve *better*: Learn to stop
picking the wrong man' (*Cosmopolitan*, February 1980).

*In what ways do their messages denote a selective filtering and
interpretation of aspects of 'the world'?*

The picture of the world presented by women's magazines is that the
individual woman is a member not so much of society as a whole but of
her society, the world of women. It is to this separate community that
these periodicals address themselves. Their spotlight is directed not
so much at the wider 'host' society, as at that host society's largest
'minority' group: females. Males exist within this feminised social
structure but are presented as supporting players. Their presence as
heroes, villains, soulmates or bosses is peripheral to the main show.

The extent to which the editorial spotlight has enlarged its beam to
encompass the wider social, political and economic world merely
serves to highlight this point. These newer, wider issues are related
consistently to the 'women's angle' just as were the earlier narrower
ones. Events, attitudes, behaviours and products are given reader
relevance through their refraction in this way. These processes help to

set agendas for the female sex and raise certain topics rather than others: the 'world' is viewed through a feminine lens.

What beliefs and values are incorporated in those messages and in what forms are they transmitted?

The women's periodical press is packed with the holy writ of female society. These explanatory parables and operational maxims offer convenient ready reference volumes continually updated with the latest revisionary doctrines. Much of this sacred knowledge is of the 'what every woman knows' kind, especially where what every woman knows implies a bond of commonality.[5] This sense of sharing and belonging is conferred at two levels: between all women as members of a broad social group, the female sex, and between some women, the members of a particular sub-group, the readers of a given magazine.

Much of what is shared is familiar. Content analysis, observation of editorial conferences, and prior experience in the field confirmed the extent to which these messages are not so much created as re-created. Each time a classic theme such as triumph over personal tragedy, or a proven sales winning subject like slimming, is reproduced, it is re-angled, re-titled and revitalised. Skilfully, ingeniously, and sometimes brilliantly, the old becomes the new. Much of what is repeated concerns the rites, sacrifices and rewards associated with female rituals. These suggest a form of sacred observance through their repetition: being 'good' at being a woman involves doing womanly things at regular and appointed times. The rituals attached to beautification, child-rearing, housework and cooking attest to this symbolic order.

In all of this the readers of women's magazines are being assembled before a sacred or totemic object. Who or what is this most venerated object within their pages? The answer is that it is not, as might have been predicted, Man. It is Woman herself. Woman is the sacred idol before whom the readers of these journals are invited to bend the knee. Does this simple act of worship, women reading about their sacred object, and following their cult practices, raise the women's magazine faithful above the everyday world to some higher, idealised plane? Content analysis shows the extent to which the secular is elevated to the sacred, notably with the 'holy' tasks of quintessential womanhood – child-care, cookery, and 'looking good'.

What individual behaviour patterns and attitudes do they foster among readers?

(a) By portraying roles and opportunities open to women? Comparative content analysis over time and between magazines shows the extent to

which their readers are offered competing or complementary definitions of the female role within a repertoire which has expanded dramatically since 1970. If there is a current consensus as to what that definition is, or should be, it is not apparent. This variety differs from the limited stereotypes of the 1950s and 1960s of the good wife and mother, or the pretty girl waiting to wed, and today's collection of car driver, student, mother, lover, shopper, working wife or home handywoman.

This range reflects more than the fact that one woman can, and does, play many roles. The hidden message here is that a woman is free to choose and can elect to be the 'kind of woman' she wants. Here an editor's perceptions of what the relevant definitions are for 'her' readers can differ markedly from those of her competitors. Two examples show the different roles and opportunities offered to women in 1980, when *Cosmopolitan* talked about 'The most powerful woman in advertising defends her industry and tells how she made it to the top' (June 1980), while *Woman's Weekly* reminded its readers about 'Loving and Needing – to find happiness and contentment we must be prepared to give our friends and relatives as much as we expect to receive from them' (22 November 1980).

(b) By portraying specifically female roles and socialising women into them? Women's magazines do more than suggest all the successful, decent, or beautiful kinds of women that a female can or should be, or that females operate within a framework of social, cultural and economic choice. Previous participation suggested, and systematic content analysis confirmed, the extent to which they also offer 'easy, step-by-step' instructions for achieving those choices and conditions which are recipes in more respects than cooking. This starts with the leading of young initiates into the desirable but demanding state of womanhood. This induction process is consistent with the unacknowledged assumption that women have to be taught femininity whereas males do not have to be shown how to become masculine.

Adolescent girls, brides, new mothers, all stages of newcomers are offered help with their *rites de passage*. 'How to' is the phrase which signals that this socialisation process is underway: 'how to' make up or find a job, 'how to' be good in bed or cook a casserole.

Such courses of instruction do not stop at the school-leaving age: continuing education is a concept long practised by the editors of the women's periodical press. Femininity as a career is a lifelong commitment. It requires frequent refresher courses and occasional updating of its central tenets.

Fledgling females are instructed and full members are given post-graduate guidance in:

LAYING FOUNDATIONS
You can ask any builder or handyman if you want to do a proper job you've got to do your groundwork thoroughly first. And it is exactly the same with make up . . . Let's show you how . . .

(*Woman*, 27 November 1979)

or:

'How to Be Thoroughly Independent Without Turning Into an Iron Maiden'
(*Cosmopolitan*, February, 1978)

(*c*) *By setting ever higher levels of achievement, as a corollary of their defining and socialising processes?* The message here is 'Dear reader, choose your female roles, learn your parts well, and then perform par excellence!' The normative role of women's magazines is most explicit and directive in the universally high standards of performance which they set. Their message is more than 'you can do it'; it is one of 'you can do it better – with a little help from us'. Which areas of her person and her life is a woman urged to excel and achieve within? From personal appearance to personal relationships, from job success to marriage success, from the mundane to the magnificent in kitchen, bathroom, boardroom or bedroom, women are urged to do more, and do it better. This relentless setting of high job performance standards contradicts the notion that women compare themselves with low-level reference groups who are predominantly other, and under-achieving, females.[6] Readers of women's magazines are presented with examples of superwomen, an endless procession of successful, beautiful and inspirational role models to envy or emulate.

Support and reassurance are also offered: not only can you do it, and do it better, but also you are not alone in your task. This is the 'surrogate sister' role of women's magazines. In offering support, encouragement and help with readers' problems, they project empathy with, and sharing of, those same problems. This 'we're all in this together' approach is both a prerequisite of, and a legitimation for, the provision of such support.

These positive messages also show how the mirror women's magazines hold up to women reflects them in a flattering and positive light. Their real world and dream world reflections are backed with the glint of powerful reinforcement. Is there something to be learned from this? Do women's magazine editors present such positive images to women because they do not exist elsewhere in the social structure? For some women, there may be nowhere outside the pages of these journals where they are consistently valued so highly, or accorded such high status. It may be that only within the pages of *Good Housekeeping* or *Woman's Realm* do some women find an easy, accessible and regular source of positive self-esteem and social support.

(d) In terms of attracting and keeping purchasers and readers? If femininity as a cult consists of a set of beliefs and practices which binds its adherents together through their common commitment to ideals and rituals, do these editors set about cultivating that commitment for their own careerist, or more purely commercial ends? The results of this study suggest that by creating and fostering images and symbols of femininity editors also create and sustain a ready-made readership for their journals, and provide a market-place for their advertisers. The sacred beliefs of the cult of femininity are not written on a *tabula rasa*, any more than they are handed down from on high. They are created in response to editors' perceptions of the female role – 'what women want' – and the imperatives of the market place – 'what will sell'.

Cultivation of the female bond involves more than journalistic techniques and conviction. It serves equally well the economic ends of the market and the rationale of publishing for profit. If the 'we females' climate were not cultivated, would individual women actively choose to buy and read these specialist journals in preference to other leisure pastimes?

Who decides the contents of the messages, and how?

In addition to all their defining, socialising and supportive purposes women's magazines set agendas of which topics are important or permissible, desirable or undesirable, worthy or not worthy of placing before the female sex. The findings of this study suggest that it is here, through their content choices, that women's magazine editors truly act as gatekeepers of the female world. It is they, the high priestesses, who decide the what as well as the when of social changes permitted to pass through the pearly gates of editorial discretion. Will abortion or homosexuality be admitted to their universe of discourse, or will they not? It is in making judgements such as these that editors demonstrate their power over content, as well as their power to confound the audience when different editors are doing different things with the agendas of their magazines.

An example demonstrates the arbitrariness with which this power may be applied. In 1979 it was possible for the editor of one of the largest women's magazines in Britain to say 'I hope we will never have any living-together couples in our fiction so long as I'm editor', while two floors away the editor of a sister publication was 'passing' a page proof which read:

Lying in bed being jealous wouldn't change anything.
All along it was only meant to be . . .

                                A CASUAL AFFAIR (*Woman*, 8 December 1979)

What social behaviour and collective attributes do women's magazines foster among readers?
Collectively and cumulatively what do these parables, rituals and totem suggest? By defining women as distinctive and separate do they help to create not only a female universe but also a bond of female solidarity? Theoretically, this question is interesting. It relates to an ideological problem for some feminists as to whether or not females comprise a sex or a class.[7] To editors, however, the question of whether or not there exists a shared consciousness based on common-sex membership amongst their female readers, does not even arise. So strong is the belief in the strength of the female bond within the corridors and conference rooms of women's magazine journalism that it forms the basis for both professional and publishing rationales.

Two assumptions implicit in these beliefs about the female bond became clear early on in the content analysis. Firstly, through being born a woman and by being a member of a particular female sub-cult, the readers of a particular magazine are blessed with a double sense of sex-based belonging. Secondly, these beliefs imply that this shared female reality is such a powerful force that it transcends individual economic, social and personality differences and provides a basis for solidarity.

Do women's magazines promote and promulgate a cult of femininity?
The questions that arose from, and the *prima facie* answers provided by, the results of this study indicate that the sociology of religion does provide useful insights into the role of women's magazines in society. The cult of femininity as defined by women's magazines does contain many of the elements of a cult as elaborated by Durkheim (1976), whereby a woman can worship her own society through its religious observances, and acquire that society's essentially social concepts through them.

These results point to readers of these journals as doubly qualified for cult membership: as females, of the cult of femininity; as readers, of the sub-cult of a particular magazine. In so far as cults have members, required rituals, explanatory myths or parables, visible 'badges' of membership, an object of veneration, high priestesses and status or esteem conferred by membership, so do the followers of women's magazines share in these things. Moreover the editors who preside over the sacraments of this cult have a vested interest in proselytising: this is one reason, perhaps, why they revise its dogmas from time to time. Their status as leaders of a particular sub-cult is at stake in terms of the numbers of followers they can attract.

Whether for reasons of conferring individual identity, inducing group solidarity, or promoting sales success, their elevation of Woman to the status of a totemic object fits well with Durkheim's view of a cult as a social institution. This is 'not simply a system of signs by which the faith is outwardly translated; it is a collection of the means by which this [system] is created and re-created periodically' (1976: 417). Re-creation presents no problem here. The collective means of worship, the shared system of signs is literally recreated at fixed periods. The ritualistic aspects of production and purchase are reinforced by weekly or monthly deadlines and weekly or monthly buying habits.

How might answers to the above questions have changed over time?
The content analysis carried out for this study probed the extent to which the messages of these journals changed over time. Interviews with editors also pin-pointed their dilemmas in recognising, leading or reacting to social change. This subject is one of such complexity, of multiple strands of influence and multiple mirroring processes that a later chapter focuses upon it. Here two examples show how constancy and change are interwoven, how supportive, understanding and reinforcing purposes remain a constant, even if the subjects towards which they are directed have changed.

In the 1930s *Woman's Own* asked its readers:

SHOULD A WIFE MAKE-UP?
This is the question every newly-wed asks herself and Mary Carlyle answers it with a wealth of understanding.

(26 November 1932)

In the late 1970s it put a newly recognised role on the agenda and provided a new line in social support:

GOING IT ALONE – AND LOVING IT
Only a few years ago if you were single we'd be telling you how to find your man. Times have changed. Singles still need their emotional attachments but today there are many women single or divorced who happily admit they prefer to be alone. There are still snags but these four pages help to smooth them out.

(15 April 1978)

This chapter has set the stage for the further investigation of women's magazines both as a social institution and as specialist periodicals within the media market place. It has pointed to some remarkable features of this uniquely specialist medium, and has raised a number of questions concerning its potential social influence, in particular the intended and unintended consequences of defining women as separate and different through the fostering of a cult of femininity.

The chapters that follow tackle these questions. Chapter 2 traces the development of the women's periodical press in Britain from the late seventeenth century to the present day, concentrating on the post-World War 2 period. It pays particular attention to the changing structure of the market from the 1950s to the 1980s and the trends of increased concentration of ownership, overall audience decline and movement from more generalist weeklies to more specialist monthlies. It notes the continued importance of advertising revenue not only to profitability but to the ways in which women's magazines distinguish and define their target markets. This chapter also presents some data on the American monthly *Cosmopolitan* which publishes seventeen international editions, mainly on a licensing basis, and thereby enables some cross-cultural comparisons to be made.

Chapter 3 discusses the categories of editorial subject matter selected for content analysis and goes on to present the results for the period 1949–74. This analysis reveals the dominant themes of the most widely read women's magazine messages in Britain and shows the female and male roles that are portrayed and the goals, values and images of social class that are overtly or covertly presented in them. Chapter 4 contrasts these findings to those of the comparative, 'follow-up' content analyses done for 1979 and 1980, and shows some significant changes and absences of change in the messages which they convey.

Chapter 5 looks at the key agenda-setting role of the editor in selecting the content and shaping the form of those messages, drawing on the extensive interviews which were undertaken. It explores the self-perceptions and professional beliefs of this elite group and the recruitment, training, status and income of these editors. Chapter 6 looks at the total publishing structure which impinges on them and on the editorial process. This structure embraces the traditions and techniques of women's magazine journalism, the examination of which shows how the shaping of the message amounts to a selective filtering and interpretation of the world.

This chapter also compares two major publishing organisations – The National Magazine Company Limited and the International

Publishing Corporation Women's Magazines Group – and presents a picture of decision-making in the editorial processes of a composite women's weekly, and how that process has changed over the past thirty years.

Chapter 7 reassesses the cultural and commercial impact of women's magazines as a social institution and as a sex-specific communications medium. It re-examines the validity and role of the concept of a cult of femininity which they proclaim, in the light of the findings of earlier chapters, and of some of the major social, economic and demographic changes which have manifested themselves within the female audience and society over the post-war period.

2

The Evolution of the Women's Periodical Press in Britain

Specialist periodicals for women have existed in Britain for almost three hundred years. Their lineage stretches back to the late seventeenth century, and their longevity and continuing viability attests not only to the dedication of their high priestesses and devotion of their followers, but also to the entrepreneurial optimism of publishers across the centuries.

This chapter traces the evolution of the women's magazine industry with particular emphasis on the period 1950–80. It sets out the historical and market context in which women's magazine editors work and produce their messages. It points to the challenges that changing social, economic, demographic, cultural and technological environments pose for editors and publishers as they define and re-define their client/target groups. From first to last this story is one of the pressure upon those who minister to the cult of femininity to make a profit from their endeavours.

From the Age of Enlightenment

The emergence of separate periodicals for gentlewomen, with the launch of *The Ladies' Mercury* in 1693, was followed by several eighteenth century variations aimed at the same social stratum (see White, 1970). Titles such as *The Ladies' Magazine* (1749), *The Lady's Magazine* (1770) and *The Lady's Monthly Museum* (1798) illustrate how the audience catered for by these publications was that of the upper or upper middle-class female. The editors of these specialised publications were intent on improving the minds of their readers, of educating as well as entertaining them. They put into their journals philosophical reflections and snippets of news from home and abroad; they were concerned with social and political ideas as well as with home management, fashion and fiction. Their tone was one of mental and moral uplift well suited to literate, leisured ladies.[1]

This upper-class tradition continued until the mid-nineteenth century when changes took place in cultural definitions of womanhood, and in the class selected as the target audience (see e.g. Welter, 1966). These shifts reflected the economic prosperity and other attributes of middle-class Victorian society, and its restricted feminine ideal – woman as a modest, pure and family-bound being, more interested in personal appearance and domestic affairs than in news of the wider world (Delamont and Duffin, 1978; Banks, 1981). The doctrines of Samuel Smiles, of self-improvement and self-help, offered a ready-made editorial platform for instructive pages on dressmaking, domestic thrift and personal hygiene.[2]

This age of Mrs Beeton was mirrored in the women's press. One of its most successful examples was produced by *Mr* Beeton: *The Englishwoman's Domestic Magazine* (1852). Samuel Beeton courted the wider potential audience of middle rather than upper-class women by the simple expedient of charging 2*d.* rather than the customary shilling charged by his competitors (Hyde, 1951). Publishers, who were often publisher–editors like Beeton, were independent entrepreneurs and magazines such as his marked a distinct move 'down market' from the elitism of their eighteenth- and nineteenth-century forebears. They offered their readers – the socially climbing wives and daughters of the professional and business classes – guidance about what to buy, wear and do to further their aspirations. As more women emerged from cloistered domesticity to pursue a social life or do good works, publishers sought to broaden the appeal of their journals to reflect these wider interests. This new editorial impetus was important for purposes of attracting advertisers as well as audiences. During the last two decades of the nineteenth century, advertisement revenue emerged as the critical factor in the profitability of the women's periodical press, as it was in the ascendance of popular national newspapers (cf. Lee, 1976; Curran, 1977, Cranfield, 1978).

The expansion of women's magazines at this time – some forty-eight journals were launched between 1880 and 1900 – paralleled this expansion of the popular press.[3] Many other factors contributed to their growth. Britain was a small, densely populated country, with a well-developed railway and retail distribution network; new technology offered cheaper paper and faster printing, and the Education Act of 1870 had led to a higher rate of literacy amongst the potential audience.

The early twentieth-century women's magazine editors and publishers were intent on capitalising on these favourable conditions. Majority, not minority, audiences were their target and reassurance not revolution their editorial credo. No trumpets were sounded for the liberation of Edwardian womanhood from the fashion-following and meal-planning laid down as the aspirational norm. Several women's magazines founded in this period were still on British bookstalls in 1982. Amongst the most venerable are: *My Weekly* (1910); *Woman's Weekly* (1911); *Vogue* (1916); *Ideal Home* (1920); *Good Housekeeping* (1922); *Woman's Journal* (1927); *Woman and Home* (1926). All these journals were launched for middle-class females preoccupied with the concerns of self, family and home – after first having found the husband who made it all possible. The first issue of *Woman's Weekly* in 1911 illustrated this class bias and domestic focus:

. . . the women of Mayfair and the lady who lives in the castle are not catered for in this paper. But . . . the woman who . . . rules the destinies of the home is going to be helped in her life, her work and her recreation by this journal.

(*Woman's Weekly*, 4 November 1911)

Some of the magazines founded in the 1920s were more outspoken about possible alternatives to such 'queen of the kitchen' editorial philosophies. The first issue of *Good Housekeeping*, for example, in September 1922, talked about 'The Law as a Profession for Women', and asked 'Some Questions on Divorce'.

The birth of the mass market
This socially adventurous subject matter contrasts with the more traditional topics covered by the generation of women's weeklies that were launched in the 1930s. Directed at a wider class audience, aiming for mass circulations, their progress was aided by the good quality, cheap printing technology and the advantages of photogravure over letterpress.[4] The launch of *Woman's Own* (1932) and *Woman* (1937) marked this further downward shift in editorial content shaped to maximise audience – and advertiser – appeal. Their editors were conscious of, and constrained by, considerations of class differences in income, employment, housing, education. 'In the old women's magazine before the war it was no good offering your reader choice because she would simply have to buy the cheapest', one recalled.

The challenge facing editors was to attract audiences that spanned both the middle and the working class. The lure that large circulations would provide for advertisers, combined with ownership of presses capable of printing millions of copies a week, were the stimuli to expansion in the immediate pre-war period.

Working-class women who hitherto had been assumed to want mainly the romantic fiction typified by *Peg's Paper* (1919), or *Red Star* (1929) as 'their' women's press, were now invited to share the messages previously reserved for middle-class females. One of the significant findings of this study is that the editorial philosophy of weeklies such as *Woman* was based on this simple, but revolutionary concept: the entertainment and enlightenment of working-class women could extend into areas of interest and expertise previously found only in the more middle-class monthlies. The women's magazine journalists who were engaged in evolving this new form of weekly periodical took their responsibilities seriously. Teams of experts were recruited – doctors, lawyers, psychologists – to answer readers' queries which came by the hundreds, then thousands, a week. Launched by Odhams Press in 1937, one year after *Mother* (1936), the early days of *Woman* were shaky – its circulation in 1937 a mere 440,193.* The appointment of a new editor, Mary Grieve, in 1940 soon confirmed that the gamble would pay off, and she recalled:

Odhams had launched this magazine to fill the printing presses at Watford. They did not know anything about women's magazines, they admitted that after their failure with the original *Woman*.

Half the board said 'let's get out of this and leave it to the AP and Newnes', but the advertising side said 'no, if we don't crack the women's market you are going to lose the advertising revenue of the future'. So they dillied and dallied and they decided to go on. They gave us six months to make a success or failure. If we had made a failure, I think the Board would have agreed 'out'.

The wartime mobilisation of the women's press

During the Second World War British women's magazines took on a new social significance and political direction. Their potential influence on the female population and unique ability to address themselves to the most intimate and the most public female activities was recognised by the Government of the day. Yet the full scope of their wartime role, and its significance for the development of women's magazines, has not been accorded the recognition it deserves.[5]

The wartime record of the female press belies any concept of media processes as passive reflectors of the social scene. Collectively and individually, women's magazines were 'the voice of women' in wartime. Editors banded together and formed The Group of Editors of Women's Magazines, as a section of the Periodical Trade Press and Weekly Newspaper Proprietors Association Ltd. They volunteered their skills, and their pages were recruited, for active service on the home front, women's division. These journals were both medium for, and mediators of, British wartime social policy, transmitting messages of sacrifice and hope to women busy keeping both factory wheels turning and home fires burning. Constrained by paper ration-

* Publishers' estimates, copy documents.

ing – the supply in 1943 was some 22½ per cent of the 1939 supply – to reduced page size and numbers, these magazines exerted perhaps their strongest ever influence on British womanhood at this time.[6]

The political power and propaganda value of women's magazines has never before or since been acknowledged or exploited as it was by the Churchill and Attlee administrations during the 1940s. In 1941, the women's press 'enlisted' for wartime service; and the Ministry of Labour Advisory Committee on woman-power was told:

. . . we feel that the women's press is above all other media best fitted to translate to women the role they must fill in increasing numbers – if production, and the servicing of the combatant forces, is to be raised to effective, winning strength.

Although we speak in different voices we must, to reach the full peak of our propaganda value, be united to saying the things which are really relevant. . . . Tell us clearly, tell us often, what you want conveyed.[7]

Handmaiden of government and handholders of the female population, this was the dual role of women's magazines in wartime. Short-staffed, bombed out – their pages still went to press. The interests of their readers were defended by editors who combined toughness with compassion, integrity with competition, determination with energy. During this time, women's magazines established their hold on a vast army of women, and in the process legitimated their authority to speak to, and on behalf of, a mass female readership. This legitimacy stemmed from audience beliefs and trust in an editorial authority invested with an ethos of responsibility mirrored in the sympathy, accuracy and hard-headed practicality of their messages. For the first time the cult of femininity promulgated by the women's periodical press cut across the structure of British society. Audience consensus and solidarity were firmly based on a common femininity and shared hardship:

We all had the same amount of rations, we all had the same amount of restrictions, we all could do only the best we could with make do and mend. It didn't matter which social class you were, this was your life. (Women's weekly editor)

The heightened political and economic importance of women and their specialist journals during the war years was acknowledged in a headline in *World's Press News* in 1943. This proclaimed and prophesied: 'The Woman's Magazine is Now an Adult Periodical – With Peace It Will Forge Ahead to New Triumphs'. Underneath, the Supervising Editor of Odham's Woman's Group wrote:

Only some forty years ago the woman's magazine was an inconsiderable factor in journalism.

Today it has won a dominant and very adult place in the periodical field, and is rivalled in sales and social influence only by the newspapers. This phenomenal growth of the woman's magazine is directly due to – and has been largely comensurate with – the advance of woman herself as a political, economic and moral force in the life of the nation.

(*World's Press News*, 7 October 1943)

Throughout the War, women's magazine editors, Government Ministers and officials met regularly in the Holborn offices of the Periodical Proprietors Association. This close cooperation between rival editors and relevant ministries in translating social and economic policies affecting women into prescriptions, proscriptions and practicalities has never been attempted on such a scale again.[8] Two prime editorial purposes were served – providing comfort and dishing out advice – when the directives of the Ministry of Food or Fuel and Power were translated into the everyday realities of women's lives. The editors of the day offered detailed guidance to audiences united as never before under the flag of femininity and the Union Jack, on how to cope with emotional (though never sexual) deprivation, while consumer goods scarcity put such intimate items as lace and knicker elastic – more for larger ladies – on the agenda for the monthly meetings of the Ministers and editors in Kingsway.

It is perhaps reflective of the status that Fleet Street then accorded to women, as well as to the women's press, that the particular authority of these journals in speaking to the female population was never seriously rivalled by the popular newspapers of the day. Only the *Daily Mirror* manifested a sustained concern with the affairs of women (Smith, 1975). During the War, its editorial matter – recalling perhaps that the *Mirror* was founded in 1903 as a paper for gentlewomen – paid considerable attention to female concerns, and the sacrifices, contribution and mode of conduct expected of its feminine readers in the interests of patriotism.[9] In doing this, the *Mirror*'s tone of voice echoed that of the women's press: friendly confidante and firm adviser.

The immediate post-war period: the implications of social and economic policy

The politicisation of the women's press during the early 1940s produced a cumulative and collective message of active female participation. Whether they involved working outside or inside the home, or both, a multiplicity of female roles were legitimated as being 'in the national interest'. Women's magazines then played their part in the opposite direction, putting across post-war social policies such as those enshrined in the Beveridge Report of 1942 (Harris, 1977;

Wilson, 1977) which firmly re-located women back in the home: both the overalled and uniformed armies of women were scheduled for rapid de-mobilisation in 1945.[10]

The contribution of women's magazines to the post-war economic and political ends of encouraging the female labour force back to kitchen concerns and the homemaker role is confirmed by the content analysis of this study (cf. Wilson, 1980).

As for the closely orchestrated cooperation between the editors of the female press and the emissaries from Whitehall, neither the open invitation to political influence nor the acting in concert long outlasted the war. The tribal loyalties and editorial rivalries of competing publishing houses reasserted themselves in the 1950s. But the high priestesses did continue to join in common cause with representatives of the emerging social services departments until the late 1940s. Together they saw through the implementation of the major social legislation affecting women and family life – The National Health Service Act 1946, National Insurance Act 1946, National Assistance Act 1948, and Children Act 1948. At a meeting in July 1948 attended by these editors, Chuter Ede, Aneurin Bevan, James Griffiths, and Arthur Woodburn, the editor of *Woman* declared in words which were prophetic for editorial development in the 1950s:

Our magazines are closely integrated with the lives of their readers. We *service* their health, home, child care, clothes, food budgets – and many other interests which make the pattern of their lives. They read our columns with their minds turned towards their own affairs . . . (emphasis added)[11]

The impact of these Acts on the daily lives of millions of women – especially working-class women – in terms of raising the quality of their life, coupled with the increasing post-war affluence and expanding consumer choices of the early 1950s, provided the raw material for mass market expansion. The editorial matter reflected this social and economic climate, Mary Grieve recollected:

When the war ended, the social Acts, the Education Act, Acts like holiday with pay – meant that suddenly vast numbers of people were interested in these new things. Whereas before the war it was a class distinction: you went for a holiday or you went for a day trip. So you couldn't write in our magazine about a week going down the French canals, however desirable and enlarging that might have been. But now you could.

The National Health Service meant that women, the mothers who'd r.ever had any doctoring really – their husbands did because they were on the panel, their children did – the mothers had very little. But when she could have medical attention, she began to be interested in the subject, and medical articles burgeoned in all the magazines. They were not there before, because medical attention was not in her experience.

From the 1950s to the 1980s: survival of the fittest
The final lifting of paper restrictions in 1952 marked the onset of three decades of competitive struggle in the women's periodical jungle. The ensuing cycles of expansion and contraction, of euphoria and paranoia, brought change and conflict to the cult, its priestesses, its organs, its owners and its followers. The story of what happened to women's magazines over this period cannot be separated from the story of what was happening to millions of women caught up in conflicts, choices and changes of their own.

Each post-war decade manifested different social, cultural and economic climates which evoked different responses in terms of the ownership, sales, titles and messages of women's magazines. First there were the 'Expansionist' 1950s, then came the 'Critical' 1960s, followed by the 'Confrontation' 1970s, and finally the early years of the 'Problematic' 1980s. These thirty years mark changes both in the structure of the market and in the form and content of the cult's messages. In the process, editorial definitions of Woman, and of the female role were first treated as immutable, then as transformable. These developments within British women's magazines are not parochial. They parallel two broad trends which have emerged and strengthened within the media of industrial societies since 1945, and which are well-documented by the evidence of the market and the analyses of communications theorists (see e.g. Katz and Szecsko, 1981). The first trend took the form of a movement away from more generalist towards more specialist products and audiences. The second trend took the form of a movement towards concentration of ownership.

The disappearance of scores of daily newspapers, and of general audience periodicals such as *Illustrated* in Britain, and *Life* in the United States attest to the long-term contraction of print media in the face of multiple changes – including increased competition from electronic media.[12] The extent to which these trends may be related raises complex questions. Are smaller, more specialised audiences the precursors or consequences of a more global pattern of media ownership – the local multi-media organisation within a multinational, multi-product conglomerate?

The changing structure of the market
Ownership, titles and sales – these are the crude indicators by which we may gauge the changes in the structure of the women's press. They provide the broad outline of the picture which records the scramble to own the big profit-earning titles, the magazines which came, stayed or departed – and the audiences which did likewise. These three indi-

cators show what a volatile, risky market women's magazines continued to be and point to a degree of increased specialisation within what was already a specialist genre.

Concentration of ownership

The global trend of media ownership into fewer and fewer hands is manifest in the tale of those British women's magazine publishers who thrived, survived or expired between the 1950s and the 1980s. Advertisement revenue was the elixir of life which they all pursued, and for which they all competed. Its pursuit was the driving force behind the ownership battles which developed in the late 1950s.

That first expansionist post-war decade saw an explosion of audience and advertiser interest in women's magazines as page and issue sizes increased and circulations soared. Sales of the brand leader, *Woman*, doubled between 1945 and 1950, from one to two million, and reached three million in 1953. Advertisement revenues climbed even more dramatically – from £1.1 million in 1950 to £2.3 million in 1953, to £5.3 million in 1958.[13] Rival publishers vied for such lucrative sums from advertisers keen to sell the wares of an expanding consumer economy to a female audience which was growing in affluence as well as numbers.

Such was the lure of profit-taking that both the least and the most successful producers became the targets of take-over bids. Daily Mirror Newspapers Ltd initiated the trend, buying The Amalgamated Press, publishers of *Woman's Weekly* in 1959 and renaming it Fleetway Publications. This move intensified competition and led Odhams Press Ltd to buy first The Hulton Press (1959) and later George Newnes Ltd (1959), publishers of *Woman's Own*, then the only real threat to *Woman*, jewel in the Odhams' crown.

The majority of women's magazines were now aligned in two rival groups whose continued profitability was threatened by the battle to raise sufficient revenue to support the high promotion costs of pitting one set of titles against the other. As speculation heightened about a merger between Odhams and Fleetway, *The Times* (27 January 1961) reported that the Government was 'gravely considering the implications not only for Britain and its press but for capitalism as a whole' (cf. RCOP, 1962, Chapter 2: 28 and 35). Odhams declined the suggestion of a joint holding company, but when an alternative arrangement with the Thomson Organisation was overtaken by a higher bid (1961) from Daily Mirror Newspapers, the once separate publishing houses of Odhams, Newnes and Fleetway were united. This coup created the world's largest women's magazine production line ever contained within one organisation. The legal rationalisation took place in December, 1962 when shares in the individual publishing houses became part of the International Publishing Corporation Ltd (IPC). In 1968, IPC assumed its present form with a magazine division which grouped like publications together: women's weekly magazines, women's monthly magazines, young women's magazines, practical and juvenile publications and special interest magazines. In May, 1970, IPC itself became a subsidiary of Reed International Ltd.[14]

Today four companies effectively control the production of women's magazines in Britain. These four, and some of their better known titles, are: IPC Magazines Ltd, publishers of *Woman's Weekly*, *Woman's Own*, *Woman*, *Woman's Journal*, *Woman's World*, *Ideal Home* and *Honey*; D. C. Thomson and Co. Ltd, publishers of *My Weekly*, *The People's Friend* and *Annabel*; Standbrook Publications Ltd, publishers of *Family Circle* and *Living*; and The National Magazine Co. Ltd, publishers of *Cosmopolitan*, *Company* and *She*. Of these four, only D.C. Thomson is fully – and fiercely – independent.[15] The other three are all linked to multinationals. IPC's parent company is Reed International Ltd, the London-based conglomerate; The National Magazine Co. Ltd is a wholly-owned subsidiary of the Hearst Corporation of America; Standbrook Publications is owned ultimately by the Thomson Equitable Corporation Ltd of Canada.

How the total women's magazine market has divided between these four, since IPC came to dominate the industry, in relation to copy sales and consumer expenditure (number of copies sold multiplied by cover price), is shown in Table 2.1. Although IPC's share of copies sold declined by 14 per cent over the sixteen years since 1965, in 1980 it nonetheless still produced a full two-thirds of all women's magazines sold in Britain. The only other producer with a sizeable share of copies sold is D.C. Thomson, with 20 per cent in 1980. The 'other' category contains several publishers including Argus Press, publishers of *True Story* and *True Romance* and Conde Nast Publications Ltd, publishers of *Vogue*.

Many have tried but few have succeeded as independent publishers of women's magazines. Two titles that did succeed as independent ventures are *Over 21* (1972) – conceived and developed by a former editor of *Honey* and *Vanity Fair* – and *Slimming* (1969), the venture of two journalists who turned it into the most successful, tightly specialised monthly of the 1970s.[16]

From the mid-1960s to the early 1980s, the oligopoly enjoyed by the major women's periodical publishers went virtually unchallenged. Unlike many other industries in Britain they did not face foreign competition, and with the exception of the threats to advertisement

Table 2.1   UK women's magazines: top four publishers' market share (%)

	1965		1977		1980	
	Copies	Expend.	Copies	Expend.	Copies	Expend.
IPC	81	79	68	65	67	63
D.C. Thomson	12	7	20	11	20	11
Standbrook Publications	2	3	4	5	3	4
National Magazine Company	1	4	3	7	4	9
Other	4	7	5	12	6	13

Source: ABC, Publishers' statements, IPC

revenues posed by commercial television and radio, women's magazines reigned supreme as the specialist medium for advertisers seeking to reach the dual-income spending power that women increasingly
commanded (see Henry, 1977). By 1981, new challenges to this
cosy market division were emerging. Competition was keener for a
woman's time, interest and money. The monopoly of the female press
on the cult's messages was threatened by alternative voices old and
new – Fleet Street's expanded coverage of 'women's topics', more
commercial radio and home video, with a fourth channel and cable
television to come. Compounding this competition were the 'free'
supplements of the popular Sundays, such as the *Sunday Express* and
the *News of the World*, launched in 1981. All these competitors were
hungry for advertisers as well as for female readers, and in the words
of *The Times* (16 February 1982): '. . . the 1980s is going to be an
exciting if not frightening decade. There is no time to assess the
impact of a new [media] development before the next has arrived.'

Volatility: the changing roll-call of titles

Births, marriages and deaths – as well as abortions, reincarnations and
apparent immortality – mark the post-war evolution of the women's
periodical press. The extreme volatility of this period has parallels
with the similarly explosive phase of development at the end of the
nineteenth century. The launch of new titles in the 1950s was exceeded only by the zeal with which others were launched, merged or
killed in the 1960s, the caution with which their successors were
launched in the 1970s (see Braithwaite and Barrell, 1979), and the
distinct reticence displayed thus far in the 1980s to commit invest-

ment of the one million pound scale which IPC spent launching *Options* in 1982.[15]

This record of long and short-stayers in the market – of seventy year olds like *My Weekly* and *Woman's Weekly*; of premature or short-lived babies such as *Nova* (1965) and *WM* (reborn from *Woman's Mirror* in 1965, and submerged into *Woman* in 1967); of those whose terminal illnesses were prolonged only briefly by merger operations such as *Woman's Illustrated*, *Woman's Day*, *Housewife* and *Everywoman* in the 1960s – all point to shifts in the supply and demand structure of the market. The first shift has to do with supply and the numbers and kinds of women's magazines on offer – as they are classified by producers into market sectors, or types of women's magazines, in relation to their client/target groups. The second shift has to do with demand and how that demand first expanded, then contracted or moved between different types of women's magazines. These supply and demand factors can be related in turn to how wider trends of media specialisation were manifest within British women's magazines.

The supply side of these journals continues to be characterised by resurgent entrepreneurial optimism. This is attested to by the fifty-four new titles launched during the period 1965–76, and the further nine between 1977 and 1982.* Such volatility is also an indication of continuing viability. Entry into the market provides its own presumptive evidence of continuing profitability. In 1981, the National Readership Survey (NRS) listed 47 weekly and monthly women's magazines.† In 1981, female consumers spent £113.5 million buying such periodicals, while advertisers spent another £113.8 million selling them their wares.*

How do publishers and editors define their client/target groups when producing women's magazines on such a scale? This question relates to how publishers divide the market into 'sectors', and how editors apply 'intuitive' and 'rational' processes to the same ends. The broadest market division is based on periodicity – mainly between weekly and monthly publication. Less distinct are demographically-based divisions making use of age or class or both. The broadest socio-economic labels applied by the publishers are those of 'up-market' – generally spinebacked, glossy monthlies – or 'down-market' – generally stapled, non-glossy weeklies. These blanket categories can be refined in terms of the National Readership Surveys' data which classify female readers along a social class scale from A to E.[17]

* BRAD (British Rate and Data) 1981; IPC, BRAD 1965–81.
† ABC, NRS, Jan.–Dec. 1981.; ABC, Publishers' statements 1965–81.

Age presents an even more problematic dividing line. The division that publishers make between 'young women's' and 'adult women's' market sectors, which generally assigns females aged 15–29 to the former, and those aged 20 and over to the latter, illustrates the extent to which these categories confuse and overlap. Yet NRS age and class data can be combined to produce 'age–class' maps (see Bird, 1977) whereby all women's magazines can be distributed around the national norms for ABC1 social classes and for age under and over 25. This method creates four sectors: 'younger–richer', 'younger–poorer', 'older–richer' and 'older–poorer' and has the advantage of allowing broad historical comparisons to be made. The 'age–class' maps reproduced in Appendix I show how the 'older–poorer' sector has declined over the post-war period, while the 'younger–richer' one has expanded.

Viability: shifting patterns of demand

Turning to the demand side – how many women's magazines are sold and read in Britain in the 1980s compared with the 1950s or 1960s? The extent to which the 1950s were uniquely expansionist is exemplified by the rise of weeklies such as *Woman* and is discussed below. The more critical 1960s and even more problematic 1970s produced a less homogenous, more segmented – and overall declining – female audience.

Between 1965 and 1981 total adult women's copy sales declined from 555.3 to 407.4 million copies per annum. During the same period young women's copy sales rose from 51.5 million in 1965, to 84.5 million in 1972, declining to 50.7 million by 1981. This pattern of falling demand for women's magazines should be set against the similarly downward trend of total consumer periodical sales overall. Despite the success stories of many smaller, specialist magazines, and notwithstanding the existence of some 1400 titles in 1981, copy sales of all consumer periodicals declined from 2,144.9 to 1,538.05 million per annum between 1965 and 1981.*†

Figure 2.1 illustrates this trend for the adult and young women's magazines and for the consumer periodical market as a whole, while detailed sales figures for 1965–81 are given in Appendix I.

The shifting patterns of audience demand over this period had an effect on the historical relationship between cover prices and advertisement revenue. Until the early 1970s, advertisement revenue had been high in relation to production costs, allowing cover prices to be kept low. Increased paper and printing costs – paper alone doubled in price between 1973 and 1974 – together with the fluctuating advertisement revenues of a 'stop-go' economy produced a shift in the

*Figure 2.1   Adult and young women's magazines compared with the consumer
periodical market in terms of total copies sold, 1965–81.*

Source: ABC, Publishers' statements, BRAD, IPC.

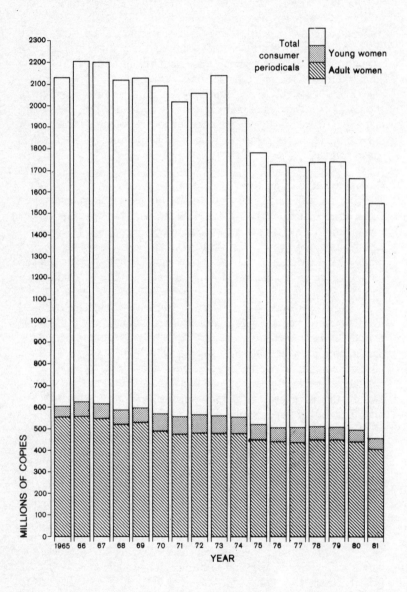

pricing and profit structure which placed a higher proportion of costs upon the consumer. Between 1973 and 1978 cover prices of women's magazines rose faster than the rate of inflation – 143 per cent as compared with 111 per cent for the Retail Price Index.[18] Yet despite this, the women's press depended as much upon advertisement revenue for profitability and viability in the 1980s as it had done a century earlier.[19] It continued to sell to two sets of clients – buyers of the magazines themselves, and buyers of the magazines' advertisement pages.

The trend to specialisation

When is a woman's magazine a specialist journal and when is it not? By definition these periodicals are specialist, their messages being directed at a specific sex audience – females – on topics that concern that sex's gender specialism: femininity. Yet the subject matter of the majority of women's magazines in Britain, as elsewhere, can be ranged along a generalist–specialist continuum of overlapping rather than discrete categories. Boundary hopping is rampant between publisher-designated market 'sectors' and their editorial coverage: fashion or family relationships creep into 'home interest', or recipes and decorating hints into 'young fashion' magazines, for example. A publishing executive's description demonstrates the difficulties of attributing specialisation within this genre:

Well, *Options* is a general interest magazine – a sort of young *Good Housekeeping* – you know, cookery, fashion, features, that sort of thing. (Publishing Director, IPC)

Thus to speak of specialisation in this context is to speak of a relatively elastic concept where subject matter duplication rather than editorial differentiation is the norm. The extent to which such repetition of the cult's messages contributes to their homogeneity or leads to their reinforcement amongst the faithful is open to investigation. More certain is the fact that within them inspiration more often takes the form of imitation than innovation – however creatively disguised. This 'sameness' reflects more than professional incest. It reflects in part the structural and cultural limitations that society places upon information and entertainment labelled 'female'. It also reflects the wariness of publishers who have counted the cost of commercial failure of determinedly 'new' publications.

The extent to which British women's magazines conform to wider cross-national patterns of specialisation within print media becomes evident when the market as a whole is examined. This study identified

five major trends and their *net* effect illustrates the degree of specialisation. They are:

● The rise, sharp decline, stabilisation and further decline of the
  mass circulation weeklies;
● The growth and relative stability of the more traditional, 'home-
  care', and 'general interest' monthlies;
● The rapid development, and subsequent slow decline, of the
  majority of young women's (15–24) monthlies;
● The revival, peak and subsequent sharp fall of the 'real life story'
  monthlies and weeklies;
● The emergence of new specific interest monthlies, alongside the
  virtual disappearance of 'pure' fashion magazines.

The first three of these trends – the rise and fall of the mass weeklies,
the continued vitality of the more traditional monthlies, and the
development of a separate young women's sector – are of particular
significance for the adult women's magazines focused on by this
study. They are discussed below under 'generalist' women's weeklies,
and 'specialist' women's monthlies, which include 'traditional' and
young women's titles.

The 'generalist' women's weeklies
The British women's weeklies have much larger sales than the monthlies in contrast to their market position in the United States and most
of Western Europe.[20] In 1981 the five largest sellers had a combined
sale of 6.1 million copies a week.* Large as this figure may seem, the
fact is that the weeklies' audience virtually halved after 1958 – when
those that sold over half a million copies each had a combined weekly
sale of over 12 million (McClelland, 1964).

This degree of decline is illustrated in Figure 2.2. All the figures
shown there refer to sales, but readership data, which show the total
numbers who read a particular issue, indicate much higher audience
levels which are classified as male, female and housewives. They also
show that readership declines at a slower rate in proportion to sales.

Why had the weeklies taken off with such spectacular speed during
the 1950s? Their rise had been foreshadowed by their wartime role.
One, *Woman*, led the field. In 1958 it reached the all-time record sale
for the British women's magazine of 3.49 million copies per week,
with a weekly readership of 11.5 millions.* Its editorial format set the
pattern for the 'service' weeklies. Designed to be a 'tradepaper for
women', the editorial concept of service was interpreted quite literally

* ABC, NRS, Jan.–Dec., 1981.

as being of 'use' or 'assistance' to women with their domestic concerns, personal problems and consumer choices.

Something of the flavour of the editorial thinking behind the decisions about topics to be placed upon the feminine agenda is revealed by Mary Grieve's recollection of those days:

> Now that it is a matter of commonality that every house has a fridge, you cannot imagine people buying a magazine to learn how to use a fridge. That was the excitement of the 1950s. What is a washing machine? What is a steam iron?
>
> You see, there was this sudden opening up of sophisticated consumer goods. They had scarcely existed before for our readers – they may have been put before the readers of *Good Housekeeping*. Now it was possible for ours to think 'Well, we could have one now that Auntie's already got one.' For the first time they were not excluded as a class.

The war changed what magazines could do in this country. What you got for the first time was a really vast number of women all with the same idea about themselves.

Afterwards, not only was the working class coming up and feeling its strength and purchasing power, but the middle class was losing money. Heavily taxed, it was quite prepared to be happy with the same kind of article

Figure 2.2   The rise and decline of women's weekly magazines, 1950–80.

Source: ABC, Publishers' statements, IPC.

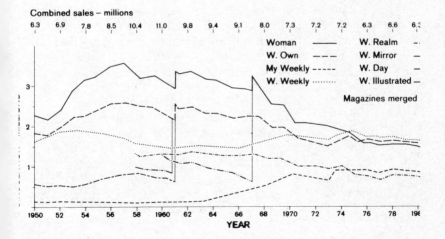

that was satisfying the women to whom the idea of, say, making a Spanish omelette was absolutely new, while to the middle-class housewife it might be a jolly nice reasonable meal she hadn't thought of. So the two could now, for different reasons, be satisfied with the same editorial content.

The editorial philosophy evolved by the successful weeklies of the 1950s was based on beliefs about audience consensus and an identity of interest amongst cohesive, primarily home-based, females – beliefs apparently confirmed by escalating sales.

These editorial rationales of female homogeneity paralleled the then fashionable *embourgeoisement* thesis of market researchers and sociologists (cf e.g. Zweig, 1961; Goldthorpe *et al*, 1969; Westergaard, 1972). Although this thesis was first criticised and then jettisoned by social scientists, it may have had a certain brief historical applicability with respect to the post-war women's magazine audience. But if it did, the declining sales of magazines for 'all' women from the mid-1960s onwards offers further confirmation of the non-feasibility of class-convergence models. The patterns of cultural differentiation in Britain were segmenting and polarising, rather than cohering or homogenising, during the social ferment of the 1960s and economic decline of the 1970s – if they had not before.

The mass female audience did not so much wither away as dissolve before the disbelieving eyes of editors and publishers accustomed to counting their followers in multi-millions. The commercial failure of attempts to introduce a 'new type' of women's magazine for a 'new type' of woman merely served to reinforce existing conventions of editorial wisdom. *WM* and *Nova* did not sell – had there really been any alterations in women's lives or tastes? The comfort of the already known, the familiar and the predictable was as soothing a mixture for editors and publishers as it was believed to be for their readers.

Yet first thousands, then millions, of women ceased to buy the titles that they had formerly purchased every week. The brand leader, *Woman*, lost sales of almost two million and experienced a readership decline of almost five million between its 1958 peak and the mid-1970s. However, sales of *My Weekly* and *Woman's Weekly* – more traditional titles with an older, more down-market audience profile, and a heavy editorial emphasis on romantic fiction – rose. The former trebled its sales between 1965 and 1974 – a success which its rivals attributed to its 'unrealistically low' price. *Woman's Weekly* sailed majestically on and on, increasing its circulation by 22 per cent between 1965 and 1972 and reaching the highest sales of any women's magazine in Britain in 1974. (See figure 2.2, p. 31).*

* ABC, Publishers' statements, 1958–1981.

Was it the 'mix', was it the price, was it more paid work, less time, more television viewing, more car driving, fewer corner newsagents?[21] Hypotheses were endless as to the fate of the weeklies.

The 'specialist' women's monthlies

The story of women's magazines in Britain in the 1960s and the 1970s is the story of the monthlies. It is they who have differentiated, innovated, and in some cases expanded, within the picture of overall audience decline. Individually and collectively their audiences are smaller than those of the weeklies. (Some comparative circulations are given in Appendix I.) Their smaller scale costs and press runs have contributed to their adaptability and have facilitated their ability to take advantage of technological changes, such as cheaper web-offset printing.[22] The social and demographic changes to which they have responded – the fact of more younger women in the population as a whole, during the 1960s and 1970s, and, of more working mothers with more money but less time to spend – were reflected in the ways in which magazines define their client/target groups and the emergence of new wisdom about doing just that.

The difficulty of ascertaining and categorising degrees of specialisation within women's magazines has been noted above. This problem is exacerbated within the monthlies, making problems of terminology and criteria of significance more acute. There is some consensus amongst the producers about the broad stratificatory system which makes monthlies generally more 'up market', and about two dimensions of segregation: age and class. When differentiation based on subject matter is added to these, any simple classification of them for purposes of discussion has to be somewhat arbitrary.

The following categories are chosen on criteria of convenience for discussion, and broad conformity with the categories in general use among people in the women's magazine world – and can be located on age–class maps: 'general interest', 'home interest', 'young women's', 'real life story' and 'specific interests'. (In a class of its own is *Spare Rib* (1972) which cannot be considered in the same league with the others as it is not so much of a commercial venture.)[23] Of these five types of monthly magazines, the traditional and young women's titles are of particular importance for the adult women's magazines focused upon by this study.

The traditional monthlies   Of great sociological as well as commercial interest is the fact that during the decade of 'Women's Lib' the most commercially successful adult women's magazines were those which were centred primarily on cookery and the home. What is more, several of them had been around for over fifty years and were still going strong. Two in this group were *Woman and Home*, the second top selling monthly in 1981 – some 603,448 – despite sales decline over the previous decade, and *Good Housekeeping*, which caters for the aspiring professional classes, and doubled its sales during the 1970s, to reach 349,196 in 1981.* Such success attracted newcomers to the home and general interest ranks. The established, carriage trade titles such as *House and Garden* and *Homes and Gardens* were joined by the trolley-pushing brigade – notably, *Family Circle* (1964), the top selling monthly, and *Living* (1967), whose owners profited from the advantages of low cover prices and novel super-market distribution. Later, they were joined by *Home and Freezer Digest* (1974) which proclaimed cookery specialisation on its cover, while covering a wider range of topics inside. Since the mid-1970s all these titles have added to their editorial agendas, yet they continue to devote the weight of their pages – and advertiser appeal – to cookery, consumer and home concerns.

The extent to which the messages of femininity continued to focus on traditional womanly concerns – and profitably so – at a time when female attitudes, behaviour and values were allegedly changing in Britain, can only be described as remarkable. The extent to which these mainstream messages persisted as both banner and epitaph of the majority of best selling women's magazines in Britain throughout this period is born out by the content analysis in Chapters 3 and 4.

The Young Women's Magazines   It was the discovery that young had money, too, (Abrams, 1959), coupled with the demographic fact of female post-war 'bulge' babies reaching magazine buying age (i.e. adolescence), that sparked the development of a separate 'young women's' sector. The young women's titles were not the main focus of this study, yet their impact on the total message of the cult – in providing an earlier form of socialisation – and their impact on the sales pattern of the women's periodical market as a whole cannot be disregarded.

IPC was the first to push the boat out. The launch of titles such as *Honey* (1960), *19* (1968) and *Look Now* (1972) pioneered and develo-ped the sales assault directed at females aged 15–29. National Maga-zine Company countered with the launch of *Cosmopolitan* (1972) (and later *Company* in 1978) – the success of which ended IPC's early monopoly in this field.

At the same time the 'down-market' romantic fiction magazines, the young women's 'real life story' titles which were also aimed at this age group, experienced a sudden revival and expansion. Between

* NRS, Jan.–Dec., 1981.

1965 and 1981, copy sales of these titles peaked at 62.7 million in 1971 and declined sharply to 28.7 million a decade later.†[24]

As for the 'specific interest' monthlies, the trend towards more tightly defined target audience groups and greater subject specialisation is reflected in the decline of one form, and the growth of others. The pure fashion monthly has virtually disappeared. In 1963 there were five; today there is *Vogue*, and to a lesser extent *Harpers and Queen*, which is as much a features as a fashion journal. Other 'specific' interest magazines include those devoted to crafts, weddings and slimming. It was during the critical 1960s that the vision of editors and publishers sharpened. Suddenly the world of women was not an undifferentiated totality, but a collection of 'target groups'.

This revelation owed something to the emergence of a new species – the marketing guru. What had been the fiercely defended territorial rights of editors and editorial directors – their sacred knowledge about the nature of the audience – came under threat. Amongst the first was an American, Dr Ernst Dichter, whose 'new woman' research allegedly influenced *Nova* and *Woman's Own*.[25] Later, when gentlemen from Quaker Oats and Heinz trod the corridors of IPC, editors of the old school confessed they could scarcely believe their ears when they were informed that 'covers are important', or 'a magazine is like a tin of beans'.

The cumulative trend of the monthlies towards specialisation and the growth of target marketing can be related to the analogy of sharp and diffuse targeting suggested by the rifle and the scatter gun. A trend within the trend can be detected: there has been movement first towards sharper targeting, and then towards more diffuse. This is evident when a greater or lesser degree of editorial subject matter specialisation is diluted by broader and more general coverage of the cult's messages in an effort to attract either a wider audience or greater advertiser support – or both.

Cosmopolitan: the cross-cultural cult message
One monthly magazine characterises many of these postwar patterns. This is *Cosmopolitan*, the most successful young women's title launched in the 1970s. Its appearance in March 1972 illustrates both the trends to multinational ownership, in this case the Hearst Corporation, and to a smaller, more tightly defined audience. Why did *Cosmo* hit the jackpot when so many others had failed? Was it the timing, was it the 'mix', or was it the target audience group?

Its editorial philosophy, which it inherited from the American mother edition, illustrates how the central messages of the cult of femininity can be transformed over time and distance, yet still remain the same. Nowhere is Woman as totem, nor Man as goal, more evident than in the pages of *Cosmopolitan*. First, in America, then in Britain, and now world-wide, its commercial success testifies to more than the powers of editorial direction or marketing expertise. It also demonstrates the processes by which social phenomena and media interpretations of them are filtered through a particular editor's audience perceptions, and are shaped to fit a particular world view.

This journal is commercially and sociologically noteworthy both for its editorial policies and for the example it presents of cross-cultural diffusion. Moreover, in the absence of comparative data, let alone a body of sociological writings on women's magazines, it affords a ready-made vehicle for cross-national comparison. The British edition was the firstborn of what has become an international extended family of *Cosmos* around the world. It is the only one which is wholly owned by the American parent company, the Hearst Corporation, through its UK subsidiary, the National Magazine Company Ltd. All the other foreign editions are produced under local licensing arrangements with carefully vetted publishers, as the Director of the International editions explained:

The reasons Hearst go to such trouble to find a publisher is, because quite simply, if you get the right publisher he'll pick the right editor. The right editor will do the right magazine, the right magazine will sell well and to the right readership. That readership will develop buoyant advertising support, which will make everybody happy, because everybody makes money that way.[26]

By 1982, the roll-call of *Cosmo* offspring around the world comprised seventeen editions published in Australia, Brazil, France, Germany, Greece, Italy, Holland, Japan, Latin America (nine regional editions; banned in Chile). Amongst these audiences, those of predominantly Catholic societies present interesting contrasts, with Italian *Cosmo* the most feminist – pro-abortion and women's rights. The Brazilian edition proscribes photographs that reveal *both* nipples and avoids the topic of abortion altogether, reflecting a culture in which virginity is still prized. Although individual editors pursue separate national identities, the extent to which Cosmopolitan International attests to the successful marketing of a globe-girdling ideology of womanhood – the cult of femininity for export – is a matter of historical and commercial record over the past decade.

Heralded as a 'bible of survival' by its British editor, the American original which spawned this far-flung, franchised family pioneered a new line in sexual openness and emotional direction, and increased its sales from an ailing 700,000 in 1965, to a healthy 2.89 million copies a month in 1981.* The editor who guided its fortunes throughout has explained her philosophy:

> *Cosmopolitan* is every girl's sophisticated older sister. . . . *Cosmopolitan* says you can get anything if you really try, if you don't just sit on your backside and gaze in on life with your nose pressed to the glass . . . we carry our profile, one piece on health, one on sex, two on emotions – we had a good one the other day on the Good Luck Factor – one on man/woman relationships, one on careers, one short story and one part of a major work of fiction, as well as our regular columns.

> (Helen Gurley Brown, quoted in *The Guardian*, 20 June 1977)

This editorial formula which combines the sex ethic of the 1960s with the work ethic of the 1970s and a strong injunction to self-help has been freely adapted yet has made this journal the most successful 'young women's' monthly in Britain. Its sales of 435,458 in 1981, and readership four times that number, suggest a degree and kind of specialisation which cuts across both age and class lines among those under 35.†

This chapter has shown how women's magazine publishers and editors of the post-war period continued to conform to the precepts laid down by their eighteenth- and nineteenth-century predecessors – precepts concerning how they distinguish their target groups in line with prevailing norms of the female role, and with perceptions of 'what women want' and 'what will sell'. Despite some changes in the class base of the audience, and the persistence of advertisement revenue as the critical factor for profitability, the processes of creating the oracles for the cult of femininity have proceeded in accordance with wider media trends: more concentrated ownership, more specialised products, more highly differentiated audiences.

These changes and persistences, together with the first rising, then falling sales of women's magazines in Britain must be set in their socio-cultural context. During the 1960s and 1970s the female audience was facing new choices and experiencing new freedoms and new conflicts. Which beliefs and practices of the cult of femininity were appropriate in an age of truly effective birth control, of doubled and trebled female economic activity rates, of increased educational chances and achievements – and what was the net effect of all this on female preferences, spending power, and relationships as lovers, wives, mothers, employees or consumers?

This changing environment for their readers brought new challenges to, and responses from, the editors in their high priestess role.

* American ABC, National Magazine Company.

†ABC, NRS, Jan.–Dec., 1981.

Should they adapt old titles and messages, or invent new ones in an effort to keep their followers faithful and to attract new ones? The problems that they faced in the 1960s and 1970s were different in kind and complexity from those of their 1950s' forebearers. The heterogeneous situations and experiences of women of differing ages, incomes, tastes and regions contrast sharply to the similar ones – however fleeting and historically specific – shared by women of dissimilar status and income in the immediate post-war period.

This points to the movement of millions of female readers from one form of the cult's messages to another – or their forsaking the gospel altogether – as more than a fact of publishing economics and audience decline. It is a significant social and cultural fact denoting changes in how women conceive of themselves, and acquire the aspirations and expectations through which they define themselves to themselves.

The evolution of the women's press traced in this chapter has set the historical and market context for those that follow. It has shown how women's magazines as a social institution and an economic phenomenon have both responded to a pattern of audience demand – and to some extent at least been able to influence it. Whether, and how, they provide a source of potential social or commercial influence depends on their messages, and what persists or changes within them over time. It is to this question, the content of their messages, that the next chapter turns.

3

The Most Repeated, Most Read Messages of the Cult: 1949–74

Chapter 1 suggested how the message of messages of the cult of femininity was that women are separate and different from men, thus sharing a common essence which transcends their differences from one another. At its most primitive this belief system perpetuates a natural law classification based on biological differences and the sexual division of labour. At a more sophisticated level it provides charters or codes that legitimise attitudes, beliefs, behaviour and institutions within the female world. At a more sophisticated level still, it reinforces the symbols and rituals that bind the female sub-culture to itself, and link it to the wider world. What form did this message take in the women's magazines that reached the widest female audience in Britain?

What were they telling their readers about the beliefs, practices and totem of the cult of femininity over the post-war period? Which topics had been put on the womanly agenda, and how had definitions of femininity and the female role changed over time? The only way to find out was to undertake a systematic, randomised and comparative content analysis – a task which hitherto has not been attempted.

The content analysis of *Woman*, *Woman's Own* and *Woman's Weekly*, 1949–74

These three weeklies were chosen for analysis because they consistently had the largest sales of any women's magazines in Britain between 1949 and 1974, and although the size of a magazine's audience is not necessarily related to its influence, there is clearly some correlation. The subject categories selected for analysis, and the creation of the analysis framework are discussed below, while full details of sampling and methods are given in Appendix II. Although sample sizes were small, this is offset by random selection, the inclusion of a wide range of variables and use of comparisons over time and between titles.[1]

The approach to the content analysis enterprise attempted to avoid the limitations of other studies. Its aims were twofold: first, to establish a quantitative base for a more qualitative analysis of the message; second, that the categories of analysis should emerge from what the magazines were saying, not from any prior assumptions or theoretical perspectives, or from empirical categories previously applied to images of women in the mass media. There was no model to apply or adapt, so it was necessary to invent one.

The procedure of working from the magazine content to categories of analysis and back to what the message was saying was adopted as a deliberate technique, to allow the magazines to speak for themselves. The starting-point was to read issues at random in search of the basic elements of a framework covering the dominant themes, roles, goals, values and social class images placed before the female audience. This framework was piloted, revised and then applied to randomly sampled issues in selected years – 1949, 1952, 1957, 1962, 1972 and 1974. A total of 196 variables were included. The complexity of this multivariable, fine-mesh approach made for time-consuming analysis, but conferred benefits in terms of providing the detailed basis for a more qualitative discussion of the dominant themes, roles, goals, values and class images that emerged therefrom. All the major findings from this study are discussed here: those relating to the visual imagery of cover photographs have been written about elsewhere.[2]

The methodology of content analysis requires that categories of subject matter be selected. It was decided to confine this analysis to four particular editorial subject categories so that a more comprehensive and deeper analytical treatment could be given to them. Two broad criteria were applied: first, which subjects would most readily reveal aspects of change and constancy in definitions of femininity and female roles; and second, which subjects would offer evidence of the persistence, growth or diminution of certain themes. Briefly, pilot analysis suggested that the most fruitful and mutually complementary areas would be: features, primarily because they deal with the world beyond the domestic; problem pages, primarily because of their high normative content and reader response; beauty, primarily because of its under-researched but powerfully prescriptive role within the cult of femininity; and fiction, primarily because of its fantasy and aspirational elements. These reasons are enlarged on below.

Why analyse features?
The term 'features' refers here to articles produced by the general

features department (as distinct from other specialist departments such as cookery or fashion). This subject category was chosen because it covers a wide range of material – from entertainers' life stories to 'real reader' dramas; from case studies of emotional and sexual problems to general wisdom about coping with life.

Since the early 1970s it has been the area of general features in which new topics relevant to social and economic change have usually made their first appearance in the pages of women's magazines. This area of discourse has widened out of all recognition, as subjects formerly taboo such as abortion, lesbianism and 'living together' have taken their place alongside old standbys like 'life at home with the stars' or 'triumph over tragedy in everyday life'. From among the several general features in a given issue of a magazine, one was chosen for detailed analysis. Two criteria guided this selection: which article was most relevant to female roles and goals, and which was most indicative of social change or continuity.

Why analyse the problem page?

Three principal reasons recommended this subject category for analysis. The problem pages are the area of women's magazine discourse which consistently strive to strike the most intimate tone of voice. Their message content is also the most intensely prescriptive; and their correspondence and readership levels remain consistently high. They also present an ideal–typical example of the multiple purposes that women's magazine journalists believe themselves and their products serve: they entertain the audience at the same time as they provide a form of psychological and social support. This is based on a bracing mixture of warmth, understanding, and practical information and advice about sexual and familial anxieties and 'worries' generally. Readers are invited to write to named persona – long-standing magazine pen names for many years, but now more commonly the writer's own – and their letters provide a prized form, albeit a self-selecting one, of audience feedback.

Until the early 1970s, the range of problems that women wrote to women's magazines about was readily classified. These included sex ('too little' or 'too much'), courtship ('he just ignores me'), and infidelity (the 'other' woman, the 'man in the office', the 'man next door'). Those letters that were printed often reflected the very subjective definitions of permissible behaviour upheld by the editors of these pages, and some of the changes that have occurred both in the message and in its tone of voice are discussed in Chapter 4. During the 1960s, for example, the problem page formula on one of these weeklies was the 'something for everybody' mix of 'young letter', 'old letter', 'sex letter' and 'mystery letter', i.e. ' "Frantic" of Tunbridge Wells, send a self-addressed envelope for a fully confidential reply'.

The 1970s brought changes both in the range of questions asked (or at least those printed) and the frankness of the replies, with the highest growth area that of correspondence concerning social services and welfare rights.

Why analyse beauty?

This subject category was chosen primarily because it has received remarkably little attention from social scientists compared with, for example, food (cf. Douglas and Gross, 1981; Deckard, 1975), and because of the very considerable attention it is given by women's magazine editors and advertisement directors.[3]

In society, as in these journals, the subject of female beauty is significant, and this significance in both arenas reflects the extent to which a woman's worth is defined in terms of her appearance. The status bestowed by the wider culture is reinforced through the cult's beliefs and practices: systematic content analysis reveals layers of manifest and latent meaning in the offerings that women's magazine beauty writers present before a high altar of female fantasy.

The goddess worshipped there is the Self, and there are prescriptive elements in the narcissistic rituals that accompany these genuflections to a mirror: there is the *duty* to beauty. But physical beauty is more than a goal in its own right; it also symbolises a separate power structure within female society. Among women, the difference lies between those who hold the scarce resource of beauty and those who do not, between the 'haves' and the 'have nots'. Within the world of women's magazines, however, all followers of the cult of femininity are *potentially* beautiful, sharing both the rights and obligations of that state.

There is a further and less metaphysical reason which makes Beauty a significant category. In the economics of women's periodical publishing, advertisement revenue from cosmetics, hair care and slimming products account for a high percentage of income. In 1981 the 'toiletries and cosmetics' category accounted for approximately one-fifth of the total advertisement revenue on *Woman*, for example.[4]

Why analyse fiction?

Fiction manifestly has aspiration and fantasy-inspiring potential (cf. Hoggart, 1957; Mann, 1974; Fowler, 1979). But there are other reasons for choosing fiction for analysis. These include the editorial importance attached to serials and short stories, the audience response that they are believed to evoke, the sameness of many fiction plots and the tight conceptual corset placed upon writers briefed 'to order'.

The importance that editors attach to fiction, the care with which they accordingly frame their requirements, and in particular the extent to which editors act as 'gatekeepers' of the feminine agenda is strikingly illustrated by the detailed brief used by a British weekly magazine in the mid-1970s:

Fiction specification. A British woman's weekly magazine, 1974a

Serials	Contemporary background. Romantic central theme, involving, especially in serials, some central conflict that is not resolved until the end. Sympathetic main characters for whom the reader can feel involvement, liking and recognition.
Age group	Central characters, especially in serials, within the 20–35 age group (in other words, the generally acknowledged 'Courtship' age). In short stories the characters' ages are not so circumscribed.
Status	Characters may be married, single or widowed.
Taboos	*Divorce*, as a central theme is not acceptable, though it can be a factor in the past that has brought about an existing state of affairs (e.g. heroine hasn't met one parent for a number of years; heroine or hero has had an unhappy childhood). We avoid *Political* or *Racial* plots, feeling that such controversy is out of place in our fiction, and is better dealt with in other non-fiction media. Plots are not based on *Class Conflict*. We try to uphold traditional moral standards, i.e. *No Sex before Marriage; No Drug-taking; No Violence*.
Promote good causes	We try to give indirect publicity to good causes through our fiction (e.g. characters rarely smoke; characters are intellectually compatible, giving greater hope for a lasting happy relationship). *Women's Lib.* is given a boost by our endeavouring to give heroines an interesting, worthwhile occupation.

a Copy document, personal communication (emphasis original)

The dominant themes of the three most widely read British women's weeklies, 1949–74

When the content analysis framework was applied to these four subject categories, it was found that dominant and sub-themes were often interchangeable; often some that had seemed minor emerged as of major significance. It was found possible to identify one dominant theme for each beauty, fiction, problem page or feature item analysed, although the number of sub-themes varied.

The themes and sub-themes that emerged from the analysis, and the frequency of their appearance in the 1950s, 1960s and 1970s, are shown in Tables 3.1 and 3.2. For convenience of discussion they have been given names which are more or less self-explanatory: 'Getting and Keeping Your Man', 'The Happy Family', 'Heart Versus Head', 'The Working Wife is a Bad Wife', 'Self-help: Overcoming Misfortune', 'Self-help: Achieving Perfection', 'Female State Mysterious', 'The Natural Order', 'Success Equals Happiness', 'Be More Beautiful' and 'Gilded Youth'. Each of these themes is discussed below.

Only two themes emerged as consistently dominant. First, there was the overwhelming star billing given to love and marriage – and the family – as the peaks of female experience and satisfaction. Second, there was the heavy emphasis placed upon the Self, and the responsibility ethic laid upon every woman to be the self-starting, self-finishing producer of herself.

The theme of themes: 'Getting and Keeping Your Man'

This represented between one-half and three-quarters of all non-beauty themes (i.e. all features, problem and fiction themes) analysed in these three weeklies – some 59 per cent overall – between 1949 and 1974. The primacy and constancy of Man as goal in the cult's messages has never been so conclusively demonstrated as in this single aggregated finding. The extent to which romantic love leading to marriage is emphasised within western societies as a particularly powerful goal for females, has attracted the attention of sociologists, anthropologists, and literary and feminist critics alike. But hitherto, we have had only limited evidence of the extent to which women's magazines define and reinforce that goal – and often that evidence has been more impressionistic or polemical than systematic.[5]

The message that romantic love was both a necessary and sufficient condition for marriage rang out loud and clear during the 1950s and 1960s. It spelled out both the condition and institution as basic entry requirements for female group membership. What was never spelled out was the competitive nature of achieving these twin goals: all

Table 3.2 Sub-themes,[a] all titles, 1949–74 (%)

	1949/52/57			1962/67			1972/74			1949–74			Total
	W	WO	WW	W	WO	WW	W	WO	WW	W	WO	WW	
Self-help: achieving perfection	28	30	14	—	—	9	23	14	5	24	17	10	17
The happy family	17	5	7	14	24	27	8	29	10	15	16	14	15
Getting and keeping your man	11	8	11	44	28	13	8	22	15	13	17	12	15
Success equals happiness	11	5	29	14	8	4	15	14	15	12	8	17	12
Self-help: overcoming misfortune	4	13	11	14	4	13	23	14	20	9	10	14	11
Gilded youth	2	5	11	—	8	22	15	—	10	5	5	14	8
The natural order	9	18	—	—	4	4	8	—	15	8	10	6	8
Heart versus head	2	8	11	14	8	—	—	—	5	3	6	6	5
Be more beautiful	7	3	3	—	4	—	—	—	5	3	3	3	3
Other	9	5	3	—	12	4	—	7	5	6	8	4	6
n[b]	46	38	28	7	25	23	13	14	20	66	77	71	214

[a] Excluding beauty
[b] n is open ended
W = Woman; WO = Woman's Own; WW = Woman's Weekly

Table 3.1 *Dominant themes,[a] all titles, 1949–74 (%)*

	1949/52/57			1962/7			1972/4			1949–74			Total
	W	WO	WW	W	WO	WW	W	WO	WW	W	WO	WW	
Getting and keeping your man	64	75	50	71	50	50	62	58	50	66	63	50	59
Self-help: overcoming misfortune	8	6	8	4	9	25	13	4	17	9	6	16	10
Heart versus head	8	5	14	8	4	4	4	8	21	7	6	13	9
The happy family	5	5	11	9	13	9	17	—	4	10	6	8	8
The working wife is a bad wife	3	3	3	—	—	—	—	13[c]	4	1	5	2	3
Self-help: achieving perfection	3	—	3	4	4	4	—	3	4	2	1	4	3
Female state mysterious	3	—	—	—	8	—	—	4	—	1	4	—	2
Gilded youth	—	—	3	—	4	8	—	—	—	—	1	4	2
Success equals happiness	3	3	3	4	—	—	—	—	—	2	1	1	1
Other	3	3	5	—	8	—	4	10	—	2	7	2	3
n[b]	36	36	36	24	24	24	24	24	24	84	84	84	252

[a] Excluding beauty
[b] n = 1 per item, 3 per issue, 4 issues per year
[c] now, 'the working wife is a good wife'

W = *Woman*; WO = *Woman's Own*; WW = *Woman's Weekly*

women were eligible for the race, but only some would win the prize. Love as a norm was a state of existence to be sought out and welcomed, just as its absence was to be avoided and feared. The woman who loved and was loved, either en route to, or within marriage, was the proto-female. The woman who was alone or unloved was not a candidate for the cult. Throughout the twenty-five years covered by this sample, there were only four instances of women who were not in the before or during marriage category: two spinsters (in the sense that they had neither hope nor scheme), one widow and one divorcee.

What forms did 'Getting and Keeping Your Man' take between the 1950s and the 1970s? Highly polemic, totally prescriptive was 'Feed the Brute' in which dutiful wives were urged to value domestic skills above book learning, and warned against straying from first duties to Him and Home:

Girls' schools don't teach nearly enough domestic science. If a few Latin lessons had to go by the board for it, what will the girl care five or ten years later when she's stirring soup, with a yelling baby under one arm, the iron burning a hole in the ironing board, the sitting room fire smoking to high heaven and her husband clamouring for his supper. . . .

As for the alternative of combining home and work tasks, there was the dreadful cautionary tale of the bride who:

. . . of course, went back to work after the honeymoon and she and her husband feed mostly out of cans or in restaurants and he can never find a pair of socks without a hole in them.

(*Woman's Own*, 25 February 1949)

The nature of 'true' love, as opposed to other forms, was – and is – a frequent theme of the fiction and problem pages. With her besotted daughter in mind, Mrs Marryat advised a mother to 'Tread warily':

It is easy for you to judge these two suitors objectively since you are not influenced, as your daughter is, by that emotion which draws her towards one of them, in spite of his faults of character.

You see, unfortunately, she only 'likes' the one you favour, whereas whatever she feels, or thinks she feels, towards the other is something far more thrilling than mere liking. . . . But try not to be too disappointed if you find she is willing to risk the ups and downs of life with a not too satisfactory partner.

(*Woman's Weekly*, 14 September 1957)

Occasionally, a less romantic, more 'down-to-earth' note was sounded – somewhat defensively – on other possible consequences of 'true love'. Ruth Martin of *Woman's Own* 'Woman to Woman Service' spoke of the chanciness of 'For Better or for Worse':

Whenever a couple marry, *the odds are against it being entirely successful* and it is only by realising this, that success can be achieved. . . . I shall be severely criticised for saying this, but just think for a moment, and see if I *am* so wrong after all.

and on sex:

The physical side of marriage is at the same time the most *important* and the most *unimportant* factor. It *must* be both. If it is one, or the other, it is fatal.

(*Woman's Own*, 17 February 1952, emphasis original)

Throughout the 1950s, 1960s and into the early 1970s, pre-marital sex was strictly taboo. The rewards of repression and the punishments of promiscuity were messages relentlessly reinforced by these weeklies. Virginity and monogamy were two cultural ideals slow to vanish from the 'getting and keeping your man' scenario. Overtly and covertly marriage and family life were set as primary goals for men as well as women. Although unselfish love and sacrifice for the loved one was a concept hammered home to females, there were occasional hints that men could give up 'all' for another:

There are many men who have built their lives around the women they love, for it is not only the wives who can make sacrifices for their partners.

Men can love as truly, tenderly, as faithfully, as women. And husbands have as much need of a loving partner, the stability and joys of family life, that inner, warm love of existence, which gives all their works purpose and makes them as worthwhile as for women. . . .

(*Woman's Weekly*, 25 February 1967)

What of romance with a capital 'R' – and the fantasy delights suggested by glittering scenarios of privileged places and people? What was their part in raising expectations of 'happy ever after'? Were the idealisations of the early 1970s markedly more 'true to life' or conducive to 'reader identification' than those of the 1950s? Not always is the short answer, and particularly not in the fictional world of *Woman's Weekly* serials. In 1974, the heroine of 'The Swallow of San Fedora' muses:

I studied that slender young man, with a profile like the head of some ancient Greek coin as he bowed low over the Australian bride's hand. Then he did the same with Kim's and then mine. A gentleman, who above all else revered women, you might have said to describe him. All sorts of romantic ideas flitted through my brain . . . as his bold dark eyes looked deep, first into Kim's and then into mine. Searching for something, I thought, romantically again. Someone, perhaps, to love him for himself, not for the title or his castle.

(*Woman's Weekly*, 28 September 1974)

However, by 1974, the possibility, nay probability, of marriage and romance turning out to be rather less of a rose-petalled bower, more of a thorny thicket, was being explored elsewhere. In a six-page special,

Woman's Own opted for openness, mutual responsibility and reciprocity:

For the many thousands of couples bewildered by the problems they face as man and wife . . . CAN THIS MARRIAGE BE SAVED?
One remark which I hear over and over again from wives in my work for the Marriage Guidance Council is: 'It's his fault. He did it. How can I be expected to forgive and forget?' Husbands tend to say the same sort of thing: 'She doesn't understand'. But is there only one person at fault in a marriage crisis?

(*Woman's Own*, 11 May 1974)

Here the turning away from sharply segregated to shared roles including mutual – not wifely alone – responsibility for marriage 'success' or 'failure' *was* a new development.

. . . And next comes 'The Happy Family'

The emergence of 'The Happy Family' as a dominant theme in its own right reflects the cultural and structural significance of the family as a sacred institution in this and other societies. It also reflects the profound social and economic implications that the family holds for females. Until the feminist movement clamoured for a re-think of sex roles in society and a change of gender emphasis within sociology itself, the family was seen as the primary location of female participation.[6] Children were the expected outcome, not only of imperfect contraception, but also of the perfect union – providing emotional and sexual fulfilment within marriage.

Within these weeklies, heavy emphasis was placed on the centrality of family life to the world of women. Implicitly and explicitly the message was clear: the satisfaction that derived from wifehood and motherhood was quintessential to the cult itself. For this reason a high normative value was placed on family solidarity and for long the message was preservation of the marital and familial status quo, at any cost – with responsibility placed particularly on the wife to maintain stability. The appearance of 'the happy family' – 8 per cent – as a theme in its own right is particularly significant when taken in conjunction with 'getting and keeping your man'. It completes a logical progression, or cultural constellation, of female aspirations and expectations, giving a combined love–marriage–family score which amounts to two-thirds – 67 per cent – of all dominant themes found outside the beauty pages.

The idealised, iconographic role model for 'the happy family' was, and still is, the royal family. The majority of British women's magazines, and especially the weeklies, have helped to create, develop and perpetuate this regal myth. No article remotely critical of the royal family appeared in any of the issues analysed. The image of royalty consistently portrayed throughout the period 1949–74 was that of the royal *family*. Year in, year out, the royals are presented as simple homebodies at heart, sharing the joys and cares of 'normal' family life – 'just like you', the female audience, 'and me', the women's magazine journalist: see, for example – 'Their Happy Marriage' (*Woman*, 22 November 1952) 'The Family At the Palace' (*Woman's Own*, 29 July 1972); 'My Perfect Granny' (by Prince Charles, *Woman*, 2 August 1980).

For less wealthy and aristocratic happy families, the guidelines for wifely and motherly performance were quite specific. In the 1950s, polemical columnists laid down the law on 'It's the Woman Who Makes the Home':

The woman of the house is the most important person in it. Her husband may be stronger and cleverer than she is. He may be a business tycoon, or a genius or a famous personality. His wife may seem inferior to him in the more obvious ways, but there is one subtle way she can outdo him every time, and that is in her influence in the home. . . .

'What is a home without a mother?' asks the text that used to hang against the florid paper of Victorian walls. What indeed? Widowers have been known to make homes for their children, but seldom very successfully. They usually have to rely on a sister, or an aunt or a housekeeper – some woman – to fill, at least in part, the gap left by the mother.

(*Woman's Own*, 11 April 1957)

'Self-help: Overcoming Misfortune' and 'Self-help: Achieving Perfection'

The second most striking finding of this study was the extent to which the weeklies' messages stress individual achievement and self-determination for women. This underground value system stemming from Victorian England flowered and flourished throughout the 1949–74 period.[7] There are two versions of directives aimed at women pulling themselves up by their own suspender belts. One emphasises individual improvements, ever striving towards a more perfect presentation and performance of self. The other holds out the carrot of hope that one's material, physical or emotional disasters can be overcome through the application of sufficient effort, courage and true grit.

If these two individualistic themes are added together, they total 13 per cent of all dominant themes. When their pre-eminence as a sub-theme is taken into account – some 28 per cent (Table 3.2) – the total strength of 'self-help' within this universe of discourse is made clear. Both versions suggest that self – not other – determination is desirable, feasible, and obtainable through the exercise of just that much more control and effort on a woman's part. Both imply free choice rather than fated 'determinism', imply active doing rather than passive acceptance, and stress a distinctly anti-collectivist, highly individualist ethic. Here, too, a competitive theory of female, 'achievement' is postulated: all women are capable of 'helping themselves', but only those who try harder win through.

The first, 'Self-help: Overcoming Misfortune', demonstrates the discipline and effort required of women if they are to transcend their personal difficulties, from the trivial to the tragic. The second, 'Self-help: Achieving Perfection', concerns a highly gender-specific form of achievement motivation. Here a woman is directed not only to try harder in the labour market, because of her historical disadvantages there; she must also strive industriously to achieve high performance standards on the homefront as well. Here the messages and advertisements directed at women set the standards of perfection; whether it's the never-fail soufflé or the perfect hair style.[8]

The recurrent melody of helping oneself to *overcome* is a classic theme. Known in 'the trade' as a T.O.T., or 'triumph over tragedy', this theme frequently takes the form of first person accounts. Journalistic drama and immediacy is invoked by a whole range of individuals who overcome a variety of physical and emotional problems – from disease to bereavement, from alcoholism to acne.

Other variations on this theme of overcoming fate include stern stuff from problem page editors or columnists: 'Do something, don't just sit down and passively accept the blows of misfortune.'

An early example came from 'The Man Who Sees':

I think it is much better, as the poet said, to 'toughen the fibre' than to harden the skin. It is better to be firm-hearted than to be thick-skinned. And that is a matter of one's faith. . . . In the manger at Bethlehem there was no sect; just the centre. And the centre is more important than the sect. . . . Make that centre firm, and keep your sensitiveness, and, whatever the world brings you, you will find a share of happiness.

(*Woman's Weekly*, 24 December 1949)

In counselling those disturbed by changes such as moving or early retirement which threaten comforting familiarities, women are urged to find security in sameness, reassurance in ritual:

In the face of impending change, it may often seem pointless to carry on with the daily routine. Yet this may be the most effective way of fighting those unsettled feelings. . . . To occupy oneself with the familiar round even if one must live from day to day, is tranquilising and strengthening.

(*Woman's Weekly*, 19 August 1972)

Outside the columns of philosopher–kings such as 'The Man Who Sees', it is in the beauty and problem pages that the emphasis on self-help is strongest. Implicit and explicit within all problem page replies is the admonition: 'Do something about it'. This was so even when 'doing something about it' in the 1950s and 1960s meant accepting what would be unacceptable by today's standards to preserve a marriage. This theme continued in the 1970s, when Mrs Marryat advised on how to learn to live with a marital problem:

> Don't try to conquer the problem [jealousy] by calling yourself names . . . say to yourself . . . 'Now I expect I shall feel jealous soon because Jim is dancing with that pretty girl. I am not going to give way to it. I'm going to smile and talk to the person next to me, and not say a single word of complaint afterwards.'
>
> (*Woman's Weekly*, 28 September 1974)

These examples demonstrate another aspect of self-help, the link between personal responsibility and individual achievement. 'Just make up your mind to do something, try hard enough, and it can be done,' is the positive message pounded home on their pages.

This setting of performance standards – of the practices that define the cult of femininity – emerged in this study as one of the most visible and constant purposes served by women's magazines. The perfection-achieving variant of the self-help theme shows how women are directed towards an ever more perfect production and presentation of self. From child-care to hair-care, from cooking to conversation, the parameters of female excellence portrayed as normative – in terms of their desirability and achievability – are universally high. This conclusion contrasts to the feminist view that women are presented with low-level reference groups by comparing themselves with other women rather than men.[9] Until recently this was true of the paid work occupational categories suggested to women as possible or desirable in these journals. It was never true of the primary occupational category – the business of being a woman. Writ large in all these messages of the cult of femininity is the exhortation to improve and excel.

Which categories of perfectability should a female strive for? Multiple forms of excellence are promulgated: *be* a better mother, *be* a better lover, *be* a better cook, *be* better dressed and *be* better looking. The urge to achieve is ever evident in women's magazine problem-solving and fact-giving – through all the editorial 'service' areas from how to paper the bathroom ceiling, to how to teach Him to be better in bed.

In counselling about marriage and the proper performance of the wifely role, attainable perfection is inclusive of 'Him':

> Do you Agree that the Average Man is Less Given to Fault Finding Than the Average Woman? If We Try to Put Our Own Failings Right, Perhaps We May Set a Good Example to Our Men Folk.
>
> (*Woman's Weekly*, 24 May 1952, capitals in original)

Learning, and especially learning by doing, is seen as important to achieving a more perfect standard of house-care, child-minding, beautifying or friendship. In 1962 a male columnist suggested flat-sharing as preparation for matrimony, as a form of apprenticeship:

SHARING HAS PITFALLS
Two girls sharing a flat may learn to be tolerant in many ways – but not when their boy-friends are involved. . . . It helps to rub off some of her sharp corners almost without realising it and teaches her a practical daily tolerance of irritating little habits . . . this could stand her in good stead in the early years of marriage.

(*Woman*, 24 February 1962)

'Heart Versus Head'

This theme captures the conflicts of the female condition and attributes which have acquired the status of secondary sex characteristics, and which reflect forms of 'cultural labelling' whereby 'emotional' or 'rational' modes of thought or behaviour become 'female' or 'male' respectively.[10] This process begins with nursery rhyme socialisation and expands to encompass philosophical and psychological distinctions between emotion and reason. It is linked to the legacy of the Enlightenment whereby the western European 'rationality' model takes precedence over other ways of experiencing and ordering the world, and incorporates a hierarchy of understanding which elevates reason (male) over and above emotion (unreason, female) which provides a legitimating logic for male domination in the process.

The tension implied by this emotion–reason dichotomy rests on more than the positing of oppositional 'His' and 'Hers' categories. It rests upon a deeper division between two incompatible sets of values. One assigns to females the role of expressive nurturers. The other locates females within the mechanics of bureaucratic and industrial processes that require logic, consistency and conformity to rules. This juxtaposing of 'thinking' and 'feeling' norms poses more acute problems for women than for men. It creates anxiety about how to conform to definitions of femininity which require that 'bright girls pretend to men that they are not' (see e.g. Komarovsky, 1946, 1973).

Within these weeklies, 'Heart Versus Head' was most often related to decisions affecting the course of love in fiction stories or in celebrities' 'own true-life' dramas. This accounts in part for the high incidence of this theme within *Woman's Weekly*, given its romantic fiction emphasis. For example, in 'The White Oleander', the heroine, Laurie, visits an exotic island to care for her wicked older sister's child. There her bad sister insists that she pretend to be the nanny, and warns her against the fascinating nobleman she meets. Laurie struggles to control her feelings:

She had allowed herself to become bewitched by his comradeliness into completely forgetting the implications of her promise to Stella. In those minutes, while Felipe stood obliterating the light from the doorway, his face dark and withdrawn, she saw the utter folly of permitting freedom to her emotions.

(*Woman's Weekly*, 6 December 1952)

Here, as elsewhere within the value structure laid down for women, individual responsibility is defined in terms of self-control. The cultural ideal is one of womanly rectitude. Typically warnings about the dangers of 'giving way' to emotions and feelings were strongest concerning sex. In the pre-pill era two groups were identified as most at risk: sexually dissatisfied wives and love-sick adolescent girls. The force with which the 'head must rule' message was delivered is shown by a dialogue between a 'real reader' and an editor. The prescription is clear – beware being tricked by passion and losing all control:

MY MOTHER DOESN'T WANT ME TO BE IN LOVE
a heartcry from a 17-year-old
Q. What is she (the mother) afraid of?
A. (*Woman's Own*) That strong emotion will break her daughter's self-control.
Q. I want to keep my self-respect
A. All that can be swept away by passion, etc. etc.

(*Woman's Own*, 4 December 1957)

This shows the unequivocal nature of moral directives handed down to females during this period, designed to serve the twin ideals of virginity before and fidelity after marriage. Eternal vigilance was the only guard against fleshly temptation – and distinctly possible pregnancy.

A much starker interpretation of the reason–emotion conflict was given in the early 1970s, in discussing abortion five years after the 1967 Abortion Act:

NEVER QUITE THE SAME AGAIN
More than for any other operation, the reason behind the decision to have an abortion is the desire to return to normal – to things as they were. But is that really possible, or does an abortion leave an emotional scar for ever afterwards? Five single girls and a married woman talk about their experiences . . .

(*Woman's Own*, 16 September 1972)

'The Working Wife is a Bad Wife'

Pilot analysis showed the early strength of this theme, especially during the 1950s. The sociological question arises, was conflict between home and work roles suggested, and how explicit was the normative direction? Historically, the extent to which the messages of the cult directed or reflected any such conflict has not been systematically explored in relation to the contribution of the women's press to the re-socialisation of the wartime female labour force towards domesticity. The virtual invisibility of this theme, 3 per cent, raises questions about the limits placed on topics put before the female audience during the 1950s and 1960s – limits created as much by exclusion as by inclusion. Which role models and reference groups were offered to the mass of the cult's followers? For the growing numbers of wives and mothers experiencing the personal, social and economic consequences of dual commitments and rewards, which satisfactions or dissatisfactions were suggested or acknowledged, withheld or ignored?

Until the early 1970s such questions were either avoided altogether or answered negatively. Female priorities were clear: a woman's world was finite, bounded by the traditional task division which assigns child and home-care exclusively to her. Editorial recognition of non-domestic female occupations within these weeklies was confined largely to 'first job' features, or glossy accounts of the successful careers of models and actresses (cf. Hatch and Hatch, 1968). One recognised females working before marriage, on the assumption that this would cease at latest with the birth of the first child. The other presented readers of all ages with idealised role models and 'success' scenarios for day-dreaming or identification.[11]

Marginally present in the 1950s, absent altogether in the 1960s, this theme reappeared in the 1970s, especially within the innovatory *Woman's Own*. There, stood on its head, altered beyond recognition it became 'The Working Wife is a Good Wife'. The extent to which Him and Home-centredness persisted as a dominant image of British womanhood within these weeklies is illustrated below. Two examples from *Woman's Weekly*, the most traditional of the three weeklies, demonstrate a slight shift, the slow filtering of social change, whereby the impossible of the fifties – a paid job for any woman who valued the quality and durability of her marriage – was redefined by the 1970s to permit some questioning of the 'captive housewife' situation. In the 1950s women were warned about 'Knowing When to Call a Halt':

The establishing of marriage values may be postponed along with that notice to the office. A young wife doing two jobs just may not have enough time, nervous strength and thought to give to this difficult business of marital adjusting.

Doing two jobs saps strength and vitality and often there is an inner conflict, which is tiring in itself, because she is occupied with one job when she knows the other is going wrong because she cannot give it her fullest attention and energy at the moment needed for it.

(*Woman's Weekly*, 14 September 1957)

Seventeen years later Mrs Marryat advised a restless housebound young mother that she was 'Not Just a Housewife' and how initiative and sharing the problem might help:

. . . as you have a young child, what about offering to help in a local play-group or starting one yourself? Information from . . .

(*Woman's Weekly*, 1 June 1974)

At this stage, the mid-1970s, no such tentative noises came from the pace-setting weekly, *Woman's Own*. The paid work vs. home duty conflict was resolved, and a five-page 'special' announced 'How to Get the Right Job at the Right Time':

At 16, 23, 35, 45 plus there's the right job for you. Whether you are just about to leave school in your mid-twenties and need a change, or in your thirties or forties and want to be trained for something entirely new, we've planned this supplement to help you make the right choice. Begin by consulting your Careerscope chart below.

(*Woman's Own*, 23 March 1974)

The 'Female State Mysterious'

Pilot analysis showed the presence of this theme, especially in the 1950s. It portrays the female condition as complex, unpredictable or incomprehensible on masculine and/or rational criteria where the terms 'masculine' and 'rational' frequently are being used interchangeably, or as logically connected. It also defines female characteristics in relation to male ones. In the event it was statistically insignificant at 2 per cent. Has this cliché stereotype of female emotionality and impetuosity disappeared? Or is it covertly held by members of both sexes, one with which women themselves have colluded?

For a woman to define herself as irrational and impulsive is to write herself a blank cheque in interpersonal relations. To state 'I am by definition changeable and unpredictable, therefore logically I cannot be held accountable for my actions' is to apply a powerful lever to the balance of power within family or interpersonal relations. As such, it offers partial redress within the conventional power structure of this period, which allocated material or psychological dependence to women. Unpredictability, when not used so frequently that it becomes the norm, can be a powerful counter to reasoned argument or choice. The conscious or unconscious adoption of such attitudes offers some support for the view of women as informal power holders. Oakley (1974) refers to the power that gossip control invests in women. Here, female 'unpredictability' may serve similar ends.

A second side to the 'mysterious female' stereotype is the echo that it provides of primitive fears of the female as unknowably threatening:

the carrier of some powerful magic adhering to her menstruating and child-bearing functions. Anthropologists and psychoanalysts have explored such beliefs and behaviours and their implications for the psyches and social roles of both sexes.[12] A third variant of feminine mystery much favoured by women's magazines involves a woman's choice of a particular female typification or 'style' as her own. These alternative images help to perpetuate a cultivated climate of delightful or disconcerting uncertainty:

WHAT KIND OF GIRL ARE YOU REALLY?
Romantic? Practical? Selfish? Generous? What are you really like? And how do others, especially your boy friend or husband, see you? Answer the ten questions below to discover your true personality – and see yourself as you really are.

(Woman's Own, 10 June 1967)

Contiguous or overlapping with the 'Female State Mysterious' is the 'Natural Order' sub-theme. It contrasts to the uncertainties or alternatives of the former and sees the female world as but one-half of a divinely ordained, because unquestionable, sexual division of society. Accordingly, men *are* this, women *are* that; men *do* this, women *do* that (cf. Fransella and Frost, 1977).

'Gilded Youth'

The Western cultural emphasis on youth as 'the best years of your life' is not exclusive to females. It reflects a long, historical, aesthetic and philosophical tradition which has influenced both sexes. In the post-war and present media market place, glistening youth was and is the ruling visual concept employed by journalists and advertisers alike. British women's magazine publishers exploited the 'youth cult' through the development of a separate young women's sector. Thus 'teenagers' or 'sub-teens' female audiences are both the stimulus for, and cash register response to, the cosmetics, fashion and entertainment industries' discovery of adolescent spending power in the late 1950s and early 1960s.[13]

Given the commercial and cultural emphasis upon youthful appearance as an ideal for women of all ages, the relative invisibility of this theme, 2 per cent, is interesting. Where it did occur most frequently was in *Woman's Weekly*, the magazine with the oldest readership profile – reaching some 4 per cent of dominant and 14 per cent of sub-themes overall. This suggests some support for the thesis that fantasy elements are involved in the identification process – or that editors believe that older readers prefer youthful idealisations to elderly realisations.

'Success Equals Happiness'

On the face of it, this theme was unimportant, but in fact it was ever present below the surface. It was insignificant in terms of the achievement-orientated nature of industrial societies, at least in terms of women gaining 'success' through a career.[14] Within the messages of the cult that define femininity itself as a career, however, achievement norms exist in abundance. They specify a range of goals and performance standards that relate to herself – love, family, happiness and 'looking good'. Yet alongside these personal goals we see happiness equated with worldly success to a considerable extent.

The material and status rewards of fame and riches, which are used to spell out the meaning of success, raises the question: how does an achieving society define 'success' other than through media role models of status visibility or symbols of conspicuous consumption? The success icons of the cult's messages are celebrities and 'personalities'. They people the pages of these weeklies, proffering their 'shared' dreams and disasters, kudos and cash to the millions:

HOSTAGES TO FORTUNE
We all dream of hitting the pools jackpot one day and abandoning ourselves to a life of carefree luxury. But what is it like to be part of the family who became rich by giving vast sums of money away? At the end of the season in which more than ever has been won on the football pools, *Woman* talks to the brothers who share in the Littlewoods millions. Each has a different kind of life and his own way of coping with the joys and problems of enormous wealth.

(*Woman*, 13 May 1972)

'Be More Beautiful'

The female duty to beautify was soon evident as this study progressed. The characteristics and internal consistency of this theme less so. Unquestionably 'Be More Beautiful' offers an archetypal example of women's magazine messages presenting the desirable as though it were the possible – just as they present the possible as though it were desirable. This particular form of the message heightens aspirations, allies them with rituals of self-discipline, and encourages every female to 'make the most of herself'. (For this reason, 'self-help: achieving perfection' was occasionally the dominant theme; otherwise 'be more beautiful' was self-selecting on the beauty pages.)

Beauty is 'taken for granted' as both means and end within the female world, and physical appearance is a highly normative cult message. Injunctions to improve the perfect – the *duty* to beautify – are proclaimed from billboard and television advertisements and are not confined to the women's press. There are latent as well as manifest meanings in these messages. Covetable and pleasurable rewards accrue to the possessor of gleaming hair, sparkling eyes and a satiny complexion – transfixed on a moonlit balcony, lolling by a palm-fringed surf and always with an adoring male attendant as the perfect prop in the luxurious backdrop.

The esteem conferred by ownership of these desirable physical attributes suggests an alternative power structure within female society, a hierarchy based upon possession of certain physical quali-ties – albeit changing from time to time, the relative importance of hair and eyes, or legs and bust. It is a social, cultural and economic fact that for some women their facial contours or body shape can deter-mine their income and status more than their life chance situation, enabling us to posit 'tit' and 'cheekbone' determinism. This is pos-sible because it concerns the distribution of a scarce resource. To be born beautiful is to be born a rarity, yet female beauty is a generalised cultural ideal.

The single-minded dedication required to 'be more beautiful' is reiterated through the same limited range of goals, values and roles. This produces a tight prescriptive package, but one packed with positive reinforcement: 'you *should* look like this', and 'you *can* look like this'. No allowance is made for day-dreaming or wishful thinking in these firm, sometimes stern idealisations that a woman should toil to emulate. 'Soft and pretty' or 'bright and sophisticated'? Simply choose this type, follow the required rituals, and the desired end is assured. Thus, second only to messages of female obligation to maxi-mise physical attractiveness, are promises of its attainability. Achievement of better looks is the logical outcome of personal effort. Comfort and inspiration are combined: any flaws in genetic make-up can always be camouflaged by the cosmetic kind, by sufficient effort – and glitter eye shadow.

Several complex and overlapping processes are at work here – social, psychological and editorial. There is goal-setting: physical beauty is presented less as an aspirational ideal, more as a holy commandment. There is reassurance: salvation can be achieved from a state of non-beauty. Then lest these aspects seem over-determin-istic, an element of free will is introduced: individual group members may choose their preferred ideal or image. Finally, once choices are resolved, detailed prescriptions follow, often requiring a greater sacrifice of time, effort and dedication than of money spent on cos-metics or consumer goods. The ritual aspects of the perfecting process are demonstrated by the 'step-by-step' instructions, the day-to-day diets, leading the initiates towards physical images and ideals which are as culturally and commercially determined as ever they are bio-logically given.

Finally, for whom and for what ends are these active, achieving beauty rituals performed? Technical advice about beautification can only relate to the female, yet surprisingly there were hardly any references to the benefits of women beautifying themselves to attract or hold a male's attention. The beauty messages largely ignored the existence of, or impact upon, men – thereby producing the 'Invisible Male' role category discussed below.

The significance of these absent males is twofold. Firstly, it emphasises the extent to which physical appearance is made integral to a woman's self concept and her femininity as such – narcissism is an explicit norm within these pages. Secondly, it confirms the extent to which the totemic object of female society is Woman, not Man. The absence of his overt presence should not be interpreted as a signal of the male's unimportance. Rather it suggests an implicit and latent meaning so powerful that it does not require explicit and manifest statement: men are the goals, not the gods.

How duty and discipline, possibility and perfection, routine and ritual form a constellation of physical prescriptions is well illustrated in the 'good-to-be-alive GIRL':

'There's more to true beauty than meets the eye' and even if you were not 'pretty really' . . . someone with verve, vitality and spring in their step is always a joy to meet. . . .

this positive thinking starts with getting up earlier to exercise, eating more fresh fruit, keeping a dry pair of shoes in the office, because:

When you feel fine, your looks improve, your work, your life: when that happens you feel even better and more pleased with life.

With a gay step and shining eyes, you can look around you and take in all the interesting facets of daily life. . . . That's the secret of a vital outlook. Look ahead to the day before you with zest and enthusiasm, and you'll look better, feel better and get much more out of life than ever before.

(*Woman*, 16 March 1957)

Another example shows the helpful, problem solving of the editorial tone. Here effort is untypically and explicitly directed at Him:

MISS WONDERFUL, THAT'S YOU
. . . it's certainly true that for a girl to score a real romantic rating in a man's eye her looks have got to be just a little special. *She* doesn't have to have a pin-up profile either . . . but she won't get far without polishing up her good points and disguising her bad ones so that he's completely befogged by glamour! It's at this stage that the romantic compliments are paid and the diamond engagement rings get shopped for!

(*Woman's Own*, 18 September 1951)

The element of hope implicit in the beauty fantasy, the urge to transform what is into what can be, is illustrated by 'New Fitness Starts Here'. The promise of resurrection goes hand in hand with reassurance where:

Almost every woman is concerned about her figure . . . The fact is, perfect bodies are pretty rare. Even model girls have their problems . . . there's no figure fault that's worth despairing over! All the help-ways in this book work and they work for everybody . . . everyone – yes really everyone – can look younger, lighter, fitter . . . and feel it too. Start now on the new you!

(*Woman*, 21 October 1967)

These examples also illustrate how the emphasis placed on individual effort and self-help, as the most rational means to the end of beauty, are persistent and powerful themes within women's magazine content as a whole.

The themes discussed above incorporate normative pictures of roles, goals and values. Any answer to the question 'What do women's magazines tell women about the sorts of women they are, can be, or should be?' involves knowledge of the roles that they specify and the aspirations that they set. Few social scientists, journalists or advertisers could examine the pages of women's magazines and disclaim that one of their most potent purposes is that of secondary socialisation: the recipes for, and values of, the female gender role.

Which were the definitive roles, goals, values and images of social class over the postwar period?

The dominant female roles
A woman plays many roles, but which does she play most often on the pages of women's magazines? The answer to this question turned out to be linked to *how* she played them. The most significant characteristic of these female roles concerns their positive nature. Women may not be entirely perfect, but they are rarely presented in grossly negative terms within the cult's messages. Rather, these confident idealisations of femininity flesh out the beliefs of the high priestesses about the inspirational and reinforcement purposes their messages serve towards the audience. These images show women bettering themselves through their own efforts, overcoming heartbreak, or holding the family together – and suggest some support for the cult's messages of female solidarity. This 'aren't we women wonderful?' approach provides shared experiences as one basis of the female bonding process.

The female roles which are labelled and listed in Table 3.3 – and the male ones in Table 3.4 – are not mutually exclusive categories. The same person or character could play several roles; classification was kept deliberately open-ended to record the maximum range presented. Sometimes these roles were defined in terms of the attributes of the person concerned, such as 'mother' or 'wife', and sometimes in terms of qualities, such as 'good' or 'bad'.

Table 3.3 *Dominant female roles, all subjects, all titles, 1949–74 (%)*

	1949/52/57			1962/7			1972/4			1949–78			Total
	W	WO	WW	W	WO[a]	WW	W	WO[b]	WW	W	WO	WW	
Wife	17	21	12	16	17	15	24	25	12	19	21	13	18
Marriage fixated	19	25	20	13	16	16	12	2	22	16	16	19	17
Mother	11	9	8	15	13	11	14	15	6	13	12	8	11
Beautifier	11	8	12	11	7	12	12	10	12	12	7	12	11
Daughter/sister	2	4	10	8	15	19	12	4	8	6	7	12	9
Female/female	8	17	14	13	5	4	—	8	5	7	11	8	9
Careerist	9	5	6	8	7	4	5	11	8	8	8	6	7
Girl-friend	7	3	10	4	7	6	3	—	7	5	3	8	5
Decent lady	2	3	4	4	4	2	7	5	5	4	4	4	4
Other	14	5	4	8	9	11	11	20	15	10	10	10	9
n	88	76	90	52	55	67	58	52	65	198	183	222	603

[a] No beauty, two issues
[b] No beauty, one issue
n = open-ended; W = *Woman*; WO = *Woman's Own*; WW = *Woman's Weekly*

The female role of roles – consistent with getting and keeping a man as the theme of themes – was that of 'Wife' – 18 per cent (Table 3.3) – a finding concordant with traditional beliefs about a woman's 'place'.[15] Here positive and supportive interpretations stress a strong element of duty and responsibility towards others, with the self-sacrificing female martyr personifying such dedication taken to the extreme. Negative portraits were few – a sprinkling of 'bad' and jealous wives condemned for failing to conform to consensual wifely behaviour, or for moaning about their lot.

Running the wife a close second was the 'Marriage Fixated Female', 17 per cent, determined to achieve marriage as her goal of goals. The crucial variable here was the degree of feminine calculation – relentlessly calculating schemers or delightfully romantic dreamers. The former could be manipulative or destructive, the latter inspired by fantasy or diverted from the chase by higher moral claims such as daughterly duty. Either way marriage was mandatory, and possession of man as object was a symbol of female achievement.

The role of 'Mother' ranked third, 11 per cent. Again, traditional role definitions prevailed with the maternal function depicted as nurturing, supportive, educative and refuge-providing (see, for example, Bernard, 1975). Warm and wise, this stereotypical paragon was the universal symbol of better British motherhood. Until the mid-1970s, neither the boundaries of this role nor its sacred nature were questioned. 'Bad' mothers occasionally intruded in the problem pages, where a few non-supportive, counter-stereotypes, neglectful of husband, children or domestic priorities, occasionally appeared.

The importance of these three roles as carriers of traditional beliefs about the female role becomes apparent when they are summed. Together they form almost half (46 per cent) of *all* female roles identified by this analysis. They are the three dominant images of femininity within the 'getting and keeping your man' and 'happy family' themes, and hereby illustrate the inter-connectedness and internal consistency of the cult's messages.

A quite different role was that of the 'Beautifier'. This icon of femininity represents the woman who makes the most of herself physically, superimposing nurture upon nature. Her image is both sexual and asexual. It is sexual in defining the female state as pleasingly attractive, as much for self-esteem as for male esteem. It is asexual in offering a polished, perfected, depiliated, deodorised object as the end-product.

Daughters and sisters account for almost a tenth of female roles identified, which suggests the significance of kinship as a basis for bonding within the world of women. Here the emphasis is on duty, loyalty and the fulfilling of obligations within sibling or filial relationships. These were positive portraits: daughters were invariably 'good', although occasionally a 'bad' sister appeared as part of a romantic triangle where two sisters battled for the same rich and covetable male.

The 'Female Female' role classifies itself as the stereotype of stereotypes. It embodies some of the cultural assumptions and prescriptions encapsulated in the 'heart versus head' theme which defines the female state as fascinating, changeable, emotional, flirtatious, dependent and submissive. The acceptability and legitimacy of this theme is historically relative: the ideal of the 1950s, the quandary of the 1960s, the jest of the 1970s and the unknown quantity of the 1980s. Likewise the emphasis on domestic roles during the 1950s and 1960s, makes the low incidence of the 'Careerist', scarcely surprising. It reflects the late in the day acceptance by these weeklies of the legitimacy of paid employment for married women, and the 'service' priority given to subject matter – and advertisement content – focused on the home. During the 1950s and 1960s, fictional accounts of working women featured the 'career girl', eyes down on her job until she contrives to be rescued from this usually tedious activity by Mr Right – who as often as not is her status and income laden boss.

The 'Girl-friend' role suggests something of the extent to which women rely upon other women for practical and emotional support. In coping with their lives, and at the same time with any feelings of powerlessness or relative deprivation which derive from that life situation, a mutual social support system can operate. In these themes, emphasis is on reciprocal loyalties reinforced by common cult membership. The overall image of these 'sisters under the skin' is constructive. The only two cases of unhelpful sisterhood were both jealous girl-friends fighting over the same delectable man.

Emergence of the 'Decent Woman', as a role in its own right, accords with the status quo-maintaining strand running through the value structure mediated to the cult during this period. Here is the decent member of society (female variant), conformist in thought and deed, being 'nice' about it, whatever it turns out to be – from house-moving to holocaust. No non-conformist or indecent woman ever appeared, no bad-mannered nose-pickers or exhibitionist houris ever leapt from the page.

Almost one-tenth of the female roles recorded were assigned to the miscellaneous category of 'Other'. This indicates the distinctiveness and multiplicity of female roles and underlines the fact that one female often performs several of them. Amongst these 'other' roles that can be defined are 'Teenage Rebel', 'Other Woman', 'Mother-in-Law', 'Queen', 'Queen Mother', and 'Princess'.

The dominant male roles

If the cult's messages supply the world of women with its prescriptions of femininity, what norms does it set for the male presence therein? Since the coming of the feminists, social science research has neglected the changing range of male roles and their media definitions. It has concentrated on two aspects – the male's 'power structure pre-eminence', or 'sex-role de-differentiation' within the family.[16] The exploratory approach used by this study asked: 'What kinds of men are presented in the cult's messages, and in what ways – positively or negatively?'

What emerged from the analysis was that whereas female roles were predominantly defined by the high priestesses in terms of relationships – wives, mothers, sisters – male roles often were not. Some, like husbands and fathers were, but others personified cultural goals, such as work achievement. Other male roles were defined rather more in terms of qualities – producing a host of good, bad and above all, desirable men who made potential husbands.

The dominant image of masculinity in these weeklies is one of social and economic success, with the majority of occupational roles fixed firmly in the middle and upper class. Office corridors, ancestral halls and hospital wards serve as hunting grounds where doctors, lawyers, architects and company directors are stalked. Such scenarios point to the persistence of the male as status symbol supreme within the female culture. Women, with rare exceptions, are still ranked by the occupation of their male partner – across the dinner table or the garden fence. This social fact is one which helps to explain why the totem of female society may be Woman, but Man remains the goal, not the god. Thus her 'possession' of a materially successful male is doubly desirable, conferring both wider social, and immediate personal, status on the woman concerned.

Table 3.4 bears this out. It shows 'Desirable Male' as the pre-eminent masculine image within these weeklies, 24 per cent. Personifying man as object of female romantic, sexual and material interest – prospective partner and provider – this idealised object is pursued with possession, and matrimony, in mind. He comes in several guises – the boy next door, the boss at the office or the attractive, mysterious, older guardian of many an orphaned heroine. His ideal–typical incarnation combines power and affluence:

His clothes, his pigskin cases, and above all his carriage, poised and assured,

Table 3.4 Dominant male roles, all subjects, all titles, 1949–74 (%)

	1949/52/57			1962/67			1972/74			1949–74			
	W	WO	WW	W	WO[a]	WW	W	WO[b]	WW	W	WO	WW	Total
Desirable male	25	36	28	15	21	25	7	23	28	17	29	27	24
Good chap	21	12	26	22	11	14	19	13	16	21	12	19	18
Invisible male	14	8	15	19	11	18	22	13	16	17	10	16	15
Husband	10	17	11	6	18	9	15	15	10	11	16	10	12
Father	11	5	4	9	11	14	15	6	8	12	7	8	9
Bad chap	8	6	5	4	5	5	7	13	6	7	7	6	7
Artistic male	—	4	3	7	5	4	9	9	2	4	6	3	4
Protector	1	1	5	7	2	5	4	6	4	3	3	5	4
Striving male	3	6	—	2	5	2	—	—	4	2	4	2	2
Other	7	5	3	9	11	4	2	2	6	6	6	4	5
n	73	74	74	46	44	56	46	47	50	165	165	180	510

[a] No beauty, two issues
[b] No beauty, one issue

n = open-ended; W = Woman; WO = Woman's Own; WW = Woman's Weekly combined to give her the impression that he had command of money and most probably had never known the lack of it.

(*Woman's Weekly*, 22 January 1949)

Occasionally these objects of female desire and stratagem are undeserving of the chase – rotters to the core. More often they reveal themselves as a 'Good Chap', the second most significant male role, 18 per cent. Who or what is a 'good chap'? Which virtues does he symbolise? Whereas pursuit-worthy males are always physically or materially attractive, or both, they may or may not manifest sterling qualities. No such ambiguities apply to a 'good chap' symbol of masculine integrity. He may not be handsome or financially dazzling, but he is reliable, responsible and trustworthy: he will never let a girl down. His hidden benefit is his utility value as latent hero – a man to fall back on when the more obvious candidate reveals himself a yob, a cad or a crook.

The role labelled 'Invisible Male', 15 per cent, emerged early as characteristic of the beauty pages. Conspicuous by their absence, these men were categorised and recorded as such in accordance with the sociological truism that social facts can be as significant through their absence as through their presence.

The 'Husband' emerged as the most ambivalent male image, characterised as 'good' or 'bad' in equal measure. Most often the 'baddies' were neglectful or philandering, whereas the 'goodies' were thoughtful and loving – and almost always well-heeled. No such ambivalence applied to 'Father', with only one 'bad dad' recorded. The remainder were idealisations of the 'good dad', a combination of natural parent and father figure, unfailing source of comfort and support.

The 'Bad Chap' was unequivocally damned. Often these blackguards were 'handsome baddies' – devilish charmers with hearts to match their raven locks. Others of the beastly breed included a few alarmingly aggressive males or 'ne'er-do-wells' – men who reneged on their striving, provider or protectionist roles. This stereotype of wickedness contrasts to the 'Protector', 4 per cent. Whatever the basis of the relationship between the female being protected and the protecting male, whether he was uncle or friend, the supplying of this service so dominated the role portrait that it was categorised as such.

Two further, opposing images are provided by 'Striving Male', 2 per cent and 'Artistic Male', 4 per cent. Given the sociological significance attached to American males as achievers (e.g. Parsons and Bales, 1955), the low incidence of striving suggests two possibilities. Either achievement norms are less prescriptive for British than American males, or – more likely – occupational and social status is already achieved by male characters prior to their appearance as 'success' symbols within the cult's messages. These heroes are busy being, not striving to be. As for the artist as hero, he is generally portrayed sympathetically, as a charming but somewhat feckless creature who requires female guidance or organisation. Amongst the 'other' male roles were 'Prince Consort', 'Inhuman Scientist', 'Older Man', 'Sporty Type' and 'Other Man'.

The dominant values and goals of womanhood

Closely linked to the social roles for both sexes which are presented by these weeklies are the aspirational goals that they set and the values they show as influencing their choice.[17]

Before discussing the highly normative nature of the values and goals found here – and expressed in terms of what women can, or should do – the distinction between them should be made clear. The term 'value' is used here to denote valued attributes of one's life-situation or behaviour facticity. The term 'goal' is used here to denote an end-state, desired outcome of a course of action. Both carry strong implications of the desirable – demonstrating their relevance to an earlier claim that women's magazines present the desirable as though it were the possible, and vice versa. If cultural norms are acquired and shared in this way by female members of the cult, the concept of 'goal' involves more individual and internal aspects. It implies action directed towards achieving a particular end or purpose, implying motivation which will help to bring about change in that direction (see, for example, Parsons, 1951).

Thus values point to routes within the female world and goals signal destinations or arrival points. Here the dual rule of women's magazines as potential – and potent – agents of secondary socialisation is apparent. They transmit the norms not only of the cult of femininity but also those that are believed to command the support of society as a whole.

Pilot analysis produced an extensive catechism of values – and a more restricted range of goals – which had been promulgated within the messages of the cult over this period. The four most dominant values were identified for each item analysed. New values which emerged were listed under 'other' and the total score aggregated to give the overall picture of dominant values shown in Table 3.5.

The dominant values of the cult of femininity

'Self-control' was the most frequent and visible value held up to females over this period – 26 per cent. No carefree abandoned femininity, no giggly girlishness here; instead self-control typified by self-

Table 3.5 Dominant values, all subjects, all titles, 1949–74 (%)

| | 1949/52/57 | | | 1962/67 | | | 1972/74 | | | 1949–74 | | | Total |
	W	WO	WW	W	WO[a]	WW	W	WO[b]	WW	W	WO	WW	
Self-control	28	29	28	25	23	26	27	17	20	28	24	26	26
Romantic love	16	22	10	23	14	9	16	20	12	18	19	10	16
Self-concept	16	10	13	12	18	12	13	12	15	14	13	13	13
Work	10	8	11	11	14	12	13	19	24	11	13	15	13
Friendship	4	6	10	5	6	9	4	5	6	4	6	9	6
Social control	8	9	7	5	3	5	7	5	7	6	6	7	6
Family life	5	5	3	5	9	7	7	8	3	6	7	4	6
Good looks	2	4	6	6	6	7	5	4	6	4	5	6	5
Wealth	5	2	7	6	1	4	5	4	5	5	2	5	4
Other	6	5	5	2	6	9	3	6	2	4	5	5	5
n	192	192	192	128	124	128	128	120	128	448	436	448	1332

[a] No beauty, one issue
[b] No beauty, two issues
n = 4 per item, 4 items per issue, 4 issues per year; W = Woman; WO = Woman's Own; WW = Woman's Weekly

discipline, calmness, courage, duty, fidelity, sacrifice, patience, responsibility, loyalty or submissiveness. Self-control was found most frequently and explicitly on the problem and beauty pages, the two most consistently prescriptive content areas. (Nonetheless, the degree to which social, as opposed to self, control is, or can be, self administered – and therefore by implication made a matter of individual choice – remains problematic.)

Within the cluster of values epitomising such control, those of duty and responsibility were particularly strong. Sociologists have commented on the significance of responsibility as definitional of female tasks, less so with duty (e.g. Oakley, 1974, 1982; Gavron, 1968). Duty was expressed dualistically here, as applying towards self and others. Towards the self it was associated with beauty admonitions against 'letting yourself go' – putting on weight or looking a mess, or sexual commandments 'not to let yourself go'. Towards others, duty was located primarily within the family and was personified by the roles of *dutiful* wife or mother (husbandly duty was both present and absent, as in the 'neglectful/bad husband' role). Duty towards society as a whole, in any sense of shared responsibility for the welfare of others, was notably missing from the individualistic ethic transmitted to British women during a period characterised by collectivist social policies and the growth of the welfare state.

'Romantic Love' was the second most dominant value, 16 per cent. Gathered under its banner were the pleasures of 'true love', 'romance', 'sexual and emotional fulfilment' – however definitions of these states changed or did not change between the 1950s and the 1970s. The negative instances of 'romantic love' were confined to attitudes and behaviours stemming from jealousy or adultery.

Two values, 'Self-concept' and 'Work', ranked equal third, 13 per cent. Here 'self-concept' denotes 'sense of self' or 'personal identity', and encompasses those aspects of femininity endorsed as important to woman's understanding and presentation of self. Certain classificatory problems arise from this definition. All the values shown in Table 3.5 arguably can contribute to a female's 'self-concept'. Nonetheless the aspects of selfhood specifically included here were self-confidence, individuality and independence which were positively evaluated, with rebelliousness, selfishness and anxiety being negatively so.

It follows that 'work' as a value can contribute either to a woman's internal self-concept or to her external occupational status and achievement or to both. Thus, ambition, initiative and work as an end in itself were all present. The extent to which limitations were placed on female ambition and achievement outside the domestic sphere has been shown by the dominant themes already discussed. Even if work as a value includes both paid and unpaid tasks, it is present only half as frequently as 'self-control'.

'Friendship', 'Social Control' and 'Family Life' were equally present, 6 per cent each. 'Family life' refers to the veneration of, and seeking after, all forms of affection between family members – parents, children and siblings. 'Social control' (as opposed to 'self-control') refers to the constraints imposed on individuals through conformity to prevailing cultural norms, such as consensus morality about what is or is not sexually permissible.

'Friendship' as a value is complex. It encompasses cultural ideals of reciprocity, generosity, understanding, kindness and forgiveness. Here the exchange nature of friendship, of giving and receiving, turns upon the giver's (friend's) expectation of return for goods or services rendered (see, e.g., Mauss, 1970). Such reciprocal expectations are applied to both heterosexual and female relationships here.

'Good Looks' as a value in and of itself was surprisingly underrepresented, 5 per cent; this is indicative of the extent to which 'self-control' and 'self-concept' are overridingly present on the beauty pages. The positive aspects of looking good included specific references to the merits of cleanliness and good health.

'Wealth' as a value was relatively insignificant, 4 per cent. Dramatised by symbols of power, property, fame or noble blood, its possession was most obvious in two content areas, fiction (especially *Woman's Weekly* serials) and features about 'real life' role models, most often successful entertainers. Generally the possession of wealth was valued highly – only occasionally does the 'poor little rich girl' theme creep in. Conversely, both thrift and minor extravagances also were endorsed. Yet perhaps in partial recognition of the unequal pay structure of the female labour force, a woman's possession or acquisition of wealth was contingent largely on the workings of fate; the 'good' marriage, the football pools win rather than on her own achievements during this period.

Finally, the 'Other' category, 5 per cent, included values such as wisdom, humour and hope.

The dominant goals of femininity

Content analysis provides one loud, clear message about the female goals presented to the woman's magazine audience during the 1950s, 1960s and early 1970s. They are tightly interrelated. What is sociologically interesting, and methodologically problematic, is their nonexclusivity. This interrelatedness suggests that the dominant themes purveyed by the women's media have a close internal consistency.

They join up, they overlap, and in so doing they confine as well as define the female world.

This is shown by Table 3.6. Mutually exclusive these goals are not. Many can be defined in terms of one another. 'Personal Happiness', for example, can be defined in terms of either 'Personal Achievement' or 'Happy Marriage/Family' or 'Male Finding/Keeping'. Methodologically, this is a positivist's nightmare; there are no tidy statistical knots to be tied. Sociologically, such contradictions are illuminating, within an exploratory study of this nature. What is clear is that these goals, however intermingled, reinforce the two strongest cultural themes manifest by these journals – those relating to the pursuit and consequences of love, and to the actions of the Self. The extent of such interconnectedness indicates the tightly interlocking – and homogeneous – nature of the symbolic order manufactured for, and marketed to, women.

The results of the content analysis for this period conclusively showed that 'Personal Happiness' was the goal of goals, 23 per cent. This end generally was realised through an emotional security based upon a 'happy', loving relationship with a man, or found within the family. Nowhere in these weeklies were the states of 'happy' or 'happiness' explicitly defined. In the cult's messages happiness exists or it does not. It is promulgated as part of a woman's obtainable existence, its possibility is rarely doubted because it is above all achievable.

Equally prominent as goals were 'Male Finding/Keeping' and 'Physical Attractiveness' – 16 per cent each. Given the extent of female folklore attached to possession of a male this incidence is relatively low. Over time guidelines for finding and keeping Him have altered. The nature of partnership is stressed and the emphasis changes, from the less closely shared experience, the complementary roles of the 1950s, to the shared family roles of the 1970s.

When we turn to the importance of narcissism within a woman's self-concept, 'physical attractiveness' as a goal is integral to the 'be more beautiful' theme. It is within the beauty pages that the prescriptions applied to all areas of female goal setting are particularly stringent, with no allowance for back-sliding.

The high value that society places on the family as an institution reflects in the 'Happy Marriage/Family' goal, 15 per cent. The keynote is one of harmony, and the blissful vision of family life is paramount. For long, the potential for conflict in unhappy marriages or families was minimised. For long, negotiation or manipulation were seen as preferable to confrontation as means to the happy-ever-after end.

The distinction between 'Personal Achievement' (13 per cent) and

Table 3.6 *Dominant goals, all subjects, all titles, 1949–74 (%)*

	1949/52/57			1962/67			1972/74			1949–74			Total
	W	WO	WW	W	WOᵃ	WW	W	WOᵇ	WW	W	WO	WW	
Personal happiness	24	26	20	27	22	17	19	24	27	23	25	21	23
Male finding/keeping	16	19	16	16	20	19	11	14	16	15	18	17	16
Physical attractiveness	15	15	17	17	16	18	16	14	17	16	15	17	16
Happy marriage/family	17	17	12	14	22	11	18	16	8	16	18	11	15
Personal achievement	11	10	18	11	11	19	13	11	12	12	10	17	13
Societal achievement	13	7	14	11	3	15	15	19	14	13	9	14	12
Social conformism	4	5	3	2	5	—	7	2	6	4	4	3	4
Other	—	1	—	2	1	1	1	—	—	1	1	0 (0.29)	1
n	144	144	144	96	90	96	96	93	96	336	327	336	999

ᵃ No beauty, two issues.
ᵇ No beauty, one issue.
n = 3 per item, 4 items per issue, 4 issues per year; W = *Woman*; WO = *Woman's Own*; WW = *Woman's Weekly*

'Societal Achievement' (12 per cent) requires clarification. The former relates to the self in terms of personal effort or emotional success in overcoming obstacles, such as physical infirmity, or achieving subjective ends within personal relationships. 'Societal achievement' involves more objective criteria, specifically the acquisition of status and monetary rewards associated with the world of work. As such it includes the attainment of economic security, material possessions, and – more rarely and recently – higher education.

Although 'Social Conformism' as a goal scored only 4 per cent, two aspects were significant: the notion that 'being the same as everyone else' is a reassuring and desirable state, coupled with strong injunctions towards 'niceness'. Not only is it 'nice' to be like everyone else, but also it is pleasant to be nice to inhabitants of that self-same cosy world.

Images of social class

What picture of social stratification do women's magazines present, either directly through the occupations portrayed, or indirectly through material symbols? Like all content messages, those of social class are both manifest and latent, intended and unintended. Thus if gender specifications are culturally prescribed and produced (see, e.g., Goffman, 1979), and femininity defined and confined within supportive, subordinate or complementary roles, what images of female social class derive from such recipes?

During the 1950s and 1960s a preponderance of secretaries, nurses, teachers, models, actresses and heiresses typified the non-domestic occupations that women's magazine writers assigned to females in both features and fiction. Whilst no direct mirroring of society can be imputed, this suggests a partial reflection of the level of female participation in service occupations during that period, and a distortion of the extent of pleasurable and prestigious occupations which are in fact open only to the privileged few. Only in the early 1970s did signs of occupational change appear. These later articles pointed to potential labour market choices which might allow females to determine their own status rather than accept male partner, or social class ascribed, life situation labels.

The findings of this study to do with social class imagery are subject to certain methodological shortcomings, but they do give us some information about a largely unexplored area of stratification – the female universe.[18] The three main categories of 'Upper', 'Middle' and 'Working' class shown in Table 3.7 are crude, their classification based on the presence or absence of two criteria – specified occupations and manifest status symbols.

Table 3.7 Social class membership, all subjects, all titles, 1949–74 (%)

	1949/52/57			1962/67			1972/74			1949–74			
	W	WO	WW	W	WO[a]	WW	W	WO[b]	WW	W	WO	WW	Total
Working class	4	2	6	—	10	—	—	14	—	2	8	3	4
Middle class	67	45	36	53	45	38	59	46	25	61	45	33	46
Upper class	6	4	6	—	—	12	3	3	9	3	3	9	5
'Consciously classless'	23	49	52	47	45	50	38	37	66	34	44	55	45
n	48	49[c]	50[c]	32	31	32	32	35[c]	32	112	115	114	341

[a] No beauty, two issues
[b] No beauty, one issue
[c] Working Class and Middle Class occupational roles in same item in *Woman's Own* 25 February 1949, *Woman's Weekly* 15 October 1949, 22 January 1949, *Woman's Own* 7 October 1974, 16 September 1972, 10 August 1974, 23 March 1974

n = open-ended; W = *Woman*; WO = *Woman's Own*; WW = *Woman's Weekly*

A fourth category, or stratum, was termed 'Consciously Classless'. This was identified on the basis of previous editorial experience, and confirmed by pilot analysis. Here the customary distinction of upper, middle and lower strata is insufficient in a context where collapsed boundaries and absent categories define the editorial approach to social differentiation (see Chapter 6). By omission or by inclusion, through an absence of the oppositional categories of upper and working class, or through the deliberate blurring or blending of class differences between women, these periodicals imply a classless female world. By incorporating aspects of uncertainty concerning status and income they perhaps reflect some wider ambiguities about female status assignment and class position – for example, the extent to which it is male-determined and related to paid or unpaid labour.

As Table 3.7 shows, where social class is attributed by occupation, the middle classes dominate, 46 per cent, with the working and upper classes barely represented, 4 and 5 per cent respectively. The editorial avoidance of social class – of different starting places in the race for success constituting a powerful factor affecting opportunity and achievement within the education and work worlds – also leaves unacknowledged its potential as a source of intra-female group rivalry or conflict. Given that female solidarity and unity is a first-order message of these journals it is perhaps unsurprising to find little basis for conflict between women (apart from battling over Him), however different their places in the wider social structure. Thus, fully 45 per cent of the sampled articles and stories revealed no specific, identifiable class image. They were 'consciously classless'.

The material symbols of status among the other 55 per cent were both prolific and unambiguous. These clarify the overt references to class situation, and show how class is imputed through images and symbols consistent with a given consumption style, or life-chance situation. Specific symbols are used to reinforce messages about ranking. Class boundaries may be blurred but status distinctions are crystal clear even when they are used as a contrived classlessness. In the symbolic sphere, as in the occupational one, this is achieved through the editorial juxtaposing or balancing of upper, middle or lower class emblems.

There is no ambiguity or messing about with the perks of the upper classes. They epitomise conspicuous display and consumption, and demonstrate a lavishly luxurious life-style in exotic or privileged locales. Accordingly, palaces, swimming pools, and servants proliferate, providing an aura of enviable existence – not just for the elite but also for the reader wanting to fantasise or identify. An early example of this Veblenesque (1970) scene-setting is given in 'Stormy Haven'

(*Woman's Weekly*, 26 January 1952) where a Middle Eastern setting provides the backdrop for expensive necklaces, white silk jackets, french milliners, cocktail parties and – eventually – a 'handsome marriage settlement'.

The wide range of statuses and occupations covered by 'middle-class' produced an equally prolific range of symbols. Typical of upper middle class spoils were the Rover car, champagne, luxury foreign holidays and castle hotel in 'The Swallows of San Fedora' (*Woman's Weekly*, 28 September 1974), or the Chelsea home, oriental rugs and child at boarding school in 'Return to a Dream' (*Woman's Own*, 21 July 1962). Symbols of the more ordinary and everyday lot typically were confined to lower middle-class domestic locations – the house on the 'estate', the housewifely chores within.

As for the working class, its rare appearance was reflected by a similar poverty of symbols. So few were they, when they emerged they imparted a certain self-conscious obviousness. For example, a highly successful and subsequently ennobled author, describing his humble origins in 'Sons and Mothers' (*Woman's Own*, 5 August 1967), refers to the shared house with no bathroom of his childhood – an image admissible as starting point, but not as final destination in the messages of the cult.

This chapter has explored the dominant themes, roles, social class images, values and goals that were mediated to the female audience by the three biggest selling women's weeklies in Britain from 1949 to 1974. It shows the dramatic – and continuing – dominance of marriage and the family within the messages endorsed by the high priestesses of the period. It reveals a disjunction between the social facts such as increased female participation in the labour force and their cultural reflection within the beliefs and practices of the cult. It also points to tension between individual and group norms, between traditional and emergent female roles, between what women's magazine words were saying and what women of many different kinds were doing. These contradictions are ones which are pursued in the next chapter, which looks at what women were doing and what women's magazines were saying during the 1970s.

4

From the 1970s to the 1980s: Change and Constancy in the Messages of the Cult

The 1970s were a decade of challenge for women, for women's magazines and for the cult of femininity. It found publishers and editors in Britain, in Europe and in America having to make new choices about the form and content of the messages carried by the women's press. This chapter looks first at the changes that were taking place in British society, in terms of social, economic and demographic change and in terms of women's changing attitudes towards themselves. It then looks at the major innovation which took place in the British market, the introduction of *Cosmopolitan* in 1972, and at the responses of American women's magazines to the 'women's movement'. It then goes on to explore the response of the three weeklies to these social changes and to the new forms of competition in the market (including increased competition from 'women's pages' in daily newspapers). It draws on the findings of an intensive study of them for the period 1975–8, and on a follow-up content analysis of issues published in 1979 and 1980 using the same framework of analysis discussed in the preceding chapter.

Demographic data and social change

Table 4.1 shows how the demographic structure of the female population of the United Kingdom changed over the post-war period, with particular reference to changes in its age structure. As the table suggests, the numbers of women were not evenly distributed through all age groups; this is in part because of the 'bulges' first of the immediate post-war baby boom, and then of the boom that began with a sudden upturn in the birthrate in 1955 and peaked in 1964. The table shows that the total number of 16–29-year-olds increased from a low of 4.8 million in 1961 to 5.8 million in 1981. The first boom 16-year-olds began to arrive by 1961 and the second boom 16-year-olds by 1971. Both cohorts have been working their way through the system ever since. Yet the number of those in the 30–59 middle range age bracket was remarkably stable over this thirty-year period, although within that bracket, the balance between older and younger women has varied as the first baby boom has fed its way through. It is the over-60s who have shown the most dramatic numerical change. Over the post-war period their numbers rose from 4.6 to 6.6 million, an increase of almost one-half in women of pensionable age.

Table 4.1   Age structure of the female population, United Kingdom (millions)

	16–29	30–59	60 and over
1951	4.9	10.8	4.6
1961	4.8	10.8	5.3
1971	5.4	10.0	6.3
1981	5.8	10.2	6.6

Source: Social Trends, no. 11

During the 1970s widespread changes took place amongst this population, in almost every area of female life – changes reflected slowly, then quickly, in women's magazines. For example, the 1970s saw the reversal of the post-war trend of increasingly early marriage. The proportion of girls in their teens and early twenties who got married fell. In addition the total number of marriages fell from 1971 to 1977, although there was a slight upturn in 1978. There was a sharp fall in the number of first marriages (both partners marrying for the first time), but this was offset to some extent by the rising numbers of re-marriages. Re-marriages amounted to 20 per cent of all marriages in 1971, and to 34 per cent in 1978. This in turn reflected the higher incidence of divorce following the coming into force of the Divorce Reform Act 1969: in 1971, some 80,000 divorces were granted in Great Britain; in 1979 the figure was 147,000.[1]

Despite all this, marriage in the 1970s continued to be popular, with 95 per cent of women and 91 per cent of men having married by the age of 40, while an increasing number of couples lived together before marriage: Nearly 20 per cent of women who married in the late 1970s had previously lived with the men who became their husbands – double the number who had done so early in the decade.[2]

Marriage at a later age has contributed to the fact of many women postponing the starting of a family – but they then have their last child at an earlier age than their grandmothers did when family sizes were on average somewhat larger. Families have been getting smaller, as well as children coming along later. In 1971 of all married couples where the head of the family was under 30, 37 per cent had no dependent children, while 54 per cent had only one child or two. In 1979 the corresponding figures were 39 and 56 per cent respectively.[3] Smaller families and a short period of child-bearing tended to reduce the length of time during which there was a dependent child in the home.

The increased number of divorced women with children was a major factor in the rise of the number of one-parent families to an estimated 920,000 by 1980.[4] The great majority of these families are headed by females, but for many the one-parent status is temporary: present evidence suggests that divorced women with children are equally likely to remarry as women without them.

The implications of these demographic changes have been succinctly summarised in a Central Policy Review Staff (1980: 103) report:

1. Women now have far greater expectations and freedom of choice about their lives. They have increased control over their fertility by means of the greater availability of effective contraception, and abortion; they are better educated and have higher expectations than ever before, as higher proportions stay on after minimum school-leaving age and go on to further education. Greater numbers choose to cohabit outside marriage and a range of work opportunities outside the home has opened up for them;

2. Social stigma has diminished for mothers who leave young – even very young – children in the care of others while they work from choice rather than necessity;

3. One direct consequence is that most women of working age are economically active as well as looking after a family;

4. Within many families the wife's income is an important element in the total family income (and expectations);

5. Over a million children are being brought up in one-parent families headed by a woman – nine-tenths of all one-parent families.

Although women were entering the labour force in the 1970s in greater numbers than ever before, and with greater numbers of wives and mothers amongst their ranks, they were not necessarily being educated better for their tasks. While it is true that the number of girls leaving school and entering full-time further or higher education rose – from 72,000 in 1970/71 to 98,600 in 1978/79 in England and Wales – they were still a very small proportion of all female school-leavers – 24.1 per cent in 1970/71, and 25.9 per cent in 1978/79. Of those continuing their education, the daughters of professional or managerial fathers were markedly over-represented.[5]

Whatever their differing educational backgrounds, the increased recruitment of women to the labour force in the 1970s increased the female contingent to 39.4 per cent of the total labour force. Of particular significance were the expanding numbers of married women entering full and part-time employment: the economic activity rate of married women, which had been only 21.7 per cent in 1951, increased to 42.3 per cent in 1971 and 51.3 per cent in 1979. For married women in the 35–54 age range the economic activity rate in 1978 reached a massive 69.9 per cent.[6]

All these demographic, social and economic changes had important implications for the way in which women saw themselves. As consumers, as partners, as adherents to – or rebels against – the cult of femininity, women were asserting themselves in new ways. New patterns and new preferences emerged in their personal and work relationships, and consumer choices of household and leisure goods.

Yet there were other equally significant – if less tangible – mechanisms of change at work. These were to be found in the realms of cultural values and sexual politics wherein women acquired their self-concepts in the process of defining their femininity to themselves. It is difficult to evaluate the extent of the social revolution fuelled by the 'women's movement' which began in America (Freeman, 1975) in the mid-1960s and made the trans-Atlantic crossing towards the end of that decade (Banks, 1981, Coote and Campbell, 1982), or to measure what its effect has been on British women other than the committed feminists. Yet public discussion of the issues shared by 'the movement', on the political and psychological planes of 'equality' or 'personhood', or on the pragmatic level of equal pay or adequate child-care, can hardly have been overlooked by all but the most dedicated of male – or female – ostriches.

Perhaps the effect of all this on the women of Britain was more covert than overt in comparison with the militancy and media coverage of the 'movement' in the United States. Yet by helping to give these issues visibility, the women's movement in Britain did play a part in leading women of different ages, classes and life chance situations to question the assumptions by which they had previously conducted their lives (see Oakley, 1982). For many, the possibility of choice was being raised, the possibility of free will rather than determinism: a woman might choose where she 'belonged', as well as make the appropriate choices to arrive at her chosen destination. This was something new on the feminine agenda, and it appeared there for the first time in the 1970s.

What part did women's magazines play in all this? Most editors busily grappling with the problems of how to target audiences more tightly, or prevent circulation decline, were aware that some changes were taking place outside their offices, but often lacked any systematic information about their nature or extent. All the transformations described above can be seen with hindsight from the vantage point of the 1980s. The high priestesses to the cult of femininity, sitting in the hot seat of their editors' chairs in the 1970s, had the problem of making sense of the flickering signals that they were receiving from the outside world. They then had the problem of deciding how much or how little of those signals to respond to in their messages – a problem which is explored more fully in the next chapter.

The mid-1970s: all change?
The years 1975–8 marked a turning-point in the ways in which the women's magazines of many industrial societies defined the cult of femininity to their readers. In Britain, for example, the journal which first dared to discuss unambiguously a range of sexual topics never before seen on the pages of a woman's magazine was the monthly, *Cosmopolitan*. From 1972 in Britain as from 1965 in America, it offered its readers this new form of psycho-social-sexual support and 'service'. Dismissed at first as a passing phenomenon devoted to the exploitation of women – and men – its full impact on the women's press can only be ascertained historically and cross-culturally as part of the world-wide family of eighteen *Cosmo* editions. In retrospect it can be seen to have had an impact on the majority of its sister women's magazines in Britain during the 1970s, comparable to that of the *Sun* on Fleet Street popular newspapers in the 1960s.

Although classified as a 'young woman's' magazine whose readership peaks in the 15–24 age group, almost half its readers are aged between 25 and 54, and its ripples of influence have reached all but the most traditional of the cult's oracles.* In the mid-1970s it was beckoning to its followers old and new with cover lines such as these: 'How to Keep Your Marriage as Sensuous and Exciting as It Was on Day One', 'Are You from the Black North? Learn how Other Northern Girls Make it in the Soft South', 'Understanding and Overcoming

* NRS, Jan.–Dec. 1981.

Guilt' (February 1975); or 'What is Happening to the Pound in Your Purse – 16 girls tell How They Fight Inflation', as well as 'What To Do About a Stingy Man', and 'How Male Dominated Are You?' (October 1975). While in 1978, *Cosmo*'s readers were cautioned: 'How is Your Marriage? Recognise the Danger Signals Before It's Too Late', 'The Pill – No One Can Decide for You but Here are the Latest Findings' (February 1978); or 'Let it Rip! How to Make Anger *Work* for You', and 'After the Test-Tube Baby, the Carbon Copy Baby – Could Cloning Ever Affect you?' (October, 1978).[7]

In bombarding its readers with cover messages such as these British *Cosmo* was following in part the lead of its mother edition but adapting them to more local needs. In the mid-1970s the cover of American *Cosmo* was telling its readers about the backlash to the women's movement which was already surfacing in America as early as 1975: 'The Total Woman – the Amazing, *Counter-trend* Best Seller That's Telling What Many Women Really Want! Can You Believe It!' (a reference to the writing of anti-feminist views put forward in the book of that name), as well as 'How Normal Are You Sexually?' (a quiz) and 'A Book That Can Really Change Your Life – *Don't Say Yes When You Want to Say No*', while addressing itself to more serious topics such as:

WOMEN'S LEGAL RIGHTS 1975: A REPORT
The law is at last beginning to treat women as responsible human beings, deserving of equal pay and equals rights. Here is a fact-filled report on the legal changes – and the legal shortcomings that still exist – in five areas that affect every woman's life.

(*Cosmopolitan*, USA, October 1975)

The five areas concerned were: 'When I Get Married', 'When I Want An Abortion', 'When I Want a Divorce', 'When I am Raped', and 'When I Go to Work' – in that order.

If American *Cosmopolitan* was the first women's magazine to get truly involved in the sexual revolution, other leading American monthlies were not slow to tune in, or respond to, the battle cries emmanating from the vocal American feminists. *Redbook* magazine began its closer dialogue with the audience by pioneering a new form of audience involvement – a questionnaire survey printed in its October 1974 issue. To the astonishment of its editors 100,000 responses were received to the question, 'How do you really feel about sex?'. Such was the wealth of material received that it was eventually entrusted to academic researchers at the Institute for Sex Research at Indiana University (generally, but inaccurately, referred to as the Kinsey Institute – and where Kinsey's research into female sexuality had been confined to a sample of fewer than 8000 women). Some of the later and more political responses of *Redbook*'s editors to their perceptions of development and transformations within the female audience are dealt with in Chapter 5.

The most outstanding example of women's magazine responsiveness to the women's movement anywhere in the world, came with the founding of a new American monthly journal, *Ms.* magazine, in 1972. This was a brave, bold and political act on the part of a few talented and committed feminists who undertook to raise the money, write the message, and sell the advertisement space themselves. The publisher, Patricia Carbine, who was a former executive of *McCalls* and *Look* magazines, said of her move from glossy magazine publishing to the do-it-yourself variety 'I think it is called putting your money where your mouth is.'

Ms. – which is written by women, as well as published and financially controlled by women – has doubled its circulation in eight years from 250,000 to 500,000 in 1981.* It has consciously sought to change the female world, not simply to reflect it: 'It is the one magazine that is both an intake mechanism for women seeking change, and a constant in the lives of women who are leading that change. It is the only magazine to sell neither home and romance fantasy (as the traditional women's magazines do) nor career fantasy and the mythical ability to "have it all" (as the newer women's magazines do).' These claims – published as an editorial credo at the start of a 1980 report on *Ms.* readers, 'The "new" Woman of the 80s' – show that the magazine, like its publishers and journalists, is still not afraid to put its mouth where its money is, in front of its intended audience – and advertisers.

These then were some of the changes that were happening to women's magazines in America and Britain as editors responded to their perceptions of social and cultural changes. Editors of monthlies were targeting their messages towards more tightly defined client/ target groups in the 1970s. What then were the editors of the more generalist mass women's weeklies doing at this time?

1975–8: *What was changing, and what was staying the same on Woman's Own, Woman and Woman's Weekly?*

By 1974, at the end of the earlier period of analysis, it was evident that the editorial approach of the three women's weeklies was becoming less protective, and the editorial tone of voice less authoritarian. In line with what was happening to women's magazines in other 'post-industrial' societies, first slowly, then quickly, the frontiers of the

---

* *Ms.* Magazine, USA.

permissible were pushed back; the range of topics that could be talked about widened, and became less inhibited by tradition or taboo. The pretence that certain 'things' did not happen – particularly to do with sexual behaviour – was replaced by a new frankness concerning what women could, and did, do. In the case of the three weeklies, whose further content analysis is discussed below, some of these newly visible questions had been treated experimentally towards the end of the 1960s. For example, in 1967 *Woman* tentatively examined 'Sex Before Marriage', (*Woman*, 11 February 1967) through the authoritative voice of its problem page editor, Evelyn Home. *Woman's Own* confronted a range of issues in its 'encyclopedia' of eight pull-out supplements on 'The Mystery of Being a Woman'. These asked questions about a woman's place in society, and her attitudes towards her family, her sexuality, her job and her*self*, stating the dilemma: 'Does she want real equality, freedom, and a say in the destiny of mankind, or just to be cherished and loved by a man?' (*Woman's Own*, 20 September 1969).

When editors discovered that they were not stoned in the streets for their daring, experimentation continued, culminating in the new trends which had emerged by 1974. These were: greater sexual explicitness, representing a wider range of the permissible; acceptance of, and hard nosed advice about, women's home and paid work roles; discussion of forms of partnership alternatives to marriage; and increased coverage of social policy issues affecting women.

The emergence of these trends in the message reflected a wider awareness on the part of editors and their staffs that for many a reader aspects of her life were changing, or were not necessarily the same as those of the woman next door. As the homogeneity of the audience continued to fragment, the problem of how much – or how little – of these changes to reflect became more critical. More fundamentally, how 'generalist' could a generalist weekly for women aged 'from 16 to 60' continue to be when confronted with changes on such a scale? For that matter, which particular age, interest, 'lifestyle', 'attitudinal' or 'aspirational' client/target group should a specialist monthly direct its messages at?

Here changes in the messages were most apparent on *Woman's Own* and *Woman*. *Woman's Weekly* continued to maintain its traditional definitions of femininity, its traditional editorial mix of cookery, knitting and escapist fiction which did not trouble its readers with those aspects of a changing world for women which they were assumed not to want to know about. Because of these strong signals of changes from its sister weeklies, an intensive study was carried out for the period between 1975 and 1978. This involved reading every issue and monitoring them for signs of changes in the roles, goals and values that they purveyed to the female audience.

The pace-setter was *Woman's Own*. Under a campaigning editor it led the way for the weeklies in showing journalists, managers – and perhaps, readers – that a 'mass' weekly caught in a downward circulation trend could expand its feminine agenda to include social policy issues such as equal pay and personal issues such as living together without benefit of wedlock; it could still cover the 'traditional' female (and advertisement) concerns such as cookery and fashion – while fulfilling its commercial goals of increasing circulation and profits in the process.

In the 1970s, there was more to the message than content alone. In Britain, quite literally there was more. There were more promotional 'free gifts' of plastic cookery and knitting aids, food and beauty samples in these weeklies – inset by hand in their multi-millions, to boost sales. On the creative side too there was more to the message than content alone. A more reader participatory approach was adopted – which was in sharp contrast to the earlier tradition of handing down the message from on high. The old forms of audience feedback provided by readers' letters and 'real readers' stories continued, but new ways of involving the audience and finding out what they were thinking and doing were also tried. Prompted by concern to discover just how their audiences were responding in terms of attitudes and behaviour towards topics such as marriage, sex or child-care, questionnaires were printed in the pages of the magazines themselves. The response letters were analysed and reported back on, initiating a more structured form of two-way communication between the high priestesses and their scribes on the one hand and the followers of the cult on the other. Alternatively special surveys were commissioned and the findings reported back in the magazine in 'follow-up' features. *Woman's Own* was the first to break this new ground. In 1975, it announced 'Your Marriage – the Truth at Last'. The conclusions arising from 10,000 questionnaire responses analysed by sociologist Robert Chester included:

. . . One wife in 10 would marry a different man if she could . . . childless marriage is a happier marriage . . . and working wives mean happier marriages . . .

(*Woman's Own*, 19 April 1975)

Following in this 'tell us what you think' path, *Woman* published the results of a commissioned survey, 'Marriage 1978 Style', based on a sample of 836 women, which claimed:

. . . one in 10 wives are unsatisfied in bed . . . nearly a quarter of husbands have hit their wives . . . only one in three women think faithfulness important in marriage.

(*Woman*, 21 January 1978)

Other women's magazines outside the analysis sample also employed the questionnaire/survey approach to sounding out audience attitudes and behaviour. Their survey responses suggest continued adherence to traditional ideals and values associated with marriage, notwithstanding some shift in attitudes towards sex. *Woman's Realm* published the results of a questionnaire on 'You and Your Marriage':

The good news is that nearly two thirds of you are happily married. But what *makes* a happy marriage? In our survey, six almost equally rated factors stood out: the ability to discuss problems, a sense of humour, sexual compatibility, friendship, acceptance of each other as individuals, and affection.

(*Woman's Realm*, 18 November 1978)

All these examples concern 'adult' women's weeklies – yet the same story is told by the young women's monthly, *Honey*. It probed the aspirations and expectations of its readers through a national survey of women aged 18–30, and men aged 20–34:

Ms Pankhurst must be turning in her grave and Ms Greer could decide to pack her bags and go home. For what you truly want, Ms 1978, is a husband, a home (preferably detached and in the country) and two children. Marriage thrives. You're extraordinarily like your mothers, and more than a little like your grandmothers. You don't much want to be a tycoon or a surgeon. You fancy a job which won't interfere with family life too much. And you are not exactly leaping from bed to bed with ever-increasing cries of satisfaction.

Men approve of this. And quite a lot of their views are, if anything, a bit more pro-Liberated Woman than yours.

(*Honey*, October 1978)

The findings of this *Honey* survey underline the strength and tenacity of the cultural ideals contained within 'Getting and Keeping Your Man' and attaching to married (as opposed to living together) partnership which persist within adherents to the cult. It also suggests that these ideals are not confined to girls and women. Romantic love leading to marriage (its ultimate fulfilment being the nuclear, two-parent, two-child family) is still accepted as the aspirational norm for both sexes.

The more hard-hitting, investigative side to this interactive approach to the audience was illustrated in campaigning articles dealing with social policy, economic and consumerist issues that were affecting women. It was in the mid-1970s that *Woman's Own* launched its 'At Your Service' section, 'the page that helps you get to grips with today's world'. Often these features were linked to questionnaires previously printed in the magazine. One such was:

HOW INFLATION IS HITTING OUR HOMES
People are usually even more reluctant to talk about their income than about
their love lives, yet more than 4000 *Woman's Own* readers replied to our July
Questionnaire about take-home pay and housekeeping money. . . . We conducted this survey in association with the National Consumer Council and the
results are being presented this week at their national congress attended by
Denis Healey, Chancellor of the Exchequer and holder of the country's
purse-strings.

. . . Husbands pass less than half their pay rises to their wives for housekeeping. . . . One in five mothers had had no increase in a year of 25 per cent
inflation. . . . Two in five wives are now finding it difficult to keep up with
food prices. . . . One in three of the poorest wives, on £10 a week or less, had
had no increase. . . .

(*Woman's Own*, 20 September 1975)

In January 1976, at the start of the year when the equal pay
legislation came into effect, this weekly published a questionnaire,
'Do we get a fair deal at Work?' for readers to complete, covering such
aspects as hours of work, reasons for working, marital status, trade
union membership and take-home pay (*Woman's Own*, 10 January
1976). Two months later it published the findings from a representative sample of the five thousand readers who responded:

NO, YOU ARE NOT GETTING WHAT THE LAW SAYS YOU
SHOULD
Women and Work – Our National Survey Results: 5000 *Woman's Own*
Readers Have Their Say
. . . One in ten women is still paid less for doing the same job as a man. The
Equal Pay Act is useless to most working women. Three out of five working
women have a job because the family needs the money. 14 per cent are the
main breadwinners. One-third of mothers at home want to go back to work
but can't find child-care. Three-quarters of husbands of full-time working
wives do less than their fair share of housework. One-quarter of working
mothers with 5 to 11-year-old children leave them without adult care during
the holidays. . . .

(*Woman's Own*, 20 March 1976)

This campaigning approach to social policy issues affecting female
readers was returned to again and again during the second half of the
challenging 1970s. In March 1978, *Woman's Own* tackled the question of equal taxation in its pages, in an open letter to the Chancellor of
the Exchequer:

DEAR MR HEALEY,
I hear you don't believe that the mass of women in this country object to the
way the income-tax system treats them so differently from men, because you
have received so few letters on the subject. I think our readers are about to
change that. Yours sincerely, Deidre Sanders (*Woman's Own*, 25 March 1978)

Three months later the magazine was able to report back:

WE'RE WINNING

More wives to get their own tax rebates. The insulting wording on tax forms 'If you are a married woman living with your husband he should complete the form as if it were addressed to him' is on the way out. The Government is now looking at ways of overhauling the tax system completely to put an end to all discrimination against women.

(*Woman's Own*, 17 June 1978)

Apart from the questionnaire or survey forms of women's magazine journalist–audience dialogue, another new way of involving readers was inviting them to participate in 'phone-ins', when their questions were answered on subjects which ranged from job finding to horoscopes. This expansion of 'reader service' also provided insights into audience attitudes and concerns as editors responded through their pages in attempting to anticipate, or at least follow, the moods and movements, of the audience.

The content analysis: *Woman*, *Woman's Own* and *Woman's Weekly*, 1979–80

It was important to ask, however, if the changes that had emerged towards the end of the earlier – 1949–74 – period of analysis were surface changes, or if there had been changes at the deeper level of the cult's message concerning definitions of the female role. Were the mid-1970s in fact the turning point which they appeared to be for the cult's adherents – or were they more of a crossroad? Were there deeper structures within the beliefs and practices of the cult – as a social institution or as a set of values – which were less mutable and more resistant to change? For example, while the signs and symbols of 'feminine dress' may swing with fashion, through their fabric or colour they rarely lose their power to signal the female gender role (cf. Barthes, 1967; Sahlins, 1976).

Only an updated content analysis using the original framework would permit any answer to such questions, or provide any basis for comparison with the earlier findings. The same framework as previously was applied to the same subject categories within randomly sampled issues, and the same advantages and constraints that applied to the analysis of the preceding chapter, also apply here. In the event, the findings of the 1979 analysis were so significantly different from those at the beginning of the 1970s – or those which had been aggregated across twenty-five years – that a further 'checking' of content analysis was done for 1980. This confirmed the 1979 findings.

The changing and unchanging messages of the four subject categories over three decades
The process of discovering what women's magazines had been telling women over the post-war period about the kinds of women they could or should be began with the selection of four subject categories – features, problem pages, beauty and fiction. These had been chosen for their potential to mirror editorial responses to – or the ignoring of – signals of social change, and to allow the magazines to speak for themselves in terms of the dominant themes, roles, values and goals which they conveyed. The broad pictures of change and constancy between these categories for each magazine are given below by way of introduction to the major findings of the 1979 and 1980 analyses which follow. All these examples are taken from randomly sampled issues of the magazines concerned.

Features – the first to change
On *Woman* and *Woman's Own* the importance attached to features increased significantly during the 1960s and into the 1970s, as was shown by the increased numbers of pages that were given to them. It was the features pages which reflected the growing concern of these journals with social issues and which first tackled a more 'realistic' approach to sexual behaviour and 'hard' subjects dealing with social policy issues such as inadequate housing, child-care, equal pay and taxation. On *Woman's Weekly*, features were never so important, and 'famed for its fiction', 'famed for its knitting' continued to proclaim its editorial priorities on the cover.

In the course of expanding the subject matter of the features pages, one regular standby that had flourished in the 1950s and 1960s passed away unmourned. Notable because of its intensely bossy, prescriptive character, these were the weekly columns of the philosopher kings and queens who offered parables of behavioural guidance based upon anecdotal or autobiographical illuminations. On *Woman* and *Woman's Own* these columnists were named: Beverley Nichols, Godfrey Winn, John Deane Potter, Monica Dickens. On *Woman's Weekly*, throughout the period of this study, anonymity was and is preferred by 'The Man Who Sees'. Until the mid-1960s this wise, reassuring father figure was portrayed in sketches – pipe in hand or mouth, casually leaning on a mantelpiece. Later, only a head drawing appeared, positioned alongside a 'mood' picture showing a tranquil mountain stream or a flowering country garden. Why did *Woman's Weekly* choose a male persona as the mouthpiece of moral guidance? Did this reinforce the traditional view of men as knowing and women as listening? No editor of *Woman's Weekly* was prepared to confirm or deny the sex of the writer of 'The Man Who Sees' – although others claimed that the column had for many years been written by a woman.

The much wider range of topics included in the features pages on *Woman* and *Woman's Own* from the early 1970s – the inclusion of consumerist and social policy issues – is demonstrated by these randomly sampled titles and intros from *Woman* over the years:

Features – titles and intros, **Woman** *1949–80*

1949   *Your Home Through His Eyes* – It's the fear everyone has of losing glamour in a young man's eyes that is apt to make for miserable embarrassment on that first visit [to her parents]. (12 February 1949)

1952   *The Romantic Life of Moira Shearer* – The real life story of Moira Shearer's progress from an adventurous childhood to success as a ballerina, film star, wife and mother-to-be makes a romance more fascinating than any drama she has acted on the screen or mimed on the ballet stage. Here . . . *Woman* introduces you to a warmly alive girl whose deepest fulfilment, despite the fact of her international success as a star, has come through a truly happy love. (15 March 1952)

1957   *This Thing Called Fascination* – Is it sorcery . . . spellbinding? No . . . fascination comes from the faith that every woman can have in her own woman's powers. (28 December 1957)

1962   *Kisses Won't Cook the Dinner* – Starry-eyed moments still count but this happy pair know there's more to marriage than honeymoon excitement. (29 June 1962)

1967   continuing . . . *Andrew, My Son*, Barbara Watson's moving story of how she built a future for her spastic child, *A Time for Parting*, 'You don't just want him to go, do you?' The doctor shouted 'You're prepared to make any excuse to keep him tied to your apron strings.' (2 December 1967)

1972   *How Can You Want Me?* – Any woman who has ever felt the foundations of her marriage shake beneath her will understand this cry from the heart. (13 May 1972)

1974   *Never Had It So Good!* – Divorced, with three dependent children, Jean Colin spent years fighting an army of niggling officials for the bare necessities of life. This week we begin her own incredible account of life 'on the welfare'. (31 August 1974)

1979   *What's So Cool About Ice Cream?* – We spend £250 million a
       year on ices and get through six litres each. But did you
       know more than half the contents of your carton could be
       air? And how many of us can tell a real dairy ice cream from a
       palm oil pretender? This week Actionwoman asks what's so
       nice about ice cream and discovers the costliest cornet in
       Britain. (25 August 1979)

1980   *Communities versus the Cuts*
       When the spending had to stop . . .
       Government cut backs started to bite. Remote figures on
       balance sheets turned into reality: nurseries and schools
       faced closure, and even lollipop men became a luxury. But
       some communities have found ways to fight back, as Gay
       Search discovered. (26 June 1980)

Problem page – *farewell to 'tut tut' and 'taboo'*
There have been dramatic changes in the manner of talking as well as
what can be talked about in the 'agony' columns of all three weeklies.
The changes began first and most dramatically on *Woman* and
Woman's Own in the early 1970s and accelerated thereafter. There was
less overt direction and more discussion about how a woman should
regard herself, her life, her partner, her children – or her lover. The
tone of voice became less formal, more colloquial over the years – less
of a diktat and more of a dialogue. The friend and surrogate sister had
become less carping, less all-knowing, more tolerant and more questioning. The stern moralising, sexual ambiguity and lofty detachment
of an earlier era had been replaced by a more direct, no nonsense
approach (cf. Makins, 1975; Kurtz, 1981).

   Some measure of the degree of change in the topics dealt with by the
problem pages in all three weeklies is given by the titles that refer to
the main letters displayed on the Mary Grant pages of *Woman's Own*
from 1949 to 1980:[8]

*Problem Page 'Lead' Letter Titles, **Woman's Own** 1949–80*
1949   The Woman with a Past (22 April 1949)

1952   I Can't Go On Like This (20 March 1952)

1957   The Danger of Marriage Without Love (11 April 1957)

1962   They Say He's Too Old For Me (3 March 1962)

1967   Mother Won't Let Us Go On Holiday Together (5 August
       1967)

1972   Suddenly I No Longer Want To Be A Virgin (16 September 1972)

1974   This 'Dressing Up' Will Turn Me Against Him (11 May 1974)

1979   I'm Fed Up With His Laziness and Demands for Sex (29 September 1979)

1980   I Am Being forced to Choose between My Boyfriend and my Children (30 August 1980)

Fiction – 'realism' versus 'escapism'
A great deal changed in the short story scenarios of *Woman* and *Woman's Own* – and not a lot in the serials of *Woman's Weekly* – during the 1970s. The short stories which formerly harped on the theme of getting and keeping your man were playing not one but several different tunes. Change was slow at first and in some cases considerable lag developed between what was being reflected by the fiction departments and what appeared elsewhere in the magazines.[9] Then almost overnight in the mid-1970s scenarios, roles, goals and themes changed out of all recognition. Heroines ceased to be heroines and heroes ceased to be heroes, not just in the text but in the illustrations: 'What I wanted was people who looked more like people in the street – men with jeans and Zapata moustaches, not finely chiselled jaws,' an editor recalled.

This fictional revolution contrasts sharply to the marginally changing world of *Woman's Weekly* serials. Across the years their titles and intros evoke the constancy of certain, classic romantic themes: mysterious but magnetic strangers, sudden but difficult inheritances, forbidding but imposing mansions – above all, the lure of love. For this reason they provide an example of constancy in the otherwise shifting definitions of the cult:

Fiction – Serial Titles and Intros, **Woman's Weekly** *1949–80*

1949   *The Young Amanda* – Take someone who has never known affection. Take someone who has always had a dream of belonging, give someone like Amanda a fortune – and see what happens! (15 October 1949)

1952   *The Frost and the Flower* – This is all that the average girl asks – a little happiness that belongs to herself, a heart to keep and a home to tend. (24 May 1952)

1957   *Island of the Heart* – Picture yourself in such a situation as this; suddenly a great deal of money and power in your hands – and yourself never quite sure whether you are loved for yourself or your possessions. It would be difficult, dangerous and puzzling. (14 September 1957)

1962   *La Vie en Rose* – Not for nothing was he nicknamed 'Lion', this brilliant, arrogant guardian of theirs! Swiftly, irrevocably he had taken possession of Viola's heart. (22 September 1962)

1967   *The Master of Torra* – The house, Torra, seemed part of the rocks on which it stood, washed by the Atlantic seas. It was a splendid, awesome place and it claimed Alison's love at first sight. If only she could have come here without deception, without the need to act out a lie. (25 February 1967)

1972   *Amalfi Love Story* – He fitted into no preconceived pattern – this man Christopher. He challenged then comforted . . . provoked then pacified. He was unpredictable and unforgettable. (1 April 1972)

1974   *All Season's Song* – Anna had never thought of herself as a schemer, even with the best of motives, yet here she was taking the law into her own hands, and waiting with quaking heart for retribution to strike. (1 June 1974)

1979   *Stowaway* – Womanlike, she wanted him to know that another man desired her. But Yves' reactions were never predictable, and she was soon regretting her impulse to provoke him! (14 April 1979)

1980   *Calling Doctor Stanton* – Seeing Alex again, warming to his reassuring presence, brought the memories flooding back. Memories of a time when she was one half whole, a woman in love. Did he hope that those happy days might return? (1 November 1980)

Beauty – trying harder than ever

The triumph of nurture over nature continued to be ever possible in the messages of the cult. With the application of a little more effort, self control or starvation – and a few step-by-step instructions – every female could become that bit more beautiful. The message of dedication to the pursuit of perfection of face and form continued unabated from the 1940s to the 1980s. Beauty is an important advertisement as well as editorial category for *Woman* and *Woman's Own*, which have always given more pages to this subject than *Woman's*

Weekly. In part this is because *Woman's Weekly* did not switch to four-colour printing until 1967, and in part it reflects the fact that it has an older readership profile than the other two. For these reasons, only *Woman* and *Woman's Own* provide the evidence of maximum constancy and minimum change in the basic message concerning the business of becoming more beautiful in fulfilling the norms of the cult of femininity.

Beauty Titles and Intros, **Woman** *and* **Woman's Own** *1949–80*

1949   *What Price Beauty?* – Helen Temple's Beauty Parlour . . . the art of beauty buying lies in learning how to choose the products which suit both you and your purse. (*Woman*, 3 September 1949)

1952   Diana Day gives you Rhonda Fleming's *10 Tips for Lovely Hair* – Here attractive screen star Rhonda Fleming, considered by Hollywood hairdressers to be one of the twelve women with the most beautiful hair in the world, tells you how to keep your hair looking lustrous and glamorous. (*Woman's Own*, 7 February 1952)

1957   *Beauty for Busy People* – These are hectic, thrilling days – parties and all the extra work that goes with them, the pleasures of entertaining and present giving crowd in on top of our normal lives. But being attractive is a fulltime business and no amount of merry panic should be allowed to play havoc with a girl's good looks . . . Helen Temple. (*Woman*, 28 December 1957)

1962   *20 Fabulous Hairstyles and How To Do Them* – 20 answers to your hair problems. (*Woman's Own*, 3 March 1962)

1967   *The Millionaire Look – For You* – Ever longed to escape to a Beauty Farm? To be re-shaped, re-vitalised made to feel like new? Ever longed to sample the glamour, the luxury, the pure pleasure of knowing a team of experts is concerned with *your* well-being; *your* looks? (*Woman*, 26 August 1967)

1972   *How to Slim in the Winter* – You don't have to give up eating all the good things. Follow our healthy diet plan and you'll lose weight, says Diana Day. (*Woman's Own*, 21 October 1972 – issue containing free gift of 5 Sucron sachets)

1974   *Why Don't They . . . improve cosmetic packaging?* – Make beauty products easier to use and handle? We're talking about the manufacturers, of course. In Beauty Box we're sitting ducks for moans about cosmetics. Those we mention are top favourites with our moaners. They don't want to stop using them, but does it have to be such a battle to get at them? Helen Temple. (*Woman*, 23 March 1974)

1979   *Can You Spot the Difference?* – One face cost nearly £7 – the other more than five times as much. (*Woman's Own*, 3 November 1979)

1980   *Working Away at Beauty* – On duty, a girl's got to look good whatever her working conditions – whether its walking a beat, flying the world, or just standing still! That's why Vickie Bramwell has been getting down to business . . . (*Woman*, 31 May 1980)

The dominant themes of the three most widely read British women's weeklies, 1979–80

What changed and what remained the same between the 1949–74 and 1979–80 content analyses? Which themes, roles, goals, values and images of social class emerged as dominant at the beginning of the 1980s? Did 'Getting and Keeping Your Man' remain as theme of themes, goal of goals – the definitive statement of femininity fulfilled? On the surface, it did not. From an aggregated total of 59 per cent across all three titles throughout the 1950s, 1960s and early 1970s (see Table 3.1), the overt supremacy and incidence of this theme was reduced to a mere 12 per cent as is shown in Table 4.2.

The diminution of this theme as overt prescription is deceptive however. Did it really topple as the ruling ideology of the female world, or did it simply go underground to flower in other forms and other places? For an answer to this we must turn to what emerged as the newly dominant theme in women's magazines in 1979 and 1980. This shows the extent to which female self-determination had become the new editorial norm – with the temporary subversion, but not the exclusion, of Man as goal.

'*Self-help*' – '*new*' *theme for the '*new*' woman?*

A considerable shift in the definitional maxims of the cult of femininity promulgated by these weeklies is suggested by the main finding of the later analyses. The new theme of themes which emerged was 'Self-help: Overcoming Misfortune', 36 per cent, backed up by its second variant of 'Achieving Perfection', 11 per cent. Together they accounted for almost half the dominant themes shown in Table 4.2 whereas during the earlier analysis period, this was only a total of 13 per cent. This amplification of the self-determination theme was as

Table 4.2 Dominant themes, all subjects[a], all titles, 1979–80 (%)

	W	1979–80 WO	WW	Total
Self-help: overcoming misfortune	35	32	40	36
Getting and keeping your man	11	10	15	12
Self-help: achieving perfection	13	14	6	11
The happy family	9	12	12	11
Heart versus head	12	8	12	10
The working wife is a good wife	9	13	7	10
Success equals happiness	11	8	8	9
Female state mysterious	—	—	—	—
Gilded youth	—	—	—	—
Other	—	3	—	1
n	24	24	24	72

[a] Excluding beauty

n = 1 per item, 3 items per issue, 4 issues per year;

W = *Woman*; WO = *Woman's Own*; WW = *Woman's Weekly*

evident in the fiction scenarios of *Woman's Weekly* serials as it was in the features pages of *Woman* and *Woman's Own*, which week after week competed with each other to find ever more moving or inspiring 'real life stories' of women who 'overcame' or 'achieved'. What did this mean? Did it represent a surface shift in emphasis from dependence on others (men?) to a more self-sufficient female self-concept, or suggest a deeper shift from outer to inner directedness?[10]

These questions relate to the wider origins of individualistic values within the world of women, which have a lengthy history and pre-date the emphasis of the Victorians on improving one's lot through one's own efforts – whichever sex one happened to be. The prior impact of the Protestant ethic on our cultural heritage is relevant – in particular the emphasis it places on the self as responsible for achieving its own destiny within the framework of the Elect (see e.g. Weber, 1958). The extent to which Puritanism's long shadow has persisted from the sixteenth to the twentieth centuries as both a surface and a subterranean value structure (e.g. Hill, 1975) raises certain questions as to its presence and pre-eminence within these weeklies at the start of the 1980s. These concern the extent to which such values are particular to, or more pronounced within, the women's media as opposed to other forms: does this medium merely supply one set of mirrors which magnify their message?

Does the increased incidence of this theme in 1979–80 suggest that the impact of the social, cultural and economic changes of the 1970s on the deeper value structures of the cult of femininity may have been less than revolutionary – and historically transitory? Whatever the degree of change that did or did not occur, much longer lines of cultural connectedness can be traced. These values which emphasise self-determination are related to Calvinism and Puritanism, as well as to Victorian individualism and self-help (see Weber 1958; Bercovitch, 1975; Smiles, 1958, respectively), and the extent to which this heritage survives and flourishes into the 1980s is illustrated below.

'Self-help: Overcoming Misfortune'

The business of *becoming* a woman, of *learning* how to be female, involves learning how to 'cope' and socialisation into the Smilesian ethic of helping yourself to cope with or overcome obstacles or 'disasters' begins at an early age. The solution of self-help cropped up in the later fiction scenarios more than it had done in the earlier ones, which had emphasised the pursuit of love, and a male. A short story showed the pervasiveness of its influence in a tale entitled 'Scrappy's Miracle' (*Woman*, 31 May 1980). This tells the story of a 10-year-old girl whose Labrador dog goes blind. The problem this creates for the girl and her family is resolved when she finds a guide dog for her blind dog – thereby overcoming her, and the dog's, misfortune.

The emphasis given to self-help in triumphing over tragedy – the TOT formula of women's magazine journalism – was linked increasingly to more topical stories. Just as the national newspapers were becoming more like magazines (women's?) by emphasising feature content in the face of television's greater news immediacy, so were women's magazines attempting to narrow the gap between the timeless and the topical on their pages.[11] An example of this, and of the theme of overcoming misfortune through self-help, concerns a wife whose husband was involved in a famous trial, and it was accompanied by the emergence of a new goal – justice:

I'LL NEVER FORGIVE, NEVER FORGET
A chance remark brought an end to my life as an unknown housewife, and led to my husband, George, lining up in the dock at the Old Bailey. Even after his acquittal the agony continued, with the loss of my much-wanted baby . . by Wendy Deakin, the wife of the fourth man in the Jeremy Thorpe trial
(*Woman's Own*, 3 November 1979)

A further topical 'news' story on the theme of self (and technological) help was 'Our Miracle Called Louise', wherein 'the parents of the first test-tube baby tell the exclusive story of the events leading up to the birth of their extraordinary child'. This particular account relates a variety of misfortunes and suggests that hope is ever-present in the ethic of self-help:

Everything was against John and Lesley Brown – her broken home, his broken marriage – yet they built up a loving relationship together. . . . They had no money, no high-powered connections, but they were chosen to take part in an historical experiment

(*Woman*, 13 October 1979)

Both these time-tested formula favourites come from the features department, the subject category which in many ways has responded the most to the impact of social change, whilst simultaneously perpetuating the 'old standbys'. Another way the inspirational elements in the self-help theme are communicated is by holding up exemplary women who symbolise the sterling qualities of that ethic:

THE COURAGE OF RUTH LINDSEY
Confined to a wheelchair for fifteen years, she could easily have allowed it to trap her. Instead, Ruth's life is an adventure. She rejected the safety of a special hospital to live on her own, and she has travelled the world to compete in international sports. Last year she had a baby, but refused to marry the father. Christine Sparks went to find out why this young woman has defied disability and convention to keep her independence

(*Woman*, 31 May 1980)

'Self-help: Achieving Perfection'
When we turn to the pursuit of perfection, the other dimension of the pre-eminent self-help theme, we find new and old ways of achieving the ever-higher standards set for an ever-more perfect female state. Learning to be a woman still involves teaching yourself to *improve* on your standards of femininity and *achieve* a better performance in all your womanly roles.

The setting of high norms of female achievement remains, and the relentless pursuit of excellence persists. Within the beauty pages, for example, there are no dramatic changes in the message between the 1950s and the 1980s, apart from increased emphasis on staying slim, trim – and latterly – healthy through diet and exercise. Fashions in emphasis on make-up shift from cheekbones to eyelids or lips, but the aim of perfection is forever fixed. It's all there as before – same rituals, same goals, same squeaky clean hair:

BE A SEXY SUMMER BEAUTY
Going topless may be on the increase on sunny beaches everywhere, but you don't have to bare all to be sexy. The secret is to have a figure that shows your loving care . . . satiny skin, squeaky clean hair and irridescent vitality. Beauty Editor Jan Collier shows you how.

(*Woman's Own*, 5 July 1980)

A new variation of the self-help/achievement theme is the pursuit, not of perfection, but of the goal of earning money while doing something you like:

MIND YOUR OWN BUSINESS
Lynne Alderson wanted to earn some money, but not to go out to work. Carol Stephens felt the same. So they pooled resources and talents to set up their own business at home. Deborah Evans has been talking to them and to four other housewives who have established successful partnerships, to find out how and why they set up their own businesses.

(*Woman's Own*, 30 August 1980)

The injunction to improve one's self and one's lot took new directions as well as taking on a new importance in women's magazines at this time. The impact upon family relationships of changing patterns of family life and of structural and demographic changes, such as more living-together young couples and more long-lived widowed grandmothers, provided another platform:

Woman's Own Family Living and Loving
Our counselling team – Mary Grant, Dr Michael Smith and Claire Rayner – have, in this three-part series, been discussing the fundamental problems facing families today and the ways they can be solved.
This Week: THE BUFFER GENERATION
If you have lively, opinionated teenagers on the one hand and maybe an ageing parent to look after on the other, it's not surprising that you and your husband begin to feel flattened between their demands. And it's at this time of your lives you're looking forwards to building a new relationship, now that your children will soon be off your hands. To hang on to yours and your partner's share of life, there are some practical steps you need to take, says Claire Rayner

(*Woman's Own*, 21 April 1979)

Although the primacy of a happy family as both cultural and emotional ideal persists as a sub-theme, here the dominant theme is one of a woman's powers of perfectability through self-help: in this case learning to put self first and not always others in her role as wife and mother. This putting of self before others was a novel suggestion for the cult's wives and mothers, but one which still places the primary responsibility for achieving that state – and family stability – upon the females concerned.

'Getting and Keeping Your Man'
Did the major finding of the later analyses – the dramatically heightened emphasis on the Self – mark the death of the earlier emphasis on romantic love in these weeklies? 'Getting and Keeping Your Man' accounted for 59 per cent of dominant themes between 1949 and 1974, yet this theme accounted for only 12 per cent of cases in 1979–80. This

evident change of emphasis should not be misinterpreted. What emerged was the extent to which 'getting', if not 'keeping' a male remains a powerful, second-order message in the pages of these weeklies. Getting 'Him' is still quintessential to femininity, and still definitional of full membership in the cult – as is shown by its dominance as a sub-theme in Table 4.3 below. This poses two sets of opposing norms for women in fulfilling their gender role. Through women's magazines' juxtaposing of messages about romantic love focused on another, and self-help and self-determination applied to everything else, emotion and reason are opposed; and the dualistic nature of femininity so defined is exposed. This reveals an emotional–rational dichotomy within the female culture which can contribute to, and reinforce, tensions between a traditional or an emergent female role structure – or within the minds of women themselves.

Table 4.3   Sub-themes, all subjects, all titles, 1979–80 (%)

| | 1979–80 | | | |
	W	*WO*	*WW*	*Total*
Getting and keeping your man	35	24	31	30
Self-help: overcoming misfortune	7	24	17	16
Heart versus head	26	8	14	16
The working wife is a good wife	18	15	15	16
The happy family	—	11	23	12
Self-help: achieving perfection	14	18	—	11
Female state mysterious	—	—	—	—
Gilded youth	—	—	—	—
Success equals happiness	—	—	—	—
Other	—	—	—	—
n	14	17	12	43

n = open-ended; *W* = *Woman*; *WO* = *Woman's Own*; *WW* = *Woman's Weekly*

What significance have these opposing signals within the 1980s versions of 'getting and keeping your man'? Previously, importance was attached to the power of love as a *means*, as much as an end. Earlier versions proferred love as a means of overcoming problems of social class differences, geographical separation, interfering relatives, uncooperative employers – love, the social mechanism supreme, resolved all.

Contributing to the force of this belief within the cult was the long
tradition of the glorification of woman as romantic heroines in fiction
(Cecil, 1974; Anderson, 1974) or as love goddesses in the cinema
(McLuhan, 1967; Haskell, 1974). Neither research nor 'realism' have
recorded any reduction in its import (cf. Gorer, 1955; O'Brien, 1976);
all the evidence points to its remaining a cultural ideal. As such it has a
long and continuing tradition within the women's press: 'the quintessential women's magazine story, like the classical novel, is structured
around the pursuit of romantic love' (Fowler, 1979, p. 106).

To what extent does love's power as a means *and* an end idealise,
legitimise, or call into question the sexual division of labour? Such is
love's strength and persistence within the symbolic order of femininity that neither the biological liberation of effective contraception,
nor the economic liberation of increased female earning capacity has
diminished its social power. The extent to which finding a male, and
forming an enduring bond of attachment, persisted as integral to a
woman's self-concept – a valued and cherished goal to be sought – is
demonstrated by its incidence as a sub-theme: 30 per cent of those that
emerged in the features, fiction and problem pages.

The extent to which the 'snare him, and staple him to the bedpost'
approach to male–female relationships had become something of an
anachronism – at least in its overt form – by the early 1980s, is
demonstrated by this array of stereotypes:

LEAP INTO THE NEW YEAR WITH LOVE
Miss 1880 fluttered her eyelashes behind a fan.
Miss 1950 learned to cook like his Mother.
Miss 1960 hitched her mini higher, and the Seventies woman rang and asked
him out.
What should Miss 1980 do to get her man in Leap Year?
(*Woman's Own*, 16 February 1980)

Ways to stalk your prey, net your catch, pin down the brute follow.
Other examples of 'traditional' approaches to processes of attraction
and attachment are to be found – particularly in the realm of fiction.
The lure of romance lingers on, never far beneath the surface –
particularly in the serials of *Woman's Weekly*. One such concerns the
recently orphaned Hilary, who helps herself over the misfortune of
losing her parents in a car crash, by taking on a job as personal
assistant to a film producer in Rome:

THE BOUGHS OF INNOCENCE
She tried to pin labels on him . . . 'Rich Playboy' . . . 'Lady Killer' . . . but
somehow they didn't fit. In that coolly quizzical glance lay some secret he was
not yet ready to share, and Hilary, new to the intrigues and intricacies of

film-making felt it safer to enquire no further. After all, their paths would probably never again cross.

(Woman's Weekly, 12/19 May 1980)

As for Hilary's job specification, the caring subordinate female role remains: 'The girl's job was to look after Henry, although she'd taken on the pelargoniums as a pleasant sideline'.

During 1979–80, the cultural ideal of romantic love crowned by happy-ever-after marriage took on new, distinctly hybrid forms from the pure bred flower of yesteryear; only selective parts of the ideal were retained. Take the case of this short story:

IF EVER I SHOULD LOSE YOU
Love wasn't only in their caresses and togetherness; it was in the way he poured the wine for her and selected the music she wanted to hear. Love surrounded them in these precious, stolen moments.

(Woman's Own, 21 April 1979)

Here the lovers concerned are married – but to other people. Here the value of self-control is called upon to maintain the twin ideals of romantic love (at a cost), and family life (to be upheld, whatever). Here is a case of role reversal of a rather different sort. Here the unfaithful wife is the good wife and mother – the dutiful one; and the bad wife is her lover's – a neurotic, selfish, incompetent woman. Similarly, the unfaithful husband was the goodie – the dutiful one; the deceived husband was the baddie – an unsuccessful, incompetent drifter. What was different and what was not different was that love should legitimise this new code of getting, but *not* keeping, a man married to another. 'Such happiness ought to be allowed', Sue thought, 'when the quality of love is this good, permission ought to be given.' Another new story approach was the acceptance of divorce as a legitimate solution to a 'difficult' marriage:

SOMETHING TO CELEBRATE
How often do you get divorced, lose your umbrella and meet the love of your life, all in one day?

(Woman, 26 July 1980)

Not very often is the short answer. This is an atypical and novel version of 'getting and keeping a man' – whilst in the process of divorcing the old one.

Again 'The Happy Family'
Despite the considerable expansion of the range of permitted male–female relationships which were subsumed under 'getting (if not keeping) a man', a related theme remained remarkably constant: the

veneration of family life. The enduring nature, continuing value and desirability of the family as a social institution remained a cultural ideal throughout the 1970s – as did marriage itself. Evidence for this is found above in the rising number who ignore Dr Johnson's dictum about remarriage as 'the triumph of hope over experience' and do just that; and by the audience surveys of the mid-1970s which showed that traditional aspirations persisted in this area, even if expectations did not.

When we look at the 1979–80 findings we see that the ideal of building and maintaining a firm family structure is still to the fore. Tables 4.2 and 4.3 show that 'The Happy Family' was present as a dominant and sub-theme, 11 per cent and 11 per cent, respectively. Examples from this period indicate how resistant to change are messages on the stability and sanctity of the family unit in an urban, technological and uncertain world. One such was:

THE TURNING POINT
Gilbert had a penchant for drink, Will kept a mistress in town, and Fred – well, Fred was her husband and, most of the time, he didn't actually do anything . . . Perhaps that was the trouble.

(Woman's Own, 2 February 1980

The plot unfolds with bored wife Lucy, mother of a 14-year-old daughter, dreaming dreams of moving to her own garden flat on the other side of town after fifteen years of marriage to the faithful Fred. One night Fred comes home and turns the tables on her, confronting her with the possibility of *his* moving out because they obviously both are bored. Lucy panics, terrified at the prospect, cries, burns the dinner. But all is well . . . Fred reveals it was a test. Really, he adores her; and they cuddle in the kitchen as the happy family is preserved.

Another short story shows how everything changes but nothing changes in the search for relationships between men and women. Everything changes in the sense that the search is now extended outside marriage, nothing changes in that the bonds of marriage and family life are still stronger than the ties of passion.

MIRAGE
She belonged to this rich and beautiful oriental world, where people were only too grateful for each new day and where love – like a pattern of light on a bolt of silk – could shift and change and perhaps disappear altogether.

(Woman's Own, 30 August 1980)

This tale involves a businessman who meets a glamorous blonde on a trip to the Far East. He fears he's falling in love, but leaves her at the airport to return home to his 'ageing wife and discontented children'. Yet even this dramatic departure from the familiar melody, this finding but not keeping the partner of the opposite sex, can still deliver a powerful latent theme which reinforces the sanctity of the happy family as taking precedence over the fleeting affair.

The happiest family of all

The strength of editorial beliefs in the 'pulling power' of the royal family is evidenced by the frequency and inevitability with which every milestone in the happiest family of all is featured on the covers, and celebrated inside the pages, of these weeklies which were once known generically as the 'knit your own royal family' journals. This belief was reinforced in August 1981, when the 'Charles and Di' wedding issues of *Woman* and *Woman's Own* sold out.

If the content of royal stories remains remarkably the same, with minimal additions and deletions to the cast across thirty years, have there been changes in the editorial tone of voice addressed to the British royal family? Is it perhaps more analytical, critical or political when chronicling royal personalities and events? There is nothing in the 1980s to match the breathless tones of 'Crawfie', the first 'inside the Palace' confidante, whose royal governess recollections increased the sales of *Woman's Own* in the early 1950s with such series as one on Princess Elizabeth (4 October 1951–29 November 1951) and another on Princess Margaret – (25 September 1952–27 November 1952).

In August 1980, *Woman* (like *Woman's Own* and *Woman's Weekly*) published a special souvenir edition in celebration of the Queen Mother's eightieth birthday with a picture of the Queen Mother on the cover and a testimonial from Prince Charles inside:

MY PERFECT GRANNY
Ever since I can remember, my grandmother has been the most wonderful example of fun, laughter, warmth, infinite security and exquisite taste . . . one of those rare people whose touch can turn everything into gold . . . bringing comfort and happiness by her presence or making any house she lives in a haven of cosiness and character. She is a figure of love and affection to young and old alike . . .

(*Woman*, 2 August 1980)

Like so much royal 'copy' in British popular newspapers and periodicals the tone of the text implies – even when it is written by a royal hand – that here is everyone's favourite granny: a woman above reproach, a pearl who symbolises all that is good, loveable and enduring in *all* of our family lives.

'Heart Versus Head'

The increased incidence of this theme underlines the switch of emphasis from the relentless pursuit of romance to the equally imperative pursuit of self-realisation. In 1979–80 the 'Heart Versus Head' theme had reasserted itself as a force in the female world. At 10 per cent it ranked close to 'the happy family', and made woman herself responsible for her own actions. This was a new variation on an old melody. The tug of emotion versus reason, of heart versus head looms large, camouflaging the more covert injunction to find – and (try?) to hold on to – a man. As before, this conflict predominantly revolves around the perils of love or sexual attraction. For example, this theme continued to crop up in the hospital corridors of power so familiar to readers of *Woman's Weekly*:

> Continuing Janet Ferguson's Heart-warming Romance Set in a Great Teaching Hospital
> THE CARING HEART
> Off duty, I'd found it all too easy to respond to this charming, good-looking man. Who wouldn't? I wondered. But Guy Fenall, back in his white coat, exacting, demanding, was a very different proposition. . . . No liberties to be taken here!
>
> (*Woman's Weekly*, 17/24 May 1980)

The professional background of the heroine, Jill, is emphasised: she is the adopted daughter of a doctor, sister of a GP and now is attracted to Guy Fenall a registrar of 'St. Mildred's, the London Teaching Hospital'. So far, so familiar . . . the unexpected twist that gives this tale the *Woman's Weekly* imprint of social change is that before she met the dashing registrar, Jill had been engaged to another, who had broken it off because 'he'd run into an old girl friend and, though she was married, he knew he still loved her'. Five years earlier, not even an ex-fiancé would or could have expressed his love for a married woman in the pages of this journal.

The trend manifest in the fiction pages – away from the breast-beating ladies of yesteryear to the headscratching sisters of today – is also to be found in the problem pages. 'Think about it' is still coun-selled as the first step towards problem solution. So even when a woman may have rushed in with her heart – or her libido – she can use her mind or her will to sort out the real or potential pitfalls in her family, work or sexual relationships. In 'A tale of two women' Vir-ginia Ironside ('Don't just sit there worrying! Share your problems') writes in *Woman* about a reader who complains 'My man friend and I worked in the same office for eighteen months and though I knew he was married he led me to believe. . . .' What he had led her to believe was that his marriage was over, until one day his wife turned up at the office showing everyone pictures of their happy family. 'This is a cautionary tale, and one I often hear', muses Virginia Ironside (*Woman*, 31 May 1980).

Woman's Own problem page editor, Angela Williams, deals with a lady whose head is ruling her heart when she asks: 'Is it safe?' This childless, 51-year-old divorcee, talks about meeting a 53-year-old widower 'who wants to make love to me. . . . Neither of us is interested in marriage – we're both too fond of our independence.' What is interesting about this letter compared with those of earlier years is neither its question nor its straightforward reply advising 'take precautions' (*Woman's Own*, 2 February 1980). What is notable is the fact that sex for the over-50s is no longer taboo; nor is sex for sex's sake. Even more remarkable is the way in which the *Woman's Weekly* advice column has responded to perceptions of change, while still keeping a wary eye on its older readership. It published a letter from a widow of 65 who asked whether or not she should accept a marriage proposal from 'a professional man twenty years younger' – to which the answer was a qualified 'yes' (*Woman's Weekly*, 22 November 1980); as well as another from a 69-year-old who complained that her 75-year-old husband 'still wants to make love three or four times a week' (*Woman's Weekly*, 7 September 1980).

'The Working Wife is a Good Wife'
The qualitative change of working wives, their transformation from bad to good was first manifested at the end of the earlier period of analysis. This trend was confirmed by the 1979–80 analysis, where this theme occurred in 10 per cent of cases. There was not a single instance of 'bad' working wives or mothers to be found. Editorial recognition of the problems posed by paid work outside the home for those with young children produced several articles filled with practical suggestions, but few as campaigning as this one:

SCHOOL HOLIDAYS WORKING MOTHERS DREAD
Fair care for children and a fair deal for mothers. That was our campaign for working mothers last year. And with an election in view, politicians fell over themselves to offer encouragement to Britain's four million working mums. What happened? Sadly, disgracefully – NOTHING MUCH. But the campaign goes on. Judith Bubbay reports on developments and ways for mums to help themselves. And experts will man our phone-in with practical advice and lists of schemes around the country.

(*Woman's Own*, 5 April 1980)

This confrontation approach was new. Although the helping hand was familiar, the emphasis on reader participation accompanied by affirmative political action marked a significant development in women's magazines' approach to social policy issues. There are no false heroics here about female responsibility to maintain the stability of family life, nor the faintest whiff of the maternal deprivation thesis

(Bowlby, 1951). Instead there is individual support offered to readers at the phone-in level, while on the wider political stage, *Woman's Own* lobbies the Prime Minister.[12]

'Success Equals Happiness'

The increased emphasis on the Self, and on achieving and overcoming through one's own efforts, was mediated in part through the increased visibility of the success theme, some 9 per cent compared with the earlier 1 per cent. However, an alternative explanation lies with the increased number of features woven around this theme as *Woman* and *Woman's Own* vied with each other to publish ever more telling revelations about ever bigger names – a succession of the rich, the famous and the powerful – of both sexes. Since by their nature elite groups are small in number, sometimes lesser players were featured as well: fifty-two issues a year require a taxing number of 'big names' to find for the star treatment.

Yet, the glitter of fame, money, social or professional status was not always purveyed as entirely covetable. There were several instances where worldly success was not equated with happiness; these were recorded under this theme as negative instances of it. An example of this less adulatory, more questioning approach is given in a story that stresses the hard work and grinding practice necessary to get to the top as a tennis star:

'I WANT TO WIN AND WIN'
Martina Navratilova, stony-faced Ladies' Champion for the past two years, is the world's worst loser. 'Tennis', she snaps, 'It's all I do.'
(*Woman's Own*, 5 July 1980)

Not only were the weeklies competing with each other for 'exclusive' rights to a celebrity's 'intimate' story, they were also competing with newspapers. A multiple mirroring process was taking place, in which newspapers were becoming more like magazines while magazines were attempting to become more topical in the daily paper sense. This produced some novel subject matter on the pages of the women's weeklies:

THE PAGE 3 GIRLS REVEAL ALL
They earn the salaries of top executives, appear daily in the national press and look sexy first thing in the morning – they're the Page 3 pin-ups. But do they simply loll around sun-kissed beaches and cash in on their curves or earn every penny through hard work? Mike Cable found out what life is really like for these sex symbols. He spoke to the girls who have been featured on Page 3 and they make a clean breast of it.
(*Woman*, 8 December 1979)

This story went on to suggest that what the British male has admired, 'no doubt almost as many women have quietly envied'. It continued, '. . . and yet as a young lady who takes off her clothes for a living, her love life turns out to be surprisingly mundane' (p. 26). What this passage suggests is that while the carriers of the cult's messages and some of their surface aspects may have changed, the deeper symbols and structures of feminine membership remain: evidence of physical charms and a love-life.

'Female State Mysterious' and 'Gilded Youth' were themes that had appeared in the earlier analysis which did not appear in the later one. One possible interpretation of this is that images of newly independent women, out in the world asserting themselves, or busy choosing new rules, roles and relationships, were not so concerned to be coy about themselves or retiring about their preferences. Another explanation could be that these three weeklies have come to terms with their status as 'adult women's' magazines and stopped overtly chasing the younger end of the market: the social, cultural and economic changes that had an impact on women's lives during the 1970s were not confined to the younger age group. The freedom to strive, to achieve, and to choose which is embedded in the self-help ethic is no longer confined to a few, late teen or pre-marital years; the technology of contraception and the expanding female labour market of the 1970s saw to that.

The old/new female roles
The extent of change and constancy in the messages of the cult is nowhere more evident than when we look at the carriers of those messages, the female role players. The extent to which overt change conceals covert durability of the archetypal feminine roles is revealed through the findings of the 1979–80 analysis, shown in Table 4.4.

As before, no limit was imposed on the numbers of roles that could be recorded for a single item. Given the standards of competence and excellence which our culture, and women's magazines, lay down for women – super cook, creative decorator, brilliant budgeter, loving mother, understanding wife, efficient office cog, sensual delight – is this surprising?

A careful examination of the pages of any women's magazine today will show how the feminine repertoire of roles has expanded. Yet if we ask which two roles outnumbered all others in the 1979 and 1980 analysis, we find again that it was the traditional ones of 'Wife', 19 per cent, and 'Mother', 21 per cent, as compared with 18 and 11 per cent in the earlier periods. This evidence of constancy and much increased emphasis on the maternal role in fact conceals a substantial shift in the definitions of both roles, allowing for greater diversity and choice. One significant social and economic factor that contributed to this has been discussed above: the emergence of the working wife or mother as an acceptable – desirable, even – member of society, no longer stereotyped as neglectful of her ill-fed husband or 'latchkey' children.

The second shift of significance concerns the transformation of previously unmentionable versions of wife and mother, such as divorcees or single mothers, into females to whom no pejorative status was attached. Again, this process of conferring visibility and legitimacy on roles and statuses that were entirely taboo until the late 1960s emerged first as 'hard reality' in the social issues probed by the features pages. The second stage of this breakthrough occurred when these 'new' role definitions and alternatives surfaced on the 'soft escapism' of the fiction pages.

Putting them on the feminine agenda produced transformations. For example, the previously censured unmarried mother became the to-be-praised single female parent, perhaps reflecting a wider cultural or an eventual matter-of-fact acceptance.[13] The phenomenon of increased numbers of women bringing up children on their own, whether or not they were married at the time of the birth, reflected amongst other things the changing family structures and higher divorce and remarriage rates discussed above.

Table 4.4 Dominant female roles, all subjects, all titles, 1979–80 (%)

	W	1979–80 WO	WW	Total
Mother	20	21	21	21
Wife	20	24	11	19
Careerist	13	14	13	13
Beautifier	13	12	11	12
Independent female	13	16	2	10
Daughter/sister	8	5	15	9
Decent lady	4	2	16	7
Marriage fixated	3	3	6	4
Girl-friend	3	—	5	3
Other	3	3	—	2
n	62	58	62	182

W = Woman; WO = Woman's Own; WW = Woman's Weekly

Four other roles were numerically significant. These were the 'Beautifier', the 'Daughter/Sister', the 'Careerist' and the 'Independent Female'. The continued appearance of the beautifier, 12 per cent, was perhaps predictable. How did the beautifier of the 1980s compare with her sister or mother of the 1960s or 1950s? In many ways her role was the most resistant to social change. Throughout the thirty-one years spanned by analysis the goals, values and central theme of 'be more beautiful' remain remarkably constant. Only the rituals change. Emphasis shifts from lips to eyes to cheeks to hair to legs – as the step-by-step solutions to a more perfectly presented face and figure are set out week by week. Narcissus remains the god of the beauty pages, and it is at this shrine dedicated to the self that the cult's adherents continue to worship – mirror in hand.

The 'Careerist' on the other hand, 13 per cent, has been revived and remodelled. In 1980, she crops up in fictional scenarios where previously the range of female occupations was confined to secretaries, nurses, or bewildered heiresses, the extent of whose ambitions were the bosses, doctors and landowners who their heads told them to resist but their hearts urged them to ensnare. Some of the most interesting examples of this transformation, this acceptance of the working girl with occupational ambitions, are found in the pages of *Woman's Weekly*. The jobs these working heroines apply for and get are often out of the ordinary – personal assistant to a film producer, winner of a fashion designer competition.

A new role category emerged in the 1979–80 analysis, that of the 'Independent Female', 10 per cent. This assertive, questing and questioning female was to be found helping herself to cope with life and love, work and play – if not on her own terms, then in accordance with a negotiated, not a dictated, settlement. These newly visible, newly identified independent ladies included several unmarried mothers, several women going on holiday alone – often to 'get over' a man – and a collection of widows, divorcees, and even a few deserted and self-sufficient wives.

The persistence of the familial bond and the 'Daughter/Sister' role, 9 per cent, as significant reflects the primary importance of 'wife' and 'mother' and suggests the subterranean persistence of 'the happy family' as an ideal state to be striven for, an institution to be returned to whatever structural changes it accommodates. Freeing the female audience from an exclusive focus on their domestic roles in no way devalues the importance of the family, where home still provides the stage where women play all their starring roles except that of wage or salary earner.

The old/new male roles

Once again the findings from the 1979–80 analysis shown in Table 4.5 demonstrate that despite the new emphasis on female self-determination, the male roles that were dominant were substantively the same as during the earlier period: desirable males and husbands are still the most frequently portrayed. In 1979–80, 'Desirable Male', 19 per cent, and 'Husband', 22 per cent, compared with 24 and 12 per cent respectively in 1949–74. What did this suggest? Were men becoming more attractive as friends, lovers and husbands to the self-helping, independent female? New characterisations of desirable men and husbands good and bad appeared alongside old tried and true favourites. Employers continued to be highly desirable males, their charm exuded a heady mixture of power, authority and sexual attraction. Owners were, if anything, even more desirable. Landowners, hotel-owners, mill-owners and shipping line-owners – these were the manly roles defined as desirable for readers of *Woman's Weekly* serials. In the other two weeklies, husbands took on newly visible tasks or activities – as helpers around the house, or as good but unfaithful dads. Even ex-husbands appeared sometimes, even in the guise of the divorced male seeking short-term sex as solace.

More consistent with the findings from the earlier period was the fact that a girl's best friend is still frequently her father. The 'Father' role, 13 per cent (9 per cent previously), is generally portrayed

Table 4.5   Dominant male roles, all subjects, all titles, 1979–80 (%)

| | | 1979–80 | | |
	W	WO	WW	Total
Husband	21	32	15	22
Desirable male	16	20	22	19
Invisible male	14	20	15	16
Father	10	14	15	13
Good chap	14	5	21	13
Bad chap	11	7	6	8
Protector	2	—	6	4
Artistic male	4	2	—	2
Other	6	—	—	2
Striving male	2	—	—	1
n	51	41	53	145

n = open-ended; *W* = *Woman*; *WO* = *Woman's Own*; *WW* = *Woman's Weekly* positively as supportive protector. Once again, the 'Good Chap', 13 per cent was the preferred model, and appeared almost twice as frequently as the 'Bad Chap', 8 per cent, as compared with 18 and 7 per cent before. While within the world of beauty, the 'Invisible Male', 16 per cent, continued to be conspicuous by his absence. At the altar of adornment he is neither made an explicit goal, nor has he any role to play.

What was interesting was the constancy of these masculine images – no dramatically new one asserted itself. There was no sign whatsoever of any masculine equivalent of the newly emergent 'independent female'. This was presumably because males were never anything else in the traditional division of labour and status embedded in the messages of the cult?

The old/new values

Does the major finding of an overall shift in editorial emphasis during the period 1979–80 towards greater self-realisation, self-determination and the presentation of a more independent and assertive femininity suggest a shift in the value structure of the cult? Or does it merely reflect the economic fact of less female dependence on the male? Perhaps this value shift implies a male in the background – preferably one whose status, income or good looks, or all three, are part of a dual-income household?

As Table 4.6 shows the dominant value during the 1979–80 period of analysis was still that of 'Self-control', 25 per cent, a finding remarkably consistent with the 26 per cent of the earlier period. The emphasis on a woman's 'Self-concept', 14 per cent also compared closely with the 13 per cent in 1949–74. A new importance was given to high self-esteem within a woman's perception of herself. A woman's sense of her own worth was part of the wider emphasis on selfhood within female society emanating from the woman's movement. Was its presence in these weeklies perhaps a partial reflection of the politics of personhood – or what Betty Freidan now calls the 'first stage' of the women's movement?[14] Fifteen years after *The Feminine Mystique* (1963) first castigated American women's magazine fiction for its glorification of 'the happy housewife', the notion of a woman's sense of self, as separate from her domestic roles, became truly visible within the value structure mediated by these British weeklies.

'Romantic Love' ranked third, 12 per cent, as compared with 16 per cent in the earlier period. As an overt value it was no longer presented as the dream, or the right, of every woman. As a more covert value, it was ever present as the necessary and sufficient condition for a heterosexual relationship. Only the question of whether or not it would lead to marriage was left unmentioned in the messages of the 1980s, particularly in the fiction pages.

The other values that the later analysis showed to be significant were those of 'Work', 7 per cent, which was frequently linked to 'Wealth' as a value, 6 per cent, where materialist aspirations were connected with getting out of the house and earning something more than pin money. 'Friendship', 9 per cent, and 'Family Life', 10 per cent (as compared with 6 per cent earlier), were also strongly represented, as was the inevitable emphasis placed by the beauty pages upon 'Good Looks', 7 per cent. The 'Other' category included a newcomer to the values placed upon the feminine agenda: sex for its own sake was posited as an acceptable, and sometimes desirable, state of affairs.

The old/new goals
It is here in the arena where women's magazines set aspirations for the female audience that the changes and constancies in the goals that they define for the cult are most clearly illustrated. Table 4.7 below shows that the goal of goals remains 'Personal Happiness', 28 per cent, just as it had been pre-eminent in the earlier analysis, 23 per cent. There are many roads leading to this state. It can of course be achieved through a successful relationship with a man, or by losing ten pounds

Table 4.6   Dominant values, all subjects, all titles, 1979–80 (%)

| | 1979–80 | | | |
	W	WO	WW	Total
Self-control	24	24	26	25
Self-concept	14	14	14	14
Romantic love	13	11	11	12
Family life	8	11	12	10
Friendship	7	6	14	9
Social control	8	11	5	8
Work	10	6	5	7
Good looks	7	8	5	7
Wealth	6	6	7	6
Other	3	3	1	2
n	128	128	124[a]	380

[a] No Beauty, one issue
n = 4 per item, 4 items per issue, 4 issues per year
W = *Woman*; WO = *Woman's Own*; WW = *Woman's Weekly*

before a holiday, or even by starting your own satisfying kind of business. The routes are multiple, but the goal is the same – personal happiness.

Second only to happiness is 'Personal Achievement', 21 per cent; this represents a considerable increase over its previously recorded 13 per cent. Here the interrelatedness of female goals is again made clear. What a woman does through her own efforts by way of achievement contributes to her sense of self, her sense of well-being and accomplishment, and thus to her personal happiness. By defining herself as someone who can achieve new competences outside the kitchen, she is doing this with the aid of her favourite magazine – but the emphasis has shifted as to who is doing the defining. She is pushing herself rather than being pushed by any obvious external authority – including the high priestesses of women's magazines.

Although the females who people the pages of the women's weeklies rate their achievements on a scale of internal as well as external satisfaction, they note the prohibitions and prescriptions of the group. 'Social Conformism', 10 per cent, is not totally disregarded in the search for goals definitional of the self. Yet this apparent increase over the earlier figure of 4 per cent is potentially misleading. Negative cases, i.e. instances of non-conformism, for example nonconformity with or rebellion against traditional social and sexual mores, were included in this category.

Two goals that retained their high priority were those of 'Happy Marriage/Family', 15 per cent (including a happy one-parent family),

Table 4.7 Dominant goals, all subjects, all titles, 1979–80 (%)

| | 1979–80 | | | |
	W	WO	WW	Total
Personal happiness	27	29	27	28
Personal achievement	20	21	22	21
Happy marriage/family	13	16	17	15
Physical attractiveness	9	12	9	10
Social conformism	9	10	10	10
Societal achievement	7	5	6	6
Male finding/keeping	6	4	5	5
Other	9	3	4	5
n	96	96	93[a]	285

[a] No beauty, one issue n = 3 items, 4 items per issue, 4 issues per year
W = Woman; WO = Woman's Own; WW = Woman's Weekly

and the goal of 'Physical Attractiveness', 10 per cent. 'Male Finding/ Keeping' as an overt goal went underground: reduced from its previous 16 per cent to 5 per cent.

Images of social class

By 1979–80 was the increased earning and spending power of women reflected in the status and income dimensions of the female world suggested by women's magazines? The earlier analysis of the 1950s, 1960s and early 1970s had revealed that the dominant social class image was what this study called 'Consciously Classless'. Whatever other new interpretations, or minimal changes of theme, the social structure of the female world remained as before, predominantly 'consciously classless', 44 per cent, and 'Middle Class', 41 per cent, as Table 4.8 shows.

Table 4.8   Images of social class, all subjects, all titles, 1979–80 (%)

| | 1979–80 | | | |
	W	WO	WW	Total
'Consciously classless'	37	50	46	44
Middle class	47	47	28	41
Upper class	8	—	19	9
Working class	8	3	7	6
n	36	34	37	107

n = open-ended;
W = *Woman*; *WO* = *Woman's Own*; *WW* = *Woman's Weekly*

As before, the 'consciously classless' image was created either by omitting any reference to occupation or socio-economic status, or by including a cross-section of occupations and incomes that places shared femininity before social differences.

Ever more lawyers, surgeons, doctors, barristers, teachers, actors, accountants and businessmen adorned the second largest social stratum, that of 'middle class', 41 per cent. As in the earlier analysis, this category was over-inclusive in the range of professions and occupations included within it. What was new were the cases of a woman's social standing being made explicit through *her* occupation, and not being dependent on *his*: university librarian, aspiring business woman, dress designer and headmistress, for example. Did this reflect not only the rising numbers of women at work, but also an assumed increase in the range of opportunities open to them, including an increase in decision-making roles? (assumptions were not born out by events: see e.g. Equal Opportunities Commission, 1981).

As Table 4.8 shows, the manual working class remained relatively invisible, 6 per cent, while the upper class appeared more frequently – all those landowners – 9 per cent. In the 1980s as in the 1950s, the privileged few were to be found in royal palaces, or adorning far away fictional backdrops, or within the 'famous celebrity tells all' feature formula. The symbols of status and wealth persist – 'priceless family rugs', Italian *palazzi*, yachts in the south seas, Caribbean plantations, Hollywood hill top hideaways.

What the content analysis categories devised in the mid-1970s did not allow for was the reflection of a new sub-class, that of unemployed youth on the dole. Editors, however, reflected this aspect of the 1979–80 social structure in telling the story of a pregnant 15-year-old and her unemployed teenage boy-friend who ran away from home and were living on the dole (*Woman's Own*, 27 October 1979). What is sociologically interesting is that no apparent stigma or sanction either personal or societal is attached to behaviour hitherto designated as 'immoral' or 'irresponsible'. The editorial tone is descriptive, not prescriptive, and the only hint of scepticism comes in the last paragraph where the journalist writing the story asks if she can come back to see how they are getting on in five years' time.

This chapter has pointed to the 1970s as a decade of confrontation, choices, changes and constancies for women and women's magazines. It has shown how directives to females during this period carried contradictory signals. These dualistic messages from three British weeklies show how many aspects of the cult's beliefs and practices were changing on the surface, but not a lot was changing underneath. They show how the importance of the totem, Woman, was enhanced, but the principal roles, goals and values used to define femininity to the audience were not so different from those of earlier decades.

What was different was the expansion of their cultural and structural framework in terms of the dominant themes from which they emerged. No longer was the message of messages 'get him and keep him'. In its place was a heightened emphasis on the cultist first helping herself – and then helping herself to find him. Pursuit of the male with marriage in mind was superseded by the priority given to a woman's power of self-direction – to pursue first her own identity, and then a male partner to complete her feminine 'identity kit' (cf. Goffman, 1961).

The values were old but the context was new. It had moved from the confines of female dependency to the wider horizons of feminine independence. These contradictions of the old within the new in part reflected conflict between traditional and emergent beliefs about a woman's 'place', as well as newly explicit tension between opposing norms of femininity as encompassing reason as well as emotion.

Despite the problems set for, and by, the high priestesses in providing such dualistic definitions of femininity, the messages of the cult did show responsiveness to changing conditions, in different ways in different magazines. In Europe, in America and in Britain, both what was said, and how it was said, altered dramatically between the 1950s and the 1980s within the pages of women's magazines. It is to those who were charged with the responsibility of resolving these kinds of journalistic problems and cultural contradictions that Chapter 5 turns in examining the role of the woman's magazine editor.

5

The Editors: High Priestesses to the Cult of Femininity

Earlier chapters have shown how editors' perceptions of social change were expressed in the dominant themes, roles, goals and values proclaimed by the three largest selling women's magazines in Britain. The part that such journals play in telling women about the kinds of women they are or can be – the wider social role of women's magazines – cannot be understood by looking at their messages alone: it is necessary to examine also the process through which those messages come into being. A key figure in that process is the editor.

Despite the constraints that the total publishing structure places upon her decision-making – emanating from managers, advertisers, staff, budgets, printers, unions, previous editorial tradition or present market position – it is still she who selects the content of the magazine and shapes its form, through dozens of large and small daily decisions. The sheer volume of decisions includes making technical or craft judgements of the order of twenty or thirty times a day, with this figure reaching fifty or sixty on press days: which picture tilted which way, which fiction illustration, with how much cleavage, and which words to choose to give immediacy and impact. These decisions are quite apart from those that concern, for example, promotional campaigns for the magazine, staff appointments and expenses, forward planning, or replying to a 'difficult' reader's letter.

Decision-making marks the professional significance of the editor's role. But this role also has a social significance. It involves the making of decisions about the current definitions of the cult of femininity – as a social institution to which all females can belong, and as a set of practices and beliefs which define the female gender role. In making such choices, the women's magazine editor's personal attributes, her perceptions of others, and her own beliefs play a major part, and these are the subject of this chapter. Chapter 6 will deal with her role and that of the publishing organisation in the wider production process which frames, and in part shapes, the message of her particular journal.

Meet the editors

Who edits women's magazines? What kind of people are they? Visual observation – and participant observation – of these editors in their natural habitat reveals no clear pattern. The majority of them are females: the few who are not surround themselves with a preponderance of females.

Some are more flamboyant than others in their dress and in the way that they act 'the editor part', and also in the way that they set the office stage for their playing of the 'star' role. The resulting *gestalt* which the majority today strive to create, emphasises a glossy presentation of self. This dressing the part in terms of following fashion trends, or trying to out-fashion fashion, is a relatively recent phenomenon. An earlier generation was characterised more by rather grand ladies in expensively cut classic suits and discreet 'real' jewellery. Increasingly, the creative, leadership and competitive aspects of the job all place a premium on projecting a distinctive personal image, and many editors appear to choose clothes that harmonise not only with their own personality, but also with that of their magazine: traditional, middle-of-the-road, or 'far-out'.

As for the office stage settings trod by the image-making editors of today, their office suites range from the opulently over-decorated to the starkly austere. Some resemble eighteenth-century salons, crowded with satin cushioned sofas, French Empire chairs, marbled tables, gilt mirrors, flowers and plants – and a tiny desk tucked into a corner. Others have wood-panelled, book-lined walls and large desks placed centre stage where they sit like the managing director of a medium-size company, receiving an endless succession of supplicants and penitents – in this case those seeking decisions about ideas, newly done or re-done copy or layouts. Attention to detail is part of women's magazine editors' customary role, and the attention that they give to surrounding themselves with the symbols of office and dressing the part attests to this.

Their individuality is expressed in ways other than their personal tastes in dress and decor. It is expressed also through their style of editing. As might be expected from such a collection of 'unique' individuals, their ways of working are various and frequently mysterious. Some conceal a will of iron beneath a mild and ladylike exterior; others stamp their personalities and booted feet over their pages in an extended ego exercise; still others project a dazzling, animated smiling self which can conceal depths of indecision or lack of confidence. This variety of editing as well as personal styles suggests there is no such thing as a 'typical' women's magazine editor.

How editors see their world

Highly motivated, highly competitive, highly skilled and highly paid – what singles out a successful women's magazine editor from her peers? What does she bring to her editing by way of conviction and experience? What does she believe herself to be doing for her readers, her publishers and the staff who help to produce 'her' magazine?

One way to find out how editors see themselves and their job, and how they perceive social change, is to talk to them and ask. The most data for this and Chapter 6 on the editorial process came from interviews and re-interviews with some thirty-four women's magazine editors – twenty-seven British and seven American – and some ninety-seven other women's magazine journalists and managers over the period 1975–81 (Appendix II details this fieldwork). Perhaps because all these people work in the publishing industry – the majority of them as 'professional communicators ' – they proved a notably articulate sample group. For this reason, many of the points made in this chapter and the next are substantiated by quotations from the editors, managers and journalists themselves – although for reasons of confidentiality only in rare cases are the individuals concerned identified. Just as the magazines were allowed to speak for themselves, so too were the editor role and the editorial process: the analytical categories emerged from the interview and observation data.

The questions that guided this part of the research focused on editors' perceptions of social change and its impact upon their audience, and upon their view of the editing task – its reponsibilities, skills, rewards and constraints. What was their source of knowledge and certainty as to what was 'right' for their client/target group? Moreover how did such guidelines help them to decide the 'when' as well as the 'what' to print in their pages?

The selection and training of editors

The interview questions concerning editors' self-concepts, agenda-setting decisions and shared beliefs were posed alongside several others about their position within the total publishing structure. For example, how did they get to be editors in the first place? What training did they have, what career routes did they follow, what selection procedures governed their appointments, what rewards are they given? There are problems in attempting to discover answers to these questions. One reason for this is that historically, the preferred routes of recruitment and promotion have been secretive and informal rather than formal and open. Another reason is that for personality or political reasons the high priestesses are often reticent about the acquisition and maintenance of their powers. For them, as for other media producers, there is no single recognised route to the editor's chair – the path is at worst uncertain and at best flexible (cf. Boyd-Barrett, 1970; Elliott, 1977).

Talent alone is insufficient. Ambition, a feeling for 'office politics', manipulative or sycophantic skills, luck – 'I was in the right place at the right time' – and even 'playing a waiting game' can influence the selection probabilities of an aspirant to the editor's chair. Of all these factors, political skills emerged as more important than charisma or creativity in getting to the top. Aptitude for the job in terms of knowing how to 'work the organisation' and 'handle people' is also a factor which influences appointment.

Turning to more universal criteria, the first and most significant one for this group is that of sex. Of the twenty-seven British women's magazine editors (past and present) who were interviewed, 84 per cent were female. In 1981, the ten largest selling women's magazines in Britain were all edited by women, whereas three of the largest American women's monthly magazines – *Redbook, Good House-keeping* and *McCalls* – were edited by men, as was the German fortnightly *Brigitte*.[1]

This positive discrimination in favour of females is in contrast to the few senior editorial positions held by women in Fleet Street. No editor of a national newspaper is female. Smith's (1980) data show only one female as assistant editor. This unfavourable sex ratio is changing, however. By 1981, more women's magazine journalists were being lured to Fleet Street, as 'the populars' stepped up competition between themselves, the women's press and the Sunday supplements for a larger slice of the female audience and the advertisement revenue consequent upon it.

A second universalistic criterion applied to editor selection is a 'good track record'. Previous sales success on a smaller journal is often the escalator to editing a larger or more prestigious one. Recruitment from within is the favoured method of the larger publishing houses. Formal procedures of open advertising, either 'in house' or in the trade press have become more widespread, often in response to union pressures, while the selection board typical of broadcasting, academe or industry is rare.[2]

The earlier pattern of women's magazine editor appointments in the 1950s and 1960s more closely resembled the handing down of a favour from on high than rewarding the striving supplicant who applies from below. Where the known 'track record' or word-of-mouth 'tip off' act as recruitment agencies, the customary courtship ritual of this pre-selection method involves an invitation to lunch or drinks where the offer is made – and generally accepted. There is no evidence of editors having to be pressured to accept a bigger star role, despite the increased responsibility – and slog – of a larger, more prestigious or more commercially successful magazine. Few turn down the challenge – and the rewards. As the then Chairman of Daily Mirror Newspapers, Cecil King, reputedly remarked when doubts were raised as to whether a candidate would accept the editorship of the then brand-leader, *Woman*: 'I have yet to meet the waiter who does not want to become head waiter.'

One of the findings of this study was that successful editor candidates can be classified into three main categories – 'Heir Apparent', (beneficiary of the heredity factor); 'Known Insider' ('better the devil you know') and 'Unknown Outsider' (talent stealing). The 'Heir Apparent' is employed by the magazine in question in a senior capacity and therefore 'in line' for appointment; the 'Known Insider' is employed by the same publishing organisation on a different magazine; the 'Unknown Outsider' is employed by another, probably directly competing, publishing organisation. An example of how such selection processes operate is given by the historical evidence in the case of *Woman, Woman's Own* and *Woman's Weekly*. This shows that the 'Heir Apparent' and the 'Known Insider' categories are the most significant.[3]

Learning by doing

Our uncertainties concerning editor selection criteria and processes also apply to patterns of editor training. What the data show is that there is no one pattern. No British women's periodical publisher operates a training school for editors as such – although both the National Magazine Company and IPC established various in-house training schemes for journalists during the 1970s.[4]

The majority of editors had worked their way up through the ranks, passing from smaller magazines to larger ones or occasionally transferring from provincial – or, more recently, national – newspapers. Here, as with other media producers (cf. Boyd-Barrett, 1970, 1980; and Elliott, 1977), the established tradition has been one of on-the-job training – or learning by doing – in the basic craft skills of women's magazine journalism. This editor's account is typical of many:

I had an extraordinary training on a small magazine. I did whatever I wanted to do as there was only a staff of about ten. One month I would do the fashion and interview and sub because they would all have to be done, and I would caption and feature write. Because of union restrictions it is not possible on many publications, and on the bigger ones it is also limited because there is greater specialisation.

I mean it was much easier when I had a staff of twenty. You could experiment there because they were all young people and they didn't really know that they shouldn't be doing X or Y and if they wanted to have a go you had them do it. If you have a staff of a hundred then it is all sort of marked out. If you come in as a trainee feature writer you might be the most brilliant sub in the world but you are never going to be able to slide over and have a little go at it. And I find that very sad because I think journalists ought to be 'all round'.

(Woman's weekly editor)

Creativity, however, cannot be learned by doing. The data show that the ability to originate, innovate and inspire – the more charismatic editor qualities – are often much less important than political and people-management skills when it comes to singling out a future editor from her journalist peers.

Whatever her route to the editor's chair, the novice high priestess has learned the positive and negative characterisations of her role from the editors whom she has worked for, observed or heard about. Her performance is guided by what she sees as the expectations that others have of her – by the norms that she has acquired from using other editors as role models, and which she reinterprets for herself – as to how a women's magazine editor should look and act. This process of anticipatory socialisation has presented her with a collection of extravagant role models. Some date back to the 1950s. There was the legendary editor of *Woman's Weekly* who reputedly unscrewed her ear trumpet at strategic moments – board meetings that bored her, or when her very ladylike young journalists hesitantly asked for a rise. There was the equally legendary gentleman who reigned at *Woman's Own*, and who threw glittering parties at the Savoy for staff and contributors where improbable things allegedly occurred. He also on a different sort of occasion greeted an editor on her return from lunch with a note saying: 'Thanks for everything, but please clear your desk by four o'clock this afternoon.' Across the Atlantic, stories of editors' escapades have been equally larger than life. The present editor-in-chief of American *Good Housekeeping* recalled that when he first entered his new office, his joy on taking up his new appointment was somewhat tempered by the knowledge that one of his predecessors had hanged himself, and another had shot himself.[5]

Thus, the processes of socialisation include more than day-to-day contact with incumbent editors – contact which increases as a writer rises through the ranks to department head, assistant or associate editor. They include absorbing the folk wisdom and fables – the mythology – of women's magazine journalism. By the time a first time editor ascends the editorial throne she has acquired the appropriate editor mystique through participant observation. She has learned well the gracious or cutting manner, and the appropriate symbols of office – potted plants, drinks cabinets, a choice antique or two – which display her status to the world in the 1980s. Surrounded by the paraphernalia of the drawing room, the editor's desk – however high the pile of page proofs – can be abandoned for the 'informal' intimacy of armchair consultations.

All of these processes are wholly consistent with Cantor's (1971) conclusions about Hollywood television producers: occupational identity is acquired through the training, socialisation and aspirations which determine role performance. The significance of such aspirations must not be minimised in this context. No women's magazine editor is crowned against her will. Although appointed by others, she wants – often fiercely – to be a 'No. 1'.

Status and income
The rewards of income as well as of status accrue to these editors. The size of their salaries often reflects the size and profitability of their circulations. Their income can also reflect the generosity or meanness of the particular organisation, and last but not least, on which side of the Atlantic they play the high priestess. At a seminar organised by the British Society of Magazine Editors on 'The Role of the Editor' in early 1980, the author publicly quizzed an American editor-in-chief about American women's magazine editor salary scales. His reply of 'I'd say somewhere between $60,000 and $100,000 plus stock options in some cases' left his British audience gasping. In 1980, so far as can be discovered, the British salary range was £10–20,000 per annum.[6] Wide as the transatlantic differential was, this nevertheless represented a considerable increase on the salaries paid to editors in the 1950s and 1960s, which so far as can be established were of the order of £2–5,000 and £4–10,000 respectively. By 1982, salary scales had increased again to between £12,000 and the 'middle twenties'. This increase represents more than compensation for inflation: it recognises that the tenure of office of most editors had shortened from a few decades to a few years.

Having acquired the belief that prestige adheres to editorship, how does working experience match such status expectation? Within the women's magazine industry editors are acknowledged as an elite group and treated as such. Theirs are the seats of honour at the top table when the advertising managers or circulation 'reps' are rallied for promotional presentations or sales conferences. Their presence provides a tangible symbol of the less tangible product the 'ad boys' or 'sales reps' are being asked to sell – and frequently they are asked to stand up and promote their magazines and, to a considerable extent, themselves as part of the selling campaign.

The degree to which deference-commanding 'inside the company' status is confirmed externally – by other media producers, or by the wider society – is not so readily discovered. Ambiguity of status is characteristic of British media producers generally because of their particular mix of elite and commercial values (Elliott, 1977). Moreover if formal education, for example, is taken as one criterion of elite status, then this group does not conform. Within the British women's magazine editor sample, only one had a university degree. This is changing. Below editor level trainee journalists increasingly are university graduates – in part a reflection of increased need for credentials in society and increased female participation in higher education (cf. e.g. Halsey *et al.* 1980; EOC, 1981). More department editors, for example, hold degrees in the 1980s than did in the 1950s. This recruitment of journalists with experience of higher education -- and perhaps with differing perspectives on the cult of femininity – may lead in time to more graduates in the editor chair.

There are other status differences that separate these editors from those of other media in Britain. In a status hierarchy which distinguishes between Fleet Street 'qualities' and 'populars', and to a lesser extent between the BBC and private companies in television, the prestige distinctions that operate within other media can be extended to include the ranking of both women's magazines and their editors. In a male-dominated media industry females generally are assigned relatively low status (Smith, 1980). In the case of women's magazines, these are, with few exceptions, 'popular' rather than 'quality', and are aimed exclusively at women. It follows that their almost universally female editors are ranked behind the exclusively male editors of Fleet Street. Within this journalistic pecking order they are located somewhere in the middle range, respected for the circulations they command, but for long regarded as producers of a mysterious product labelled 'women only'.

How they see themselves

The interview and observation data show how the women's magazine editor, or editor-in-chief, has a wide range of responsibilities but also enjoys a wide range of discretionary powers in carrying them out. She carries creative, ethical and legal responsibility for every word or illustration that appears in 'her' magazine. Like other editors her tasks include dreaming up ideas, selecting those of others and directing the shaping of the chosen messages through the editorial process.

This directing of editorial policy, process and staff implies accepting *inter alia* brickbats and bouquets for the errors and talents of others. Her lines of responsibility, of command and accountability, run in three directions and three ways: upward towards management, in the sense that she carries the can for producing a successful commercial product; downward towards staff in the sense that staff depend on the editor to guard their interests and represent their needs and grievance to management; and thirdly, towards the audience. This is seen as requiring that the faithful be given a message that they will want to hear and buy, whilst also being given useful services of personal guidance, social support and consumer advice.

Every editor interviewed had a different definition of her role, yet a general consensus emerged about the norms and expectations that they and others applied to it. The question was to discover to what extent editors set their own norms, and decide for themselves whether or not the demands made upon them are legitimate and compulsory.

The major point on which all thirty-four editors agreed entirely was that their role was central. They were the pivot around which the entire editorial process swung. Without them, 'their' magazine would not happen the way it did – or possibly at all:

As far as I am concerned an editor is a dictator, possibly a benevolent dictator. I do not hold with committee think. If you've any good ideas and you discuss them with more than three people, you end up with either a bad idea or a watered down good idea. Therefore, if you're a *real* editor, in the old sense, such as Ross of the *New Yorker*, you actually know what you want.

Hopefully, you're in the right framework – if you're not you're out of a job quite sharpish – and you do what you intend to do. Never do any reader research, or market surveys, because that is just asking for your audience to tell you what they think they think. Probably, sometimes they don't even understand the question in the first place.

If you know what you want, and you are able to get the best out of people, do it. It is a kind of dictatorship, definitely. It's also a relationship. I can tell by picking up any publication (a) if it has an editor or if it has a committee, and (b) if it is loved or unloved.

(Women's monthly editor)

An editor is a mixture of a really bossy chef in a great big kitchen, who knows exactly that someone has put the wrong ingredient in a sauce; a conductor of an orchestra who can hear if the violin right in the back row has just done it wrong. It's just a sort of gathering together of the whole elements of producing something within a framework. I mean if I were editing *Autocar*, which I would do very well because I like cars, I would obviously be in a different framework but there's still the same sense of direction towards it.

(Woman's fashion monthly editor)

Managers are not so inclined to political, artistic or culinary metaphors. They often describe editors in terms of strength or status: editors are strong or weak – and occasionally great. They have, or do not have, creative talents, people management skills and commercial flair. A great editor is one who combines creative with commercial flair, and succeeds in producing a magazine which sells both copies and advertisement space. The importance of editors to company profitability was stressed by many publishing executives:

The people who matter in a publication are essentially the editors. If the editors are good the magazine will be good and the advertising will be good, and unless you do something really violently stupid, the profit will be good. If your magazine editors are no good, the rest can be absolutely 100 per cent and you still get nowhere. The editors are the essential people.

(Cecil King, former Chairman, IPC)

As far as I am concerned, editors are number one in the organisation, bar none. If you have an editor that can produce you a magazine that sells very healthily on an increase, then they're worth their weight in gold. You might get rid of anybody else, but not them. In this business I can't see how you can operate any sort of management structure without the editors having a significant say in the editing of their magazine. Not necessarily the economics of it.

(IPC publishing executive)

The editor mystique

The self-concept of editors concerning their pivotal role in the editorial process is enhanced by the 'mystique' which surrounds its performance. The 'mystique' view of editing is not confined to the high priestesses or their staffs. It is held also by editors and journalists of other media who believe themselves to have special or sacred knowledge about the nature of their particular audience and the messages it wishes to read, listen to or watch. Moreover the mystique of the editing process is held not only by editors who are appointed to office on the understanding that they have it, but also by those who appoint them, managers who reinforce the view by acting on the basis of it.

This stance can create difficulties for others within the total publishing structure – such as advertisement directors, promotion experts, accountants and lawyers – who cannot make such claims but whose professional expertise may lead them to a judgement that runs counter to that of the editor. Whose magic or mystique is the more powerful? When such questions are asked, it transpires that the mystique is a variable concept. Beliefs in its possession are contingent upon its reaffirmation by the most recent ABC circulation figures. These act to confirm or disconfirm an editor's special powers and elusive ability to 'know what they want, when they want it and how'. Yet in certain situations, the mystique can be acquired by those outside its circle through processes of transmission akin to those of sympathetic magic (see e.g. Frazer, 1959). Thus elements of the mystique can be acquired over the ritual of the business lunch, or by the touching of certain symbols of creative power such as 'visuals' or 'layouts'. Thus mere association with the mystique holders, the editors, may impart aspects of their sacred knowledge and its authority to those endowed with more tangible powers – financial or hierarchical.

Do beliefs in their own mystique and its power predispose women's magazine editors towards being 'taken over' by their role? Is it internalised like that of the priest, or is individuality defined in terms of it like the rock star? Empirically, this is difficult to discover. Editors are experienced in controlling themselves in interview situations, so the accounts of others, together with the insights gained from previous participation, were useful in this regard. Total involvement undoubtedly is a prerequisite for the dedicated editor who reads every word, 'OKs' every title and illustration, chooses every cover-picture and writes all the cover lines – or gets others to rewrite them. This total involvement is here called the 'Stanislavsky method of editing' – or the living-out of the role.[7] All aspects of one's experience, the whole of life and society, family and friends are used as sources and sounding boards; they provide the background for the serious business of editing:

Once you become an editor you put yourself second. I don't feel there's any other way. Everybody told me when I took over this was going to happen and I said 'No, not with me it isn't. I've got a lot of other interests.'
Not now. Sometimes I don't know what 'me' is any more which isn't very nice, but still that's beside the point. You have to do it. And X was like this, it was job first, self second. I think married men, married women, their married lives, their personal lives, suffer with a magazine the size of a major weekly. I think it is possible on the smaller ones not to immerse yourself so totally.
(Women's weekly editor)

As a result of this high personal investment, many women's magazine editors experience 'their' magazine as an extension of themselves, or speak of it as their 'baby' or as a personal possession. They frequently use the possessive case – stories, staff or audience become 'mine' – as in 'when I had the *Realm* it was a different kind of magazine'.

The editor's personality and editing style
Enthusiastic, controlled, blasé, impulsive, brisk, warm or distant – the personality traits of the women's magazine editors interviewed for this study ranged across a wide spectrum. All were skilled politicians

down to the tips of their ringed fingers, almost all were masterly in their 'presentation of self' (cf. Goffman, 1959). This made the identification of specific personality traits and their impact on the editorial process more a matter for observation, or one to be checked against the accounts of others.

What emerged was that an editor's personality impinges on her editing style. This affects the production process, and it can work both positively and negatively within that process. The temperamental editor, however talented, is often counter-productive in her caprices, and the 'she never knows what she wants until you've done something else' syndrome is universally decried as negative. The editor who can inspire others and has the ability to create a close working atmosphere is the universally desired, positive role model. Many editors claimed 'we were a team, no other word for it', or 'we are like a big family fighting and making up all the time', or 'we are a community'. Not all team, family or community members experience a particular editor's reign in such happy terms. One ex-editor unknowingly contradicted his predecessor who had claimed his regime was a 'community', describing him thus: 'He was a bastard, no other word for it. He taught me a lot, though – mostly what not to do.' This referred to a legendary editor of the 1950s whose staff management techniques included the tactic of regularly inviting senior editors in at 6 pm to tear apart a layout, before saying he would be back after the theatre to see how they had got on with its revision.

While this is an extreme example of editing style, it does not contradict the finding that there appear to be only two variants, autocratic and not-quite-so-autocratic. The editor's word 'goes' in the 1980s just as it did in the 1950s, despite the majority surrounding their decision-making with the trappings of democracy, elaborate consultation and conference systems which did not exist in the more blatantly imperious regimes of earlier times. It is through her performance of a particular editing style that an editor communicates her personality and her philosophy about 'her' magazine to the entire editorial team. By exerting a particular kind of authority – covertly persuasive or overtly arbitrary – she can indoctrinate newcomers to the fold, or subjectively shape the message to her personal handprint. The impact of differing editing styles on those who are on the receiving end is evoked by two participants:

As far as the Editor was concerned, I was green when I joined and needed to learn the magazine's philosophy. She never spelled it out for me. It was obviously something you were supposed to soak in through the pores because she couldn't express it. She said, 'It's the mix, it's just like a jar of pickles, you've got to get the right mix', and she regarded each of her sections as an individual ingredient that went into the mix.

Also she hated sensationalising things. I had a tendency to sensationalise given half a chance, and it was always knocked right back. You weren't to oversell. It was always *tone* that she was worried about: 'It mustn't sound glib.' That was her real term of disapproval, you know, 'like an ad'.

(Women's monthly editor)

This more delegatory, learn-by-osmosis style of editing contrasts to the more subjective and do-it-myself approach of another editor:

She honestly believed that an intro was a good intro only if she wrote it. That a feature was only a good feature if she liked it. That a story was only a good story if it had the kind of ending she enjoyed. Everything in the magazine had always got to be what she liked, and although she's a fairly typical woman, she couldn't be typical of millions of women. You've got to get away and say 'OK, I don't like that, it's not what I want, but it will probably please somebody', but she was always trying to please herself.

(Women's weekly associate editor)

The high priestesses: agenda-setters to the female world

The significance of the editor's role within the editorial process is dwarfed by comparison with its potential social significance in the world outside. For it is these editors, in deciding what their magazines will deal with, who are also deciding what will be included or excluded from the agenda of feminine concerns. This general power subsumes a number of specific powers. They are able to confer status upon – or withhold it from – individuals, issues and events by rendering them, or refusing to render them, visible on their pages (cf. Lazarsfeld and Merton, 1948; Cohen, 1981). In all these respects women's magazine editors confirm their setting of boundaries on the female world. This is what invests their agenda-setting with social significance: the extent of their potential influence upon the female audience, in promoting historically specific interpretations of 'appropriate' female roles, is very great.

All editors of specialist periodicals exercise a degree of power in terms of defining the boundaries of their constituencies, be they of gardeners, fishermen, educationalists or women. The editors of magazines whose special realm is femininity itself exercise greater powers than most in this regard because the boundaries of their sphere of potential influence are less self-evident, and because they have such a large potential client/target group for their constituents. They are also powerful in that they exercise influence over their readers to the extent that women rely on them for information, support, guidance, direction about – or distraction from – those things which they equate with their womanliness, and which they choose to read about in that connection.

Earlier chapters showed the ways in which the largest selling women's magazines in Britain turned the mirror that could reflect social change towards the world, or towards the wall, at different times – the consequences being reflected in the messages that they purveyed. In making decisions about which way to turn their mirrors, what were the issues that most exercised the editors of the day?

There were two topics that were particularly problematic. They concerned the cult's totem – its particular view of Woman – and the sacred taboos surrounding her social location and sexual behaviour. Was the 'proper' place of Woman inside the home as wife and mother, or outside it as paid worker? What responses should the faithful be making in the face of more open female sexuality inside and outside wedlock? The extent to which editors of women's magazines in Europe, America and Britain confronted these questions, or chose to ignore them, points to the exceptional range of discretionary powers which they exercise in acting as agenda-setters to the female world. The content analysis of earlier chapters, which showed how some were concerned to keep new topics off the agenda to 'protect' their readers, emphasises how the priestesses assume pastoral powers over their flocks. In making choices of this order on behalf of the female sex, these editors are acting in ways more complex, active and prescriptive than the classic model of media gatekeeping suggests (cf. White, 1950; Breed, 1955, Bass, 1969, Donohue, 1972; Chibnall, 1975, Smythe, 1975).

Choices, changes, and conflicts

Every editor was asked for her views on the most significant social changes for women that she had identified. The responses were remarkably consistent between both the British and the American editors. To a woman – and man – they replied 'more women going out to work, especially married women'. After that, came the influence of the 'sexual revolution', and in the case of the American editors, the impact of the 'women's movement'.

How did these perceptions of social change influence their decisions about what to put into their magazines? How responsive were the high priestesses – and through them their messages – to the information that they were taking in about what the world and their readers were doing during the 1960s and 1970s? Only a comparative, randomised content analysis such as was done for the three British weeklies would go some way towards an individual answer for every editor and her magazine – a scale of content analysis beyond the scope of this study. Yet insights into the ways in which editors responded to their perceptions of changing female attitudes and behaviour came from the interview data itself. These indicated the additional problems created by beliefs about the more rapid rate of change in the 1960s and 1970s, as compared with the slower one of the 1950s. The quandaries posed by putting working mothers and increased sexual freedom on the agenda, also involved professional skills of getting the 'timing' and 'tone of voice' right. These skills are analysed in Chapter 6 along with other professional practices of women's magazine journalists. Here they are relevant to the editor's pace-setting role only in the sense that knowing 'when' and 'how to put it' can be as important as the knowledge of 'what' to reflect, ignore or anticipate.

The big decisions that editors of women's magazines make concern the new topics that they will make visible, or about which they will engage in public debate. The extent to which these topics are contentious or consensual, and whether they deviate from – or conform to – what are deemed the currently 'appropriate', 'proper' or desirable roles, goals and values for femininity is revealed within a given magazine's world view. Which were the issues that made the biggest impact? The reply of this British editor was typical:

Work, of course, going out to work was the biggest change. The acceptance of women working who have families, that's probably the biggest one.

The sexual thing was very big as well – that's late sixties, really. It's taken an awfully long time, but they do have orgasms, and they are supposed to enjoy them, and if they don't 'what are they, and why aren't I getting one?'

(Women's weekly editor)

The 'more working wives' phenomenon was equated with a more clearly defined identity, independence and spending power:

Earning your own money, even a few pounds a week, that's made all the difference in the world. The acceptance of the fact that you are not doing a wicked and immoral thing, or that you've [not] got an inadequate husband because you go out and earn.

Whether you go out and earn it cleaning my house, or editing a magazine, it doesn't really matter how much you are bringing in. The point is you have got a say in what's spent and how it's spent. If you want that new dining room table, you have it. You don't have to spend long hours thinking how it's the best thing for your husband's career that you should have it.

(Women's monthly editor)

Some editors related women going out to work to diminished 'time' and 'need' for women's magazines:

Then there is the business of women going out to work. Once you go out to work you have less time; your needs are different, and they might have been answered by either television, newspapers or by the television programme paper. Have you seen what is happening to *TV Times* lately? My God, they are all on my back.

(Women's weekly editor)

Assessing the impact of the mid-1970s women's movement on her audience and her approach to what the magazine would say one editor stressed the turning away from the old soothing recipe of 'happy ever after':

It isn't making glib assumptions that all your lives are going to be happier as a result of anything. Young women are going to find life more difficult in the future but they will get more compensations, which is an adult situation. When you are a child you just require happiness, when you are an adult you realise you can't be happy all the time. It's admitting that life is not a bowl of cherries.

Women have always been offered the sop of happiness. If you have a baby you'll be happy. If you get married you'll be happy. If you have pretty clothes and wear nice makeup and smell nice you will be happy. Now nobody's offering these promises any more – they were never true – but now you admit they are not. They are compensations. It's nice to have pretty clothes and makeup and babies but it does not automatically make your life happy.

(Women's monthly editor)

Another editor reflected on how some magazines in the early 1960s had perpetuated arbitrary or anachronistic social rules about behaviour, manners or dress long after they had outlived their utility or meaningfulness for their readers:

I don't think we had realised how many people were going into first class restaurants who'd never been there before. That it was no longer a case of saying 'If you are fortunate enough to. . . .' We were over-acknowledging our C-rating readership. After all people don't like to be C-rated. I think its much more flattering to say 'When you go to the best restaurant in your town . . .' instead of 'If you are lucky enough to be invited by your husband's boss's wife to go with them.'

No, it was not talking down, it was bending over backwards to make them not feel bad if they never did. But hardly anybody doesn't get to something, sometime. If you've only been on one package deal to Paris for two nights, you at least have been abroad – and you know you've done it – and you are a very different person from the person who has never ventured out of East Finchley.

(Women's weekly deputy editor)

The content analysis of the preceding chapters showed the extent to which the cult's perceptions of and prohibitions towards sex had changed. This transformation began slowly. An editor recalled her battles over the introduction of sex topics into a young women's magazine in the early 1960s:

Most of our management were middle-aged men, or men on the verge of retirement, and they just could not face up to us telling teenagers about contraception, abortion and living in sin – you never hear that phrase now, do you?

So we had those sort of battles. Sometimes if we talked about relationships between men and women as though they were married, people would say

'This isn't really a teenage magazine. It's too grown up.'

(Women's monthly editor)

In part, editors' decisions to put more open and controversial articles about sex into their pages was prompted not so much by their perceptions of social change as by their felt duty to respond to readers' letters asking for more explicit help:

A lot of features actually come from readers' letters. The whole business about 'too scared to make love' was readers' letters. They were all still writing in about how, when, if – you know, all that sort of thing. I thought, 'Blimey, so a lot of them are doing it and don't know how to, and are scared stiff.'

(Women's weekly editor)

Several editors felt that too much attention had been paid during the 1970s to the topic of sex within their pages, and pointed out how women's magazines had responded to changing attitudes towards other areas of the permitted or the permissible:

Sex is not necessarily the area that reflected more change. It's just more sensational, so you notice it. Every time anybody wants to say how have magazines changed, you find yourself having to trot out this business of 'We did abortion' as if this was the only thing that has changed. Sex wasn't the only thing, it was one of them.

(Women's weekly editor)

By the mid-1970s such were the plethora of articles on 'How to get more from your sex-life' or 'How to have a happy marriage' that one editor recalled a predecessor calling a halt:

One day she came in and said, 'Can't we do something? I feel there must be a lot of women who are fed up reading about sex, bored with sex, can't we do a kind of anti-sex piece for those women?'
We had a lot of fun talking about, laughing about it and trying to work it out. It became known as the 'eff off, Fred' piece – we could just see this lady saying, 'No, eff off, Fred.'

(Women's monthly editor)

Apart from consideration of the increased spending power and decreased leisure time of working women, and debates about how much sex to put in their magazines, editors made other kinds of decision that related to their perceptions of change. There are examples of editors' reluctance to anticipate rather than reflect, or even to keep pace with, changes, including status changes which are linked to consumption styles:

Cars were something she never wanted brought into anything. Suddenly you realised that cars had got to be brought into things. Towards the end of her regime she was beginning to acknowledge that ordinary people had cars – within about three years of her leaving we had a car column. But we're talking about the late fifties and the pace of change hadn't accelerated that much then, but I do think she kept pace on the whole.

(Women's weekly chief sub-editor)

The importance of 'pace' and 'timing' was reinforced by an editor who compared another magazine with her own:

I think they kept trying new gimmicks, trying desperately hard, and in fact throwing away the majority for the minority readership. They just couldn't find a plateau, and I think you've got to have a very firm basis and change on that.

Our magazine always kept its plateau, always has, and has been happy to go on developing the theme, changing the theme as time demands – imperceptibly and almost unnoticeably.

(Women's weekly editor)

The measured or erratic degree of responsiveness of individual editors – bound or unfettered by previous editorial traditions – to perceptions of change has to be related to further questions of overall policy direction, of anticipating future audience 'needs' and 'wants', as well as satisfying established ones:

She'd got to please management, please the advertisers, cope with the personnel side, all the immense amount of paperwork that's involved with hiring and firing in union matters and so on, and thinking ahead was not something she wanted to do as well.

One day management forced her to. I mean quite literally sent her home and told her that she had got to work out a statement of intent as to what she felt the philosophy of the magazine should be in the future.

(Women's monthly editor)

There are production contingencies – total issue size, number of colour and advertisement pages – which also are linked to the editorial handling of perceptions of changing, and unchanging, audience demand:

The decision to have God only once a month was frankly a physical problem. We were having fewer editorial pages and the regulars were taking up far too much space. So I took out the pets column – but what else could you take out? You can't take out the doctor's diary, or the letters page, it's very well read. You can't take out horoscopes or problem pages, very well read. Can't take out any of my editorial, in fact I've made that bigger. The one thing that doesn't get that sort of readership, and is there in a sense as a placebo, was the God column.

(Women's weekly editor)

The kind and pace of change in American women's magazines differed from many of those in Britain. In part this was because the largest selling American titles were monthlies, more glossy and more middle-class. In the mid-1970s the editor-in-chief of *Ladies' Home*

Journal, commented on how her competitors were responding to the changing audience scene:

I think some of us responded more than others, and some over-responded too. *Cosmo* was the first to break the ground on the sexual revolution. *Ms.* broke the ground on the feminist revolution. I think all of us incorporate material now which incorporates those changes. *Good Housekeeping* less than the others – on the other hand they are doing very well with the traditional woman. *Redbook* has done very well by going more into political involvement. They ran that sex survey which has been very successful.

This contrasts to the firmly apolitical stance adopted by the majority of British women's magazines and their editors throughout most of the post-war period. After their treatment of social policies affecting women and family life in the late 1940s there was a long pause until public discussion of the Sex Discrimination Act and Equal Pay Act forced related issues onto the pages of most of these journals in the mid-1970s. This contrasts to the earlier and more active involvement of major American women's magazines and their editors with the political issues of the 1960s and thereafter.

Two editors, both of them male, spoke publicly and in our interviews about the relationship between the women's media, social policy and political action. The editor-in-chief of *McCalls*, made these points:

In 1963 I got a group of women's magazine editors together because I was very concerned about the possibility of nuclear war. We persuaded ourselves that we could make a mass effort, that we would have a joint interview with President Kennedy and try to raise the awareness of large numbers of women that the threat was real – and to get them to support the nuclear test ban treaty ratifications. But that was an exception. I suppose even the reason I was able to suggest it was that the possibility of 'power' over the readers was latent. We didn't make it happen, we influenced.

I think the picture of any mass media as being sort of a conscious manipulation of people's opinions is really way out of line. But there's an interplay between what's possible and whether you test the limits of what's possible or not, or whether you simply reinforce what you think people want to hear and have a sort of retrograde action.

The editor-in-chief of *Redbook* – the American monthly which counted anthropologist Margaret Mead as a contributor for seventeen years, and which heralded a turning point in the received wisdom of the women's movement with the first publication of extracts from Betty Friedan's *The Second Stage* in January 1980 – mobilised the leading women's magazine editors to support the Equal Rights Amendment (ERA) as early as 1975.[8] Speaking to a Conference on Women in Public Life that same year, the editor stated his beliefs about the role of women's magazines and the changing role of women:

I'm the editor-in-chief of one of the most important women's magazines in the country. I'm in a position to have some effect on the image of women and on the women's movement. What do I see as the function of a magazine whose very image as a woman's magazine seems to re-enforce the cliche and stereotyped view of women? What we *can* do at *Redbook* – and *do* do, I think – is to try to present for our readers the very startling – *still startling* – notion that women are powerful, that women have potential, that women are equal to men.

Sixteen years ago we raised the question of why women feel trapped – and since then have consistently probed the consciousness of ourselves and our readers all the way up to this month's issue which carries Liz Carpenter's article on the six women – three of them Texans, of course – who could be President of the United States. *Redbook* thinks a woman *can* be. And it is right for a woman's magazine to raise the possibility.[9]

Do these editors share any beliefs about their editing role?

Decisions about the form and content of the message in relation to their perceptions of social change are influenced by the role of the editor within the editorial process, as well as by what she (or he) may believe to be the new gospel for the cult of femininity and its adherents. Were there any particular beliefs about the editing role that they shared as an occupational group? The first question was: did such a collection of professionally 'unique' individuals constitute a group in any wider sociological sense? If they did constitute a group, were there any beliefs about themselves, their tasks, or their readers that they held in common?

The interview data confirmed that women's magazine editors can be said to comprise a group for two reasons: they share certain broad ethical and work norms, and they form a fairly cohesive and increasingly international social and professional network.[10] Being bound by ties of clientship and patronage, linked by threads of intrigue and gossip, and engaged in competitive struggles requires that they know what one another are doing. It does of course help that they share many of the same production routines and constraints, and share much of the same 'recipe knowledge' of what constitutes the female world. This sharing of procedures and symbols facilitates the development of common ideas (cf. Berger and Luckmann, 1967). It helps to create homogeneity in their messages – as does the fact that their careers take them from one magazine to another.

There are problems in exploring the shared ideas of any occupational group. The professed beliefs, from which the analytical categories derive, are not always easy to ascertain. This is especially so where the beliefs expressed in interviews and observed in action consist of judgments, rationalisations, intuitions, attitudes and convictions. To speak of women's magazine editors as holding or adhering to a set of beliefs as cohesive or consistent, as the term 'ideology' implies, would be to impose sociological and categorical nicety upon this jumble of judgements, rationalisations, etc.[11]

However, five beliefs emerged that were sufficiently strongly held and widely shared to qualify as a women's magazine editor 'group belief': the commercial success of their magazines; their responsibilities towards the audience; the rightness of their approach to the editing task; the degree of autonomy that they exercised in controlling the production process; and and their self-concept as professional journalists (cf. Tunstall, 1971; Christian, 1980). Each of these aspects is discussed in turn below.

The commercial imperative

The first and most important belief shared by these editors is that professional success is to be defined in economic terms, namely steady or rising circulations and healthy advertisement revenues (cf. Curran, 1980). The importance attached to this demonstrates the close fit between the career goals of individuals and the economic goals of their publishing organisations, an identity of interest which takes precedence over any acclaim or prestige accorded to them by their peers for creativity or innovation. Moreover, most editors define achievement for themselves and their competitors – and have it defined for them by their employers – in accordance with what is here termed 'the commercial imperative' (cf. Cohen and Young, 1973). Support for this belief is pragmatically based on self-interest. Occupational status, career mobility and job security all revolve around a 'good track record' in terms of copy sales, advertisement revenue and overall profitability. These provide criteria for assessment and comparison of an editor's performance by managers, advertisers, peers and competitors. The extent to which commercial success defines this group's 'taken-for-granted world' is illustrated by remarks such as this:

The important end of your market is always your youngest. If you've got somebody of 60 you might possibly keep them for ten years before they die, and that is a very non-productive advertising area. Now let's not kid ourselves. Magazines are produced to make a profit, and they make a profit out of advertising. Therefore the younger end of your market is vital.

(Women's weekly editor)

Acceptance of the commercial imperative as a belief which unites at a group level does not disguise its divisiveness at the individual one. It separates the achievers from the non-achievers. It confers personal and occupational status. It gives rise to positive and concrete expression through managerial and budgetary support. Through its imperative aspects, by making sales success the ultimate arbiter of editor performance, it provides the most pervasive and influential group belief of all, because all other rewards derive from it.[12]

Responsibility to the audience

The belief that they have a duty towards their readers comes second only to editors' beliefs about their duty to their employers and the commercial imperative. Many claim that 'the reader comes first'. Many feel so strongly about being fair to the audience that they are prepared to argue with their masters in terms of opposing cover price increases, or asking for more editorial pages in a thin issue where there are insufficient advertisements to justify them.

These editors see their wider social role as one of guardianship towards the audience. This concept is prescriptive. It involves ethical overtones of what an editor should do in her readers' best interests, and causes her to set norms for herself and her staff in respect of audience responsibility. The majority of editors defined their 'reader service' ethic in terms evocative of the 'service ideal' of the traditional or caring professions. The importance attached to the idea of 'giving' the reader something – practical advice, entertainment, value for money – is demonstrated by these editors, one British, one American:

It was never consciously worked out, as 'let's make the public think that we have all the answers'. She said that no successful magazine was ever founded on cynicism, and she managed to gather about herself a group of mainly women who'd got a kind of missionary zeal about putting across their message. Their message seemed to be that, with their help, a woman's life could be that little bit better.

(Women's weekly associate editor)

Well 'service' defines as help, and the magazine is not designed primarily for pastime, nor as controversy or for general education. We do not have the space, we do have deadlines, we are restricted in various ways from covering some kinds of events and subjects and the like, so that we're talking about help when we're talking about service.

(Editor-in-Chief, *Woman's Day*, USA)

In voicing their aim of providing a helpful service these editors subscribe to the similar ideals and ethics claimed by television and newspaper producers (see e.g. Windlesham, 1969; Whale, 1980). Yet there are distinctive ways in which such beliefs are applied within women's magazines. In talking about audience responsibilities, the high priestesses often use language that is more typical of family, partnership or pastoral dialogue than media communications channels. Many espouse a concept of 'caring' for their readers, with caring applied in emotive or affective terms as much as ethical or cognitive ones. The strength of an editor's caring about the audience is shared by, and expressed through, her editorial team, and their degree of dedication to the job. Caring in this context implies that there is audience dependency on the one hand, and editorial reinforcement of positive self-esteem on the other:

It's a support role really, and encouragement. Our policy – we don't actually spell it out – is you can do anything you really want to, if you want to, here's how. And so we sort of push and push and say, 'Yes, you can, yes you can. Yes you can do a job, yes you can get a degree, yes you can be prettier, yes you can be a better lover, yes you can travel abroad.'

All the time we keep on titillating their appetites, and then built into all that entertainment surface is a lot of fact and further addresses and help.

(Women's monthly editor)

Thus the collective sense of care and duty towards the female audience is fulfilled through the belief that women's magazines provide services for their audience – information, support and guidance. In doing this they support Brown's conclusion (1969: 156): 'It may be extremely difficult for literary intellectuals to believe that popular journalists consider their work to be of social importance, yet there are grounds for suggesting that this is indeed the case.'

Approaches to the editing task – the 'thinkers' and the 'feelers'

If beliefs about publishing for profit and audience responsibility link women's magazine editors to the wider world, what beliefs do they share about themselves and their work approach inside the editorial walls? Previous participation suggested, and interview data confirmed, that women's magazine editors fall into two classes: the 'thinkers' and the 'feelers'. Alternatively, they may be defined as primarily rational or primarily intuitive in their job approach, where 'rational' in this context means an editing mode which seeks to apply evidence or 'factual' criteria to decisions about content, whereas 'intuitive' refers to one which employs experiential insights or subjective feelings as a basis for decisions. Not all editors could be assigned neatly into one or the other category. Some blur the dividing line between the two approaches unconsciously, others quite deliberately. If 'gut feel' does not come up with an answer, then they may consider looking at some research findings. In choosing whichever stance suits their strategy of the moment – 'I just have this feeling that women are getting all romantic and broody again' – they perhaps call upon the alternative approach, consulting marriage, divorce and fertility tables only when the favoured one does not give any definite answer.

The extent of consensus between many editors – and their managers – about the utility, validity and legitimacy of intuition as a guide for action is one of the most significant findings of this study:

You do get down with editing sometimes to what for want of better words is gut feeling. It's also something that you feel with your fingertips.

(Women's monthly editor)

When old X asked me how I did it, I'd learned a bit by then and so I pointed to myself and said 'with my belly – it's all in here'. He reported back to management that I did it by magic and I was never troubled again.

(Women's monthly editor)

I think it's a total ego trip. It's very self-indulgent in that you put things in that you care about and want to read yourself. If you do it as an intellectual exercise I don't think it comes off in warmth. I'm not sure that I can put it into words – all I know is that I literally measure everything by me, always have done.

At the same time I just think that there are lots of people like me that want to learn a bit more about something, that often have vague stirrings to do something different, either knock over the traces, or run away from every-body, or be prime minister, or else just go home and knit. You have all these feelings.

(Women's monthly editor)

In contrast to this emotive approach is the altogether cooler and more analytical style of other editors:

I think editing can be a very objective process. I think it is in my case. I'm perfectly objective about this magazine. I'm perfectly clear about what those stories are doing – I wouldn't read those stories myself for pleasure.

When I got the job and had to think about editing, the starting point was: here's a magazine, it's successful already, let's see what it's doing, what it provides – vicarious excitement, reassurance. What kind of woman would need that? Well, they must be lonely, uncertain and bored, otherwise they wouldn't need it.

After that I actually used titbits I picked up from sociological research. It was a book – an account of what happened to families that had been living in the East End. I thought it was an absolute bible. It went on for almost three years to a most literal extent. In fact we actually ran a story series about a new estate.

(Women's monthly editor)

The 'gut feel' approach suggests that the concept of purposively rational conduct (Weber, 1968a) needs to be revised if it is to be applicable here. The type of instrumental rationality used by most of these editors is one that employs intuitions about the audience as a means to an end. Where these intuitions are accepted, confirmed and thus legitimated by staff and managers within the total publishing structure, using intuitions as a means to the end of making a message decision can be seen as rational, and may be appropriately described by the term 'intuitive rationality'.[13]

Where the 'gut feel', 'just knowing' or 'I get a feeling' approach is believed to be, and is acted upon as, the most appropriate means to immediate ends such as content decisions and to the ultimate end of achieving higher sales – is its appropriateness legitimated by default? Is it the most appropriate means because there are no other guides to decision, just as there are no satisfactory explanations of differences in journalistic or sales performance between competing editors.

Intuition emerged as the strongest source of editor certainty both in choosing message content and in creating its form. As such, it is associated with, and is integral to, the editor mystique:

Editors know by instinct. You're paid to be right, this is what I always say, and the minute you're wrong you deserve to be fired – and you will be. So, finally, it's your instinct which, if you've been doing it long enough, you can rely on.
(Women's monthly editor)

Feedback about the readers is valuable because it gives you new things you didn't know about – but you must rely on instinct first. Feedback in a sense bolsters up what you already know.
(Women's monthly editor)

It's a hunch, it's a feeling, that's what editing is about. If you haven't got it you should do something else.
(Women's weekly editor)

On closer scrutiny, however, the editing process turns out to be not quite so totally based on the editor's own 'gut feeling' as many claim. Other intuitive sources of content inspiration and decisional validation emerge. These include the impressions and feelings of partners, friends and colleagues, with many an editor's secretary standing in for an audience of millions as to whether a photograph is 'right', or a 'special offer' dress liked. Other more 'factual' sources of information and confirmation are provided by readers' letters, press hand-outs, 'contacts' inside or outside the business, television, newspapers, other women's magazines – even the findings of market research. Thus decisions are based on material or factual evidence – however impressionistic or fragmentary – as much as on, or prior to, intuition, which determines what importance is attached to these bits of evidence.

All that consumerism stuff – we've analysed ourselves out of our minds with readers' letters on that. Really, the questions are all legal, pensions, tax, careers – whereas they used to be 'how do I get stains out of my carpets?'

The letters have got worse about pensions and things. We're a last resort now. They've been to their Pensions' Office, the lovely lady there who was going to sort it out hasn't sorted it out. They've been to the Citizens Advice Bureau and they sent them back to the Pensions' Office . . . they come to us as an absolutely last resort.
(Women's weekly editor)

I suppose I use readers a bit like I use market research: to reassure me that what I am doing is running along similar paths. I have a breakdown every month of which correspondence comes in to each department. The report then deals specifically with the roses and the bricks – and I pass them on to the department heads.

(Women's monthly editor)

Many editors claimed disdain for audience research and marketing studies. Whether what editors *say* they do in respect of audience research is the same as what they *actually* do is difficult to discover. Typically, they are dismissive or ambivalent: 'They only tell you what you already knew all along', or 'I only take any notice when they say what I knew anyway'. In practice, selective perception turns out to be the favoured approach. Market research findings are accepted or rejected according to whether they reinforce or contradict the editor's pre-existing attitudes, values, beliefs or intuitions:

I never needed feedback. I only ever used market research or reps' reports to confirm to other people what I knew all the time. The only exception was when old X taught me the secret of the thorough readership. If on a boom issue the market research shows a very high thorough readership – this means they didn't just read the sub-titles, intros and bits, but they actually read the features and fiction to the end – then you know it's going to go.

(Women's weekly editor)

The uncertainty of the 1980s has brought a slight swing towards audience research. Some editors welcome it in their search for new insights into, and information about, their client/target group, especially if they specify the research topics and select the relevant findings.[14] In addition, as content analysis showed, increased use is made of surveys and questionnaires in the magazines themselves as a means of monitoring audience attitudes and behaviour. There is an interesting comparison between the attitudes of American and British editors to research. The attitude of American editors is generally more favourable to audience research – especially on the part of male editors. Is this perhaps because of their 'honorary female' status within the women's magazine world? Does their being male limit the extent to which they can employ the empathetic self-reference open to born female high priestesses?

With or without benefit of market research, the editor as symbol of sacred knowledge and holder of a hotline to the Almighty, conveys certainty: she knows what the audience wants to read. Whatever private doubts she may have about her personal or creative capacities, whatever credit she may give to the talent or hard work of others, her public face is the face of certainty. Standing Descartes on his head, she and her peers collectively suggest: 'I *am* [editor], therefore I *know*.' An editor, unlike a philosopher, cannot afford the time for doubt.

Editor autonomy: freedom from and freedom to

The editors of women's magazines, like other 'sovereign' editors (see especially Tunstall, 1977), hold strong beliefs about their areas of autonomous action and spheres of personal control. These beliefs embrace the normative concept of autonomy as much as the empirical one. They refer to what 'ought' to be as much as what 'is' within their editorial domains, and are supported by reference to what may be termed the 'Divine Right of Editors'.

What these editors typically mean when they use the word 'autonomy' is that when they come to determine the form and content of their magazine's message, they are free *from* external pressures, and free *to* take decisions on these matters. This power to determine content refers primarily to editorial subject matter but carries an implied power to veto advertisements which are judged potentially offensive, fraudulent or not consonant with a particular magazine's identity. The fluctuating power of an editor to resist external pressures – from managers, unions, manufacturers or advertisers – in shaping the total message of her magazine points to the relative and contingent nature of the autonomy which she enjoys.

The most influential factors in determining an editor's freedom relate to beliefs about the commercial imperative and audience responsibility discussed above. Similarly, in the way that her special knowledge of what the audience wants to read – her 'just knowing' what they want – is testified to (or not) within the editorial team and the total publishing context by her current ABC sales figures, so are her powers to determine the editorial message or resist unwelcome advertisements equally conditional on market success.

Editors' beliefs in the divine right to control what gets printed in their magazines are tested during times of crisis. This is explored in chapter 6 in relation to the period when things 'went wrong' on 'Her Weekly'. The extent to which editors believe their powers should encompass to the vetoing of disliked advertisements is less clear cut or universally upheld. The reasons for this uncertainty are complex. They relate to the degree of personal and professional integrity that individual editors apply in translating their beliefs about responsibility to the audience – as well as their beliefs about responsibility to their employers – into practical actions. In attempting to exercise her sacred rights over what gets printed in the pages of her magazine, the editor is caught between the two markets her product is intended to sell to: on the one hand, the audience, and on the other, the advertisers who seek the attention of that particular audience, and whose revenue still subsidises the production cost of that magazine product. Does this mean that women's magazine editors are both manipulated by, and manipulators of, a materialist ideology which purveys a crude consumerism to the audience in the form of an ever-escalating level of consumer aspirations and expectations?

The answer to this is that women's magazine editors are acutely aware of their female audience as consumers, but primarily as consumers of their own magazine. One area of content over which they claim autonomy is coverage of new products. They *are* courted and pressurised by manufacturers, advertisement and public relations executives, and the extent to which an individual editor resists or succumbs to such pressures when they are in conflict with her judgement is as much a function of personal integrity in terms of perceived audience responsibility as it is of the constraints imposed by a particular editorial ethos, or by a poor climate for advertisement revenue. For example, during the reign of Mary Grieve on *Woman* in the 1950s, when advertisement revenues were at their most lucrative, there was an absolute ban on the mentioning of a manufacturer's name with reference to any product 'featured' in the magazine. The same stern injunction was not applied by editors of competing journals (and indeed staff members attempted to argue that withholding of brand name information was a positive disservice to readers who might seek out those particular articles to buy).

On this question of individual integrity, this study yielded several instances where editors whose freedom to resist disliked advertisements was reinforced or legitimated by sales success. For example, in the 1960s the editor of *Woman* refused to accept advertisements for a fraudulent 'bust developer' which ran in other magazines; in the early 1970s the editors of several IPC women's magazines carried their resistance to vaginal deodorant sprays to boardroom level on the ground that they were potentially harmful; in the early 1980s some editors of IPC magazines demonstrated their autonomy over total content by accepting advertisements for abortion clinics, others by refusing them.

Do such instances exonerate editors from charges of collusion with advertisers, or at the very least of condoning the raising of unrealistic audience expectations in relation to the consumer goods that they 'feature' in their editorial pages, or carry in their advertisement ones? As the above examples show, this question is empirical as much as it is ideological. It relates both to the shared beliefs of women's magazine editors and to the actions and situational constraints of individuals.

'She's a real pro'

The fifth belief that editors share is that they are 'professionals'. Like other occupational groups, women's magazine editors combine ideas about the 'right' way of working, professionalism, with those of professional occupational status. These editors and those who make up their editorial teams have a strong self-concept of themselves as professional working journalists. This is equated with taking an endlessly painstaking approach to the job in applying their craft and creative skills, in the context of their specialist knowledge about the specific traditions and techniques of message making for the cult of femininity. Being professional also involves personnel management skills in running what are often large staffs: moreover it involves the political skills essential to survival in a competitive environment, the business management skills required of editors to sell merchandise through their pages, and skills of promotion and public presentation – exposure on other media, addressing advertising conferences, and sometimes publicly meeting the readers.

Many writers (cf. Goode, 1969; Pavalko, 1971; Johnson, 1972; Halmos, 1973) agree that an occupational group's claim to professional status invariably rests on three elements – a claim to autonomy, commitment to the ideal of service, and a claim to a specialist knowledge base. Goode also points out 'that the claim to autonomy or trust loses its point unless the client or society can *in fact* be *harmed* because of unethical or incompetent work by the practitioner' (1969: 296, emphasis original). In so far as these editors do share a specialist knowledge base – the rites, rituals and dogmas of the cult of femininity – and in so far as their claim to autonomy rests on a prior claim of offering a service to the public, they do conform to this agreed definition of professionalism. On the criterion of being able to harm society by unethical or incompetent work, however, the answer is less clear-cut, but it is difficult to see how they could do active harm in the way that an incompetent surgeon might do.

In addition to the traditional 'caring' or 'personal' professions, which sociologists have looked at, there are other, less studied types of professional. For example, there are professional, as opposed to amateur, footballers. The captain of a team may resemble the editor of a women's magazine in being relatively highly skilled; in possessing the ability to 'read' a game, just as women's magazine editors 'read' their audience; in putting in long hours without complaint when duty calls; in acting by turns the role of inspirer and slave-driver; and in sometimes playing dirty (committing a 'professional' foul). In some respects editors resemble these kinds of professionals more than those of the traditional professions such as doctors. At all events, the belief in professionalism, and the perception of themselves as professionals is so strongly held by editors that the ultimate accolade to an editor's ears is 'she's a real pro'.

This chapter has introduced the key actors in the editorial process, the editors themselves. It has examined the attributes, practices and beliefs of this group of individualists who share certain broad work and ethical norms, but whose selection, training and career trajectories differ widely.

This chapter has also pointed to the powers of these editors and the decision-making criteria that they call upon, distinguishing between 'the thinkers' and 'the feelers' in directing their editorial teams. In the performance of their editing task they also wield wider social powers. It is they who decide which beliefs and practices will be included in, or excluded from, the message. It is they who decide what will be inscribed upon, or struck off, the feminine agenda. It is they – in their role of high priestesses to the cult of femininity – who determine the holy writ of women's magazines.

In making decisions about what to include in or exclude from their pages they act in accordance with a set of group beliefs identified by this study as belief in the commercial imperative; in responsibility or service towards the audience; in rational or intuitive task approach; in autonomy and in professionalism. All these beliefs are brought to bear on the production process by which the messages of women's magazines come into being, and how they respond to a greater or lesser degree to changes in the world outside. Chapter 7 considers the relationship between that production process, the editorial process, and the total publishing structure – the organisational and 'political' context within which editors' beliefs are brought to bear on message content.

6

Shaping the Message: The Impact of Organisation, Tradition and Process

This chapter deals with the publishing organisation and editorial process which provide the context for the editor's role – and through her, influence how the message comes about, what it says, and how responsive it is to what is happening in the outside world. It begins by comparing the structure of two publishing organisations, and explores the impact of their scale and hierarchy upon the respective editors in their selecting and shaping of the feminine agenda. It does this by looking at the way the message is moulded in accordance with women's magazine traditions and by the efforts of the editorial team. These processes are then examined historically through a composite picture of a typical weekly production line in action – that of 'Her Weekly'.

What impact does the wider publishing organisation have upon the editor, and through her on the message? To what extent do women's magazine editors feel that they belong within, or are distant from, the centres of power and authority of their employing organisation? It is a fact of everyday working life for any media producer – however individualistic, timid, temperamental or tyrannical – that he or she must operate both within the larger structure and with smaller groups. To realise their creative and career goals these women's magazine editors work with many sets of experts inside and outside their editorial domains – writers, sub-editors, artists, photographers; advertising, marketing, publicity, and circulation specialists. They also have formal and informal links with the wider organisation – lines of accountability, networks of communication, ties of political allegiance or clientship. Through these formal and informal links they act as the main channel for information in both directions between the editorial team and the organisation as a whole.

From the editors' accounts working relationships inside their teams tend to be of three kinds, competitive, cooperative or conflictual. Outside them, relationships with promotion or advertising specialists, or with line managers generally were seen as more complex. The degree of complexity was perceived as scale-related: they are governed by bureaucratic or paternalistic norms, by whether the management ethos is one of impersonality or direct involvement, by how many layers of authority intervene between them and 'the top' (cf. Udy, 1959; Webber, 1970; Blau and Schoenherr, 1971). The interview data suggest that editors' beliefs about the relative autonomy or powerlessness that they feel when they compare their own degree of administrative or creative freedom with those of other editors, are influenced by factors such as these.

Editors' views illustrate three factors that affect the way in which management is seen to impinge on the role: the gulf of comprehension between the 'editorial' and 'management' sides, the different values of management, and the sheer size of the organisation.

I've got to admit that I've never yet met a magazine management that I can respect as a journalist. They see a magazine as something to be exploited. Most managements that I've dealt with didn't in fact read. Consequently it's very hard to get them to understand why a piece of copy has taken four days to produce, why it's been rewritten three times, because to them it was perfectly okay after the first time.
Photography is a bit easier except that they all think they know what makes a good picture. You've got to sometimes pander to them . . . his favourite colour is green, let's give him green, kind of thing, where it doesn't matter.
(Women's monthly editor)

The parent company of *Vogue* is in New York. The separate companies are autonomous in so far as they have their own board of directors, of which I am one – a statutory one! Management has never been a problem, but remember that this is a very small company. I mean, when you get into the biggest, you're practically in an inverted pyramid with the tiny editorial bit at the bottom.
(Women's monthly editor)

The modern structure of very large companies was doomed to destroy the editors. It might produce a viable financial commodity for a time but it's bound to destroy editors because no editor can take a risk. They don't know who they are placating or impressing, and these are both impossible emotions in an editor's life.
(Women's weekly editor)

Organisation and process: the impact of structure and scale
In an attempt to explore the validity of editors' accounts of how they were affected by the size of the publishing organisations that they worked for, two publishing structures were examined in the light of the considerable literature devoted to complex organisations (see e.g.

Levinson, 1957; Etzioni, 1964; Bittner, 1965; Pugh *et al.*, 1968; Hall, 1968; Argyris, 1971; Perrow, 1972; Salaman, 1981). These publishing structures were those of IPC's Women's Magazines Group and The National Magazine Company Limited.

The large-scale: IPC Women's Magazines Group
The formation of this company was traced in Chapter 2. Following the take-overs of 1958–61, central control and coordination were achieved gradually within the three pseudo-autonomous houses of Odhams, Newnes and Fleetway. On the most successful titles overt interference was minimal at first: no one wished to upset the geese who were laying the golden eggs. Above the editor of *Woman*, for example, was the editorial director of several magazines, who sat on the Odhams board and remained in office for a time. Later, an editorial overlord of women's magazines was appointed for a brief period by the Mirror Group, but by and large the three company structures functioned semi-independently.

With the formation of IPC Magazine Division in 1968, these earlier lines of command were swept away. During the following decade, there were frequent structural changes. In the five years between the autumn of 1968 and December 1974 five changes of management structure occurred.[1] These changes involved different groupings of different types of magazines – the present Women's Magazines Group was formed in April 1971 – and different arrangements into tiers of main and subsidiary boards of directors. By and large the same faces stayed at the top, providing a measure of continuity, with some moving between advertising, promotion or circulation, creating a ripple effect of re-appointments beneath them each time. Between 1975 and 1980, there were four further alterations to the management structure, and the one current at end-1981 is shown in Figure 6.1.

Over the years, what did all this mean for the high priestesses, their editorial processes and the form and content of the cult's messages? The changes, which were of greatest significance for editors within the organisation which has acquired the colloquial label of 'the Ministry of Magazines' (*The Times*, 25 May 1982), were the introduction of the publisher system, the centralisation of ancillary service departments and the formal (in terms of status) recognition of outstanding contributions by editors to the company's profits. The first of these – the introduction of 'publishers' in 1968 – created an additional level of hierarchy between editors and the IPC Magazines Board (who themselves came under the main IPC Board, which in turn came under the Reed International Board). The publisher was responsible for meeting a magazine's profit, promotion, advertisement and circu-

Figure 6.1   Board Structure: IPC Women's Magazines Group, 1981

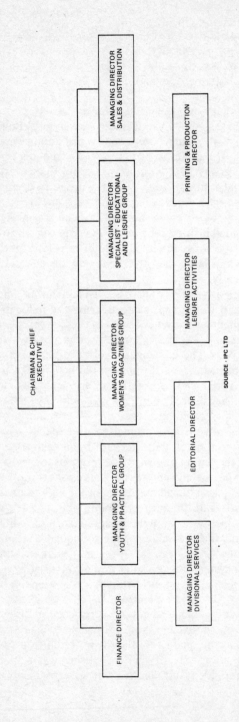

CHAIRMAN & CHIEF EXECUTIVE

FINANCE DIRECTOR

MANAGING DIRECTOR YOUTH & PRACTICAL GROUP

MANAGING DIRECTOR DIVISIONAL SERVICES

MANAGING DIRECTOR WOMEN'S MAGAZINES GROUP

EDITORIAL DIRECTOR

MANAGING DIRECTOR SPECIALIST · EDUCATIONAL AND LEISURE GROUP

MANAGING DIRECTOR LEISURE ACTIVITIES

MANAGING DIRECTOR SALES & DISTRIBUTION

PRINTING & PRODUCTION DIRECTOR

SOURCE · IPC LTD

lation targets, as well as for 'editorial policy and its anticipated effect on the readership profile'.[2]

In 1971 these responsibilities were split between publisher and publishing director, the former concentrating on the business side and the latter on overall editorial policy. For editors of smaller circulation magazines, the publisher was of greater day-to-day importance. On the larger weeklies, it was the publishing (later, editorial) directors who exerted the greater impact on editors and through them on what the magazines were saying. Theirs was a watching brief; they monitored the form and content of the message at all times. By and large, direct intervention was reserved for situations where sales were falling, or editorial matter deemed to have violated the canons of consensus morality or good taste. When problems arose, they had the authority to call the editor to account or suggest changes in policy or presentation.

In practice the publisher system can work for, as well as against, an editor's will, since the pressures are not always applied only in a downward direction. Editors can cultivate publishers and publishing directors as allies, or consult them about risky decisions. Editors with good working relationships with their publisher or publishing director – who might have previous editor experience themselves – know they can argue an editor's case for extra resources: more staff, more money, or more editorial pages in a slim issue where low advertisement sales have reduced size overall.

The second significant structural change for editors took the form of centralising certain ancillary or 'servicing' departments, such as advertising and promotion, within the Women's Magazines Group. For example, the advertising departments of individual magazines were amalgamated and a policy of 'Group Sell' inaugurated in October 1976. Editors of individual magazines lost their 'own' ad-man and other specialists, becoming instead clients of 'group' managers. Several editors deplored the loss of 'uniqueness' in being herded together with their internal competitors, and from mid-1979 this system was modified to allow the major titles and groups more advertisement autonomy, although they continued to function within a form of 'Group Sell' throughout the period of this study.[3]

A third significant structural change was the formal recognition of editor importance. In 1976, the two editors commanding the two highest circulations, those of *Woman's Own* and *Woman's Weekly*, were appointed to directorships on the two ancillary Women's Magazine Group boards (subsequently disbanded) which reported to the main IPC Magazines Board. (These appointments increased to five the number of directors with prior editor experience who have served on Women's Magazine Group Boards since their inception.) This was the first time that sitting editors, with no other management functions, had been awarded this distinction and their prestige was heightened in the eyes of both peers and staffs in consequence. By 1980, the situation had changed again: one editor moved into management and off the board, the other retired and was not replaced. This left one female representative, the Editorial Director, on the IPC Magazines main board.

The medium-scale: National Magazine Company Ltd
In terms of history and organisational structure, the medium-scale National Magazine Company presents an interesting comparison. Throughout the period of this study it had an unprecedentedly stable management structure. It had the same managing director from 1963 to 1982. Perhaps because of this continuity and perhaps because of its smaller scale – it publishes only five women's magazines in comparison with IPC's seventeen – an editor's line to the top has always been shorter, more open and more clearly defined.

National Magazines introduced its version of the publisher system in 1969. In this company that role is really that of the business manager: 'it says "bus man" on my payslip', one explained. In practice the relationship between editors and publishers is a working partnership, with both responsible directly to the top. A publisher clarified how this works in practice:

The publishers' function is to be responsible for their magazine as a profit centre and, at the same time, to be the top advertisement salesman of the magazine with an Advertisement Director or Manager and advertisement representative under them.
In fact, the publishers have not got total control. Most importantly, they do not control the editors. They are level with their own editor and work by cooperation and, hopefully, agreement as to the development of the magazine.

Until the late 1970s, there was no British board structure as such. The management hierarchy consisted of a managing director and company secretary, as well as seven American directors from the Hearst Corporation. In 1979 a new board structure was created. Five new British directors were appointed – including the publishers of *Cosmopolitan, Good Housekeeping, Harpers and Queen* – which raised the 'local' board members to seven, while the American directors were raised to eleven. The only other structural changes that occurred during the period of this study were the board appointment of the (female) publisher of *Company*, the resignation of the Assistant Managing Director and appointment of a Deputy Managing Director (who subsequently succeeded to the top position in 1982). The board structure which was in operation in 1981, at the end of this period of study, is shown in Figure 6.2.

In the medium-scale National Magazine Company, as with the larger IPC, the content, form and short-term policy of their magazines are largely left to editors if they maintain a satisfactory sales performance. The editors in 'Nat Mag' claim that shorter lines of communication allow them to initiate contact with the Managing Director, or to receive feedback, more easily and directly – they can simply pick up the phone. Another factor, that was thought to be conducive to openness of communication at the time of this study, was the managing director's previous role as an editor and editorial director. His editors saw this prior experience as a great asset. Not only did this managing director provide continuity during the nineteen years he held his post, but he had also shared in the editing mystique, and understood the nature of its special knowledge. Yet despite this, no other editors have been appointed to the National Magazine Board.

Although, they differ in scale and hierarchy, the two companies are similar in certain respects that directly and indirectly bear upon their editors. For example, the medium-scale National Magazine Company and the larger-scale IPC Women's Magazines Group conform to the post-war pattern of media ownership discussed in Chapter 2 in that they both are part of multinational, multi-media conglomerates. A conclusion of this study was that the 'contingent autonomy' of publishing companies within much larger organisations is in many ways analogous to that of the editor. Degrees of freedom – and levels of esteem – are equally conditional upon a successful record as a profit producer. The satisfactory contribution of a National Magazine Company Ltd or an IPC Magazines Ltd to the annual accounts of their ultimate owners – the Hearst Corporation or Reed International plc – determines their standing and autonomy within the corporate pecking order – much in the same way as her current circulation and advertisement sales rating determine the standing and autonomy of a women's magazine editor.

If editors are controlled by beliefs about the commercial imperative is this because it is the ruling rationale of their employers, busy meeting the short-term goals of the annual profit plan? This question is relevant to the wider issue of who is manipulating whom in the corporate owner, publishing manager, women's magazine editor, female audience exchange, and raises further questions concerning consumer versus producer sovereignty. Is the female audience exercising the former and in part creating its own image of self – a particular variant of the cult of femininity – by actively choosing to purchase a particular women's magazine? These wider issues are ones

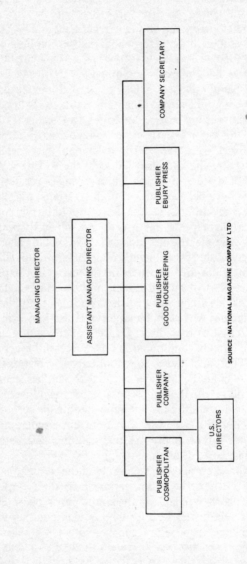

Figure 6.2   Board Structure: National Magazine Company, 1981

MANAGING DIRECTOR

ASSISTANT MANAGING DIRECTOR

COMPANY SECRETARY

PUBLISHER EBURY PRESS

PUBLISHER GOOD HOUSEKEEPING

PUBLISHER COMPANY

PUBLISHER COSMOPOLITAN

U.S. DIRECTORS

SOURCE : NATIONAL MAGAZINE COMPANY LTD

which have been discussed by, amongst others, Schumpeter (1954), Galbraith (1958, 1969), and Marris and Wood (1971).[4]

The editorial process: traditions and techniques

If the publishing organisation is one factor which affects the cult's messages, a second factor is the tradition and technique of women's magazine journalism. To a remarkable degree the form is the message as well as the content with these journals. Content analysis attests to this. The visual and verbal symbols they use impart meaning as much as the subject matter does, through the way in which content is categorised, conceptualised, shaped and delivered. Cover photographs on women's magazines the world over – in the developing societies as well as those of the industrialised world – are an illustration of this. They demonstrate how pictures of ever-smiling females are chosen to suggest that femininity is a desirable and pleasurable state. Such images convey, and help to create, homogeneity within the cult. By looking at the journalistic traditions and conventions employed to create a symbolic order intended to synthesise beliefs and practices about 'how best to be a woman' (i.e. smile), insights are gained into why the message takes the form it does, and why that message's consistency has persisted in so many respects over time.

One reason for continuity in the central tenets of the gospel has been the relatively secluded nature of women's magazine journalism in the past. In Britain, for example, until the mid-1970s, 'women's journalism', like 'women's things' and 'women's place' was a set apart and circumscribed affair. It was a decidedly mysterious and somewhat curious activity carried on – in the case of what is now IPC's Women's Magazines Group – in three main centres: the marbled halls of the Amalgamated Press/Fleetway Publications in Farringdon Street, the backrooms facing the white tiled wells of Odhams Press, 189 High Holborn, and the winding corridors behind the big clock and open cage lifts of George Newnes, Southampton Street. All three were a five-minute walk from Fleet Street, but a world away in terms of professional practice, ethos and salary scales. Perhaps their most visible difference was in the reversed sex ratios of their staffs. In these offices, men were a minority group, ghettoised in art departments or perhaps features, but never to be found within the female-only domains of cookery, beauty, fashion, knitting or home.

By the mid-1970s, this professional segregation by type of journalism and by sex was lessening. Recruitment from newspaper and other periodical genres became more common, with more men and more 'famous name' writers coming from outside the specialism. The geographic location of these three particular centres of women's magazine journalism also shifted. In 1976, they were 'rationalised' into the same building; they are now located 'across the River' in the open-plan offices of the King's Reach 'low rise'. There the mysterious ladies of the women's press quickly reverted to type by privatising their office corners with banks of filing cabinets and potted plants, and were soon demanding walls where none had been intended. This 'privatisation' of women's magazine journalists is evident even within the open-plan, primary colour offices of the National Magazine Company titles. The *Good Housekeeping* offices are sectionalised into 'something resembling Hampton Court maze' a publisher commented. This is in marked contrast to those of *Cosmopolitan*, where the editor, a former Fleet Street journalist, has re-created a wide open newspaper-style office where she sits in full view of the staff – and they of her.

Yet women's magazine journalism remains qualitatively different in many respects. It does not deal in the immediacy of news; its content is rarely dictated by overnight events. When it is, for British women's magazines, this is usually in response to a sudden royal event. Time and technological constraints imposed by long advanced printing deadlines are one reason for this. They involve forward planning some three to nine months before publication, and dispatching finished text, illustrations and lay-outs to the printer two to three months before the 'on-sale' date for monthlies, and three to six weeks for weeklies. Such constraints reinforce what is already a predisposition of the women's periodical press to a pre-packaged product of customary and expected subject matter.

Why should there be this predisposition when other periodicals, such as Sunday newspaper colour supplements, also work to advanced deadlines? The first reason why women's magazines are pre-packaged with customary and expected subject matter is that they are *culture-bound*; the second is that they are *category-bound*. They locate themselves within the boundaries of consensual definitions of the female culture, and confine themselves to the categories of experience that society, and these journals, assign to women. Consequently, those who act as scribes to the high priestesses, and to the cult of femininity, themselves become prone to ritualisation in their professional practices in promulgating its pre-ordained writs and rituals.

This ritualisation is consistent with the way in which women's magazine editorial processes operate. First comes the time-honoured division of sections or categories of subject matter. Next come the 'ideas' to fill each category week by week or month by month. Last comes the shaping of the message to fit the cult's maxims, a particular editorial tradition or company marketing strategy, and a given editor's personal preferences. (The latter can sometimes be very personal indeed: 'Get that fat actor, what's his name, for that fashion feature – fat men turn me on', an editor once instructed the author.)

Pre-determined categories

Several implicit assumptions can be discerned on the part of editors and journalists which predispose women's magazines towards culture and category boundedness. These assumptions can be observed not only in British women's magazines, but also cross-nationally. The first, and most pervasive, assumption is that women's magazines by definition are a separate, specialist genre devoted to 'female interests', and that their devotions accord with the presumed homogeneity of the exclusively female culture they reflect. Their second implicit assumption is that women's magazines provide the female sex with a unique voice, one which will simultaneously proselytise new members to the cult of femininity whilst sustaining old ones in the faith. From *Elle* to *Brigitte* to *Grazia* to *Family Circle* and *Good Housekeeping*, women's magazines contain their subject matter within the parallel tracks provided by cultural and professional tradition. Like the majority of advertisements directed at women (see e.g. Millum, 1975; Langholz-Leymore, 1975; Goffman, 1979), they too reflect the areas of interest that are customarily assigned to females.

The content categories of the traditional division of editorial specialisms – cookery, fashion, personal problems and home – reflect this him, home and appearance-centredness. These divisions also create within the production structure teams of specialists with organisational interests in preserving those self-same separate categories. Content analyses confirmed the extent to which these subject divisions have remained constant, not only in Britain, but cross-nationally, throughout the period of this study. Does this consistency reinforce the shared norms and values which make for similarity in the cult's messages and a sense of solidarity amongst the faithful? The contents pages of the three British women's weeklies reproduced on page 160 show the prominence still given in 1980 to the 'service' areas of home, beauty, knitting and health, in addition to the perennial 'regulars' such as horoscopes, readers' letters and the problem pages. These 'regulars' are just that, familiar in form, content and positioning: readers' letters on page three and horoscopes and problem pages at the back throughout the periods of content analysis.

What is remarkable is how little expansion has occurred in the subject categories presented to the audience. Amongst the few categories which have been added to the feminine agenda during the

woman

WHO WE ARE

EDITOR	Jo Sandilands
ASSOCIATE EDITOR	Penny Radford
ART EDITOR	Nick Overhead
ASSISTANT EDITORS	Wendy Henry George Cannon
SENIOR EDITOR	Billie Figg
FASHION	Willa Beattie
BEAUTY	Arline Usden
HOME	Andrea Spencer
KNITTING	Lesley Stanfield
COOKERY	Frances Naldrett
FEATURES	Davina Lloyd
ACTIONWOMAN	Jan Walsh
FICTION	Rose Wild
TRAVEL & MOTORING	Jean Barratt
YOU & US	Kate Mahony
PICTURES	Barbara Peevor
CHIEF SUB-EDITOR	Linda Belcher
CORRESPONDENCE	Terry Austin

WHAT'S IN IT FOR YOU

Cover Chris Grout-Smith. Hair and make-up: Martin at Harı & Friends.

WHERE WE ARE

KING'S REACH TOWER
STAMFORD STREET, LONDON SE1 9LS.
TEL: 01-261 5413.
Advertising inquiries: 01-261 6770.
VOLUME 87 NUMBER 2250

Prices—including VAT at current rate—quoted in this issue are correct at time of going to press. © IPC Magazines Ltd., 1980.

CONTENTS

Cover by John Shelley/ Overseas Photo and Feature Agency

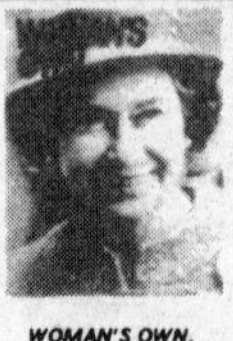

WOMAN'S OWN, KING'S REACH TOWER, LONDON SE1 9LS. JULY 5, 1980 Reader Service: 01-261 5823/5797/5843 Editorial: 01-261 5474. Offers: Medway 404221 Advertisement Manager Ian Cooper: 01-261 5198 Prices quoted in this issue were correct at time of going to press. The Editor reserves the right to shorten or modify any letters or material submitted. We regret that we cannot answer letters unless they are accompanied by a stamped addressed envelope. © IPC Magazines Ltd., 1980

WOMAN'S WEEKLY

KING'S REACH TOWER,
STAMFORD STREET, LONDON SE1 9LS
01-261 6617 and 6131
Knitting: 01-261 6317
Advertising: 01-261 6660

CONTENTS

© IPC Magazines Ltd., 1980

Figure 6.3 Contents pages, three British women's weeklies, 1980
Reproduced by kind permission of IPC.

post-war period are travel, money management and consumerism. In some cases – notably fiction, problem pages and features – existing categories have changed out of all recognition, whereas the home-based and self-centred categories, such as cookery or beauty, have bent with fashion but retained their sacrosanct status. They are doubly sacred as categories of female experience defined as essential to female group membership – and to women's magazine advertisement revenue.

Interviews with journalists, editors and publishers revealed an unquestioning acceptance of this world view. For them, these divisions of feminine concern were pre-ordained, 'natural' in fact: 'every woman has a home to care for, even if she lives alone', was a frequent explanation. This world view is here called the Gertrude Stein, or 'a woman, is a woman, is a woman' approach to women's magazine journalism.[5] This primary division of subject matter into 'female interest' or 'service' areas also extends into a secondary classification of all content as entertainment or information.

Creating the bright ideas

The pressures of inspiration, desperation and production fuel the creative brainstorming sessions of women's magazine journalism. These conclaves – alternately 'laid back' or frenetic – differ little from those of other media in many ways, yet the generation and application of ideas in this medium has implications for some of the wider questions raised by this study. Firstly, it offers indications of changing conditions – in terms of a magazine's responsiveness to internal organisation and production pressures, and to external changes in what women are doing within society, and within a particular magazine's client/target group. Secondly, the choosing of ideas for publication places a great deal of power in the hands of the editor whose decisions can be quite arbitrary, or whimsical, or both.

'Where do ideas come from?' was a question put to all the journalists, artists and editors interviewed. Their replies confirmed the extent to which media producers feed off one another – not only cannibalising their own species, but also devouring the output of others. This editor's comment was typical:

I read a lot. I see all the papers before I leave home in the morning. I listen to the radio on my way in, in the course of the day I'll leaf through maybe half a dozen other women's magazines from here, or around the world. When I get home I switch on the television – or I've got one in the office if I'm working late.

'Contacts' are another source of inspiration. The ideas they spark can range from the impressionistic to the factual, from an editor who says, 'My charlady buys only frozen dinners . . . don't know why we go on giving them balanced, budget meals' to one who observes 'I see sales of home computers have gone up, so we're trying one out and doing a feature on them.' The fact that these journalists know a priori the categories they must fill with ideas is reinforced by their corresponding specialisation of function within the editorial process. Fashion departments tend to produce only fashion ideas. Everyone wants to score as an idea person, and creativity is equated with the ability to produce a burst of ideas either spontaneously or on demand. Whatever their range, ideas are customarily submitted in writing by those whose union membership entitles them to do so. Only the editorial elite – the National Union of Journalists (NUJ) and Society of Lithographic Artists, Designers, Engravers and Process Workers (SLADE) members whose union card classifies them as such – are enfranchised to make a direct creative input.

Rarely, however, is the production of ideas as carefully orchestrated and categorised as in the content index reproduced as Table 6.1. This specifies the areas for which ideas are required to fill a single issue. Although these detailed guidelines provide the structure for this journal's successful editorial formula (an American women's monthly magazine), its philosophy is created by its editor in her selecting and shaping of those ideas that will carry her message.

Such detailed specifications are unusual, whether as a guide to 'ideas' to order, or as a guide to message shaping. Most women's magazines operate with similar broad divisions of subject matter but rely as much on *ad hoc* as on scheduled ideas. The 'tear sheet' is one common source of instant inspiration. These are pages torn from other magazines and used as a source of 'ideas', a routine form of plagiarism within one medium of a communication industry notable for its ability to 'rip off' the ideas of competitors. Tear sheets – which are literally ripped out – provide visual or written references for journalists, artists or photographers. Sometimes they are used as a springboard for a 'new idea'; at other times they are blatantly copied, as closely as copyright laws will allow. Spotting the ideas of others for adaptation or replication is learned early in the career of women's magazine journalists and done routinely as 'part of the job'. As such, it offers a case study of unintended value migration, where 'tear sheets' from *Elle, Brigitte, McCalls, Grazia* or *Damernas Värld* act as a form of instant, if unintended, cultural diffusion.

Shaping the message

When the bright ideas have been grasped from wherever and whomever, the editor makes her decisions as to which will be used, how they

*Table 6.1   Ideas scheduling outline: American women's monthly
magazine*[a]

---

1. Major emotional piece
2. Major sex piece
3. Profile
   a. Major
   b. Minor
4. Minor emotional/psychological/self-help pieces
   a. 'How to . . .' (answer the telephone/be more assertive in your job/etc.)
   b. Man/woman article (not about sex)
   c. Negative emotions (e.g. fear, anger, jealousy, etc.)
   d. Maturity/coping
   e. Friendship/family
5. Career story
6. Medical, health, or body piece
7. General piece
8. Gossip/celebrity piece
9. Strong visual piece
10. Quiz
11. Fiction
12. Regular services features
13. Supplement or bonus extra.

---

[a] Personal communication, copy document

will be 'handled', and when they will be printed. These are the critical editor actions, ones that have a particular social significance for these editors who act as high priestesses to the cult of femininity, and agenda setters for the female world. The fact that such decisions are usually made in conclave with senior or department editors underlines the sex-specificity of this communication process – overwhelmingly from females to females and back again – and its dualistic message which stresses both the separateness of, and solidarity between, women.

In translating editor decisions into words and pictures, women's magazine journalists employ an armoury of professional skills and techniques. These mould the message to fit the editors's prior briefing, her known predilections ('have you noticed how she chooses cover models that look like her?'), and the editorial traditions and marketing policies aimed at reaching a particular magazine's client/

target group. The skills and techniques that these journalists share with others include those of 'treatment', 'angling', 'editorial balance' and 'timing'. The techniques that they have advanced to the status of an art form within their own genre include what this study identifies and terms 'the reader test', 'write speak' and 'personalising' – and the creation of a 'consciously classless' female world. Examples of all these techniques abound in the content analysis quotations of earlier chapters. They are relevant here to the working of the editorial process as to how they assist or impede the responsiveness of the message to changes in the world outside.

'Treatment', 'angling', 'balance' and 'timing'

All these concepts are familiar journalistic devices employed for pragmatic reasons of achieving intended visual and textual effects and arousing specific audience responses. How do women's magazine versions of these techniques differ from those of other media? Here as elsewhere 'treatment' and 'angling' denote the choice of every word, picture, illustration and type face according to a set of professional and policy criteria. But here, superimposed on these criteria, is the prior consideration that every treatment and angle be relevant to *women*. This means choosing the symbol or stereotype of *feminine* courage, enterprise, true love, beauty or worldly success and then dramatising that aspect, however many times the copy has to be re-written or the layout re-drawn. Here, the medium truly is the message where form is as important as content, where every picture encapsulates or idealises an aspect of femininity, and every article is tightly tailored to 'the women's angle'.

'Editorial balance' and 'timing' are also techniques which women's magazine journalists share with those of other media, but practise in a different way. Considerations of balance concern not only the issue to hand, but also those which precede or follow it. They involve avoiding too much visually or verbally similar material, getting the right 'mix' of information and entertainment, and above all putting the whole recipe together in ways that will 'make the readers love the issue, and want to buy the next one'. The American monthly whose formula is shown in Table 6.1 presents a cameo of a precision exercise in editorial balance. More typically, the office walls of the editor, production, chief sub and art editor of every women's magazine are lined with detailed plans which show where the ads 'fall' and what can and cannot be moved in a given issue.

If balancing skills are learned through experiment, imitation or experience, the acquisition and exercise of a successful sense of 'timing' is more elusive. Timing, both in the sense of forward planning and in the ability to forecast trends, draws more upon judgement than experience. It is a critical aspect of the editor role in relation to her agenda-setting purposes, and her regulation of the rate at which social and cultural change will be filtered to the audience.[6]

Timing also refers to the ability to transform 'hot' news into the 'warmed up', reactive news of women's magazines. These journalists can not take the simple decision to report what happens today, as is the case with newspaper and television journalists who operate with audience–producer consensus that their purpose is to report the topical. However 'news' is defined, selected, created, reported, amplified, distorted, or censored it presents accounts of events deemed as demanding immediate audience attention.[7] Any illusion of immediacy in women's magazines is perforce constructed, crafted and timed. The kind and degree of timing skill required by women's magazine journalists is further constrained by the category boundedness of their subject matter and by their long-hold printing dates. This predisposes their messages towards the timeless rather than the timely, and is a further aspect of the homogeneity and continuity of the message. Typical 'timeless' features include 'Which personality (or beauty) type are you?' quizzes, deliberately non-seasonal recipes or knitting patterns, emotional or health 'think pieces', and articles on the mysteries of palmistry, astrology or numerology.

'Write–speak' and 'personalising'

One differing feature of women's magazines is their persuasive, woman-to-woman tone of voice, which skilfully and tellingly reinforces their supportive – and normative – stance towards the audience. This sisterly, companionable tone of voice permeates more than the editorial messages: it is echoed in the copy styles of their advertisers, and in the promotion language of press and television advertisements for the magazines themselves. Two techniques which typify the women's magazine tone of voice are those identified by this study as 'write–speak' and 'personalising'.

It is not clear whether write–speak is a language invented by women's magazine journalists, but the richness of its imagery and the fluency of its grammar have surely been perfected by them. In a medium which conveys a sense of belonging and group membership as a second order message of all content, the written word strives to evoke the intimacy of the spoken. So pervasive is this sense of talking to the audience that it carries over unconsciously into the language of the production process. An art editor asks of a cover transparency 'Does it talk to the reader?' The editor asks a knitting editor of a pull-over, 'What does it say?'

Novice journalists learn the craft of writing speech within this chatty communication context. They learn to use active verbs in the present tense and second person pronouns:

Don't let wet hair dampen your holiday. Take a few tips, use a few tricks, knots and clips, while your hair's still limp and ratty, and you have a head start on style when evening comes.

(*Woman*, 26 July 1980)

This approach means words are styled according to a short list of maxims. The most important precept is 'don't talk down to the reader'. This apparant egalitarianism (which in and of itself assumes a social distance between the scribes and followers of the cult which implies a deliberate denial of the influence of class) emphasises shared association. The sweet voice of persuasion is encouraging, helpful and hopeful – being female is a positive thing. The high priestesses can prescribe, but they must never patronise or punish. In giving advice they take the hand; they do not twist the arm.

Write–speak also lends itself to 'personalising', a technique used to inject familiarity, directness and intimacy into the tone of voice and what it is talking about. Personalising takes two forms. One uses first person accounts of a celebrity or reader's 'own' story as a means of conveying immediacy and commonality: for example, 'Fame was my Enemy' (*Woman*, 3 March 1962) and 'Drinking was Ruining My Marriage' (*Woman*, 15 June 1974). This use of real people, either famous or unknown, is intended to make the reader feel that there are aspects of these individuals lives that correspond with hers and those of her relations or friends. The second form of personalising involves frequent use of second person pronouns, singular or plural: the 'you' form of address is pointed directly at the reader as are similar you-directed advertisements, because it is believed to be effective.[8]

'The reader test'

This is where the audience also plays a significant part in moulding the message, albeit in absentia, when women's magazine editors apply highly individualised concepts of 'their' readers in making content decisions. Feedback from readers' letters, contacts with reader competition winners and meeting readers on promotional or photographic tours around the country all contribute to an editor's ideas about 'her' readers. 'Will they like it?', 'Will they understand it?', 'Will they relate to her (or it)?' are questions applied when making the 'reader test'. This test is used to determine the closeness of fit between an editorial subject or object and the client group responses it will evoke: and it is put to self, staff, secretary or friends. In making judgements of this order editors reinforce their own beliefs and those of others in the validity of their powers – the sacred knowledge of the audience which is the basis of the editor 'mystique'.

In translating their ideas of reader relevance into print, four types of potential models for 'identification' are used: anonymous professionals, fictional heroines, 'real' readers and celebrities. The repeated use of real readers and celebrities demonstrates deeply held professional beliefs about the audience gratifications assumed to derive from satisfying curiosity about, whilst supplying bases for feeling the same as, quite other people. This is the vicarious living or voyeurism syndrome of popular culture and is not confined to women's magazines.

Thus, employing famous names to 'sell' newspapers and periodicals is a common enough practice, and this has attracted the attention of social historians, for example, Boorstin (1961) and Eliade (1963); the latter talks about 'the mythicisation of public figures' and 'the obsession with 'success' which is so characteristic of modern society' (p. 20). Candidates for the 'success' spotlights of these journals are mauled over in editorial conferences as to their availability or desirability for subsequent 'mythicisation': 'No, she doesn't want to talk about having his baby, and her agent says she's gone to Palm Springs', or 'Who's ever heard of him? Who wants to know?' The message that such rich, powerful or beautiful people are employed to communicate is that 'you may not be exactly like me, but there are aspects of me that you as a woman may wish to share or emulate'.

Fascinating as the royal, rich and beautiful are, they present problems of economic and social distance which do not arise when 'people like us' are given the 'treatment'. Processes of media visibility and amplification (cf. Cohen, 1981) differ in social and symbolic terms when 'ordinary' readers share their everyday triumphs and traumas with other members of the cult. Shaping the message to foster this sense of common identity and understanding is a technique which owes a considerable, unacknowledged debt to social psychology, where George Herbert Mead's (1934) concept of the 'generalised other' is invoked unwittingly through the frequent references to 'a woman like you', or inferences of 'as every woman knows'.

This generalising approach lends itself to stereotyping, and the application of the reader test involves reaching into the editorial store cupboard of time-tested symbols and stereotypes (cf. Manstead and McCulloch, 1981). These can be based upon sex role, physical or personality types, or upon material or emotional conditions – almost always presented positively rather than negatively. Thus, the bad mother rarely appears, ugly ducklings are almost always turned into swans, and the talented and beautiful are rewarded with fame and riches whatever their 'private' heartaches.

Journalists justify the use of stereotypes on pragmatic grounds. They form a sign language of instant meanings whereby typical individuals and situations are believed to facilitate the communication process (see e.g. Hall, 1970). An editor briefs a features editor: 'get some sad, lonely, bereft pictures' (of a female pools winner whose marriage has ended). Or a writer telephones a contact (in this case, the author) to help to find a 'reader':

. . . What we want is a woman, late thirties or forties, alone, children; after splitting up trains for a fresh career; difficulties, emotional and financial.

Editorial specifications as tight as these raise questions as to whether such 'typical' individuals and situations exist a priori in the culture. Are they invented by women's magazine journalists? Or do they exist within society before being selected out, reshaped and reflected back from whence they came?

'Consciously classless'
A further journalistic means of putting across 'we women are all in this together' is the covert stratification system women's magazines promulgate. It is a social structure which trainee writers learn early by osmosis; it is not indoctrinated as such. The extent of its influence, and pervasiveness of its methods, however, were revealed only through extensive content analysis. Evolved by women's magazine journalists through a combination of benign neglect and clever construction, this invisible, social structure in the mind has been termed 'consciously classless' by this study. Two techniques are employed. One eschews social class differences by omission rather than inclusion, avoiding any mention of stratification as such. The other propounds a 'classless' female society by the inclusion of a 'representative' cross-section of individual occupations and social strata (in line with the magazine's readership profile), either within a given article, or across an entire issue, or both. The net effect is to suggest homogeneity within the cult. There is only one class of membership, that of woman, where the badge of belonging is supplied by sex and gender, not by status or income.

'Her Weekly' – the editorial process in action
The impact of organisational scale and hierarchy, and of journalistic tradition and technique on the cult's messages can best be understood by taking a closer look at the dynamics of the editorial process.

Earlier chapters dealt with the content analysis findings from the three largest selling women's magazines in Britain – all weeklies. Data from interviews with the former and present staff of these magazines give some insights into the impact of social and organisational change on the process of editing a women's weekly. The findings of these various sets of interviews were broadly consistent and are presented here as a composite picture of 'Her Weekly'. The events described all took place.

A typical weekly production line, such as the one on 'Her Weekly', is actively engaged in creating up to four issues simultaneously while forward planning a dozen more. There have been some changes in these editorial processes, particularly in the roles of the sub-editing and art departments, aimed at reducing printing charges. In 'Her Weekly's art department, for example, between 1968 and 1978 there was 'an almost 100 per cent increase in the prepreparation of colour artwork for the printers' without apparent restrictions of creativity – although some artists complained that the extra work meant less time for inspiration.

There has also been a move towards more centralised, hierarchical control and away from delegation and quasi-autonomous departments. Despite these changes, throughout the period covered by this study, 'Her Weekly's production structure has remained remarkably stable in its professional ethos, production practices and journalistic techniques.

In the 1980s, the editorial division of labour is organised much as it was in the 1950s, carried out by much the same kinds of specialists. The extent to which this structural continuity reflects professional assumptions about the nature of the messages the audience wants to hear, or reflects the vested interests of specialists in maintaining the continued importance of their own areas of expertise, is explored below.

In very many ways women's magazine journalism has remained a relatively unchanging skill-based craft, as yet barely touched by new technology. The creative aspects of production remain less amenable to rule-governed bureaucratisation than their subsequent processing turns out to be (cf. e.g. Schlesinger, 1978, and Stinchcombe, 1959). Despite the few changes introduced to meet the demands of more sophisticated printing technology or closer cost accountancy, the editorial process has altered only marginally in terms of who does what, and who sanctions what. The twin principles of 'the editor's word goes' and a division of labour founded on 'female interest' categories such as cookery, home and beauty with specialist editors reigning over their miniature empires, still typify production lines

Figure 6.4 'Her Weekly' editorial staff structure, 1980

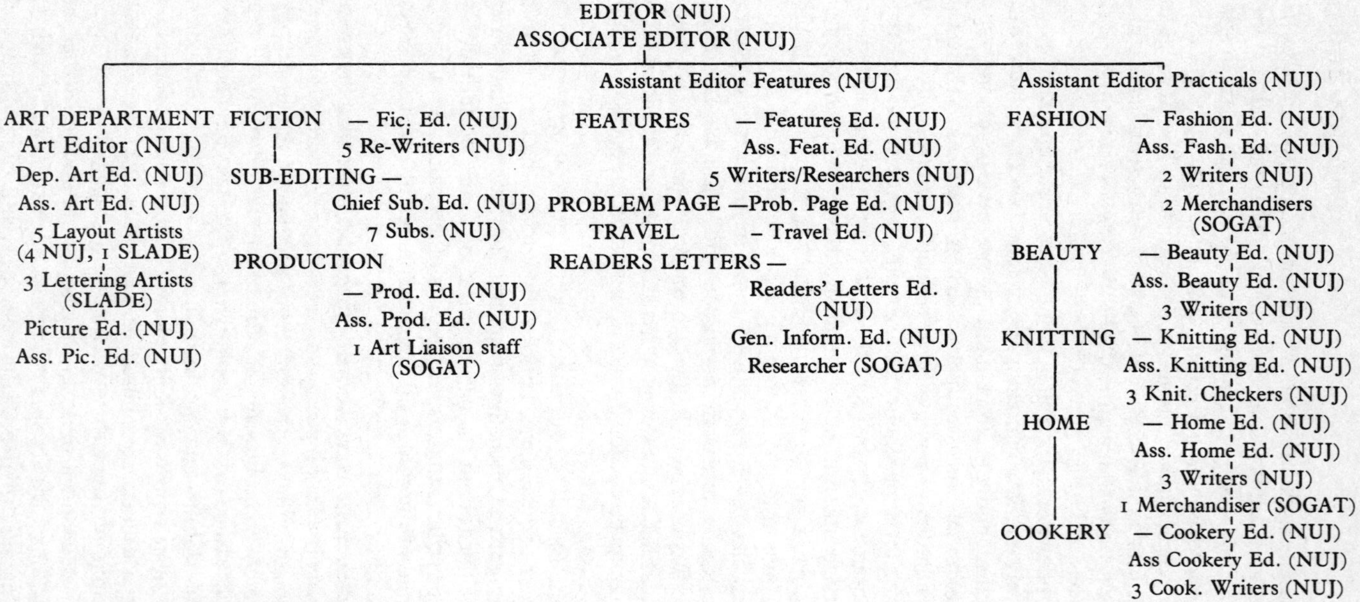

EDITOR (NUJ)
ASSOCIATE EDITOR (NUJ)

Assistant Editor (NUJ)

ART DEPARTMENT
- Art Editor (NUJ)
- Dep. Art Ed. (NUJ)
- Ass. Art Ed. (NUJ)
- 5 Layout Artists (4 NUJ, 1 SLADE)
- 3 Lettering Artists (SLADE)
- Picture Ed. (NUJ)
- Ass. Pic. Ed. (NUJ)

FICTION
- Fic. Ed. (NUJ)
- 5 Re-Writers (NUJ)

SUB-EDITING
- Chief Sub. Ed. (NUJ)
- 7 Subs. (NUJ)

PRODUCTION
- Prod. Ed. (NUJ)
- Ass. Prod. Ed. (NUJ)
- 1 Art Liaison staff (SOGAT)

Assistant Editor Features (NUJ)

FEATURES
- Features Ed. (NUJ)
- Ass. Feat. Ed. (NUJ)
- 5 Writers/Researchers (NUJ)

PROBLEM PAGE
- Prob. Page Ed. (NUJ)

TRAVEL
- Travel Ed. (NUJ)

READERS LETTERS
- Readers' Letters Ed. (NUJ)
- Gen. Inform. Ed. (NUJ)
- Researcher (SOGAT)

Assistant Editor Practicals (NUJ)

FASHION
- Fashion Ed. (NUJ)
- Ass. Fash. Ed. (NUJ)
- 2 Writers (NUJ)
- 2 Merchandisers (SOGAT)

BEAUTY
- Beauty Ed. (NUJ)
- Ass. Beauty Ed. (NUJ)
- 3 Writers (NUJ)

KNITTING
- Knitting Ed. (NUJ)
- Ass. Knitting Ed. (NUJ)
- 3 Knit. Checkers (NUJ)

HOME
- Home Ed. (NUJ)
- Ass. Home Ed. (NUJ)
- 3 Writers (NUJ)
- 1 Merchandiser (SOGAT)

COOKERY
- Cookery Ed. (NUJ)
- Ass Cookery Ed. (NUJ)
- 3 Cook. Writers (NUJ)

Note: This figure shows the 71 editors, writers, artists, merchandisers and researchers with their relevant union membership. It does not show the 22 secretaries or the 14 other Readers Letters Department staff.

like the one on 'Her Weekly'. This structure predisposes the entire editorial process towards hierarchical decision-making.

From idea to printed page
Figure 6.4 shows the editorial staff structure on 'Her Weekly' in 1980. This shows that there were seventy-one editors, writers, artists, picture researchers and 'merchandisers' (who find the clothes, furniture, accessories and props for photography). In addition there were twenty-two secretarial staff, and fourteen people answering readers' letters in the correspondence department. Figure 6.4 also shows the hierarchical lines of command and accountability between the top tier of editorial responsibility, specialist departments and the general processing departments of production and art.

The editorial process of 'Her Weekly' is highly labour intensive. It combines a creative with a bureaucratic work-flow. It is both a process of papers being shuffled from one desk to the next, and the creation of the pieces of paper in the first place. Here, chaos, crisis and 'adhocery' overrule order, routine and the 'best laid plans'. When a feature collapses at the last minute – in the 1980s as in the 1950s because the beautiful film star modelling the maternity clothes has had a miscarriage, or the famous singer writing about 'our happy marriage' decides to sue for divorce – the ability to make decisions fast is more important than their quality. An editor who 'knows what she wants' is ever preferred to one who dithers deadlines away.

Does the editor personally read every word and approve every picture that appears in 'Her Weekly'? Many editors cited this as their most important task – one whose meticulous performance separated the 'real' editors, such as themselves, from the rest. On 'Her Weekly' the verdict of the editor or her deputy results in copy and pictures going either forward for processing or back to the department from whence they came for a rethink and rewrite. It is symptomatic of an individual editor's personality and editing style – warm or cool, involved or remote – as well as a function of her day-to-day work load, whether or not such instructions are delivered personally, or deputised.

It is here – at the top – that certain key staff relationships exert maximum impact on the internal working of the editorial process. These relationships display varying degrees of interdependence and power-sharing. Editors have weaknesses as well as strengths, and some are more forthcoming than others about admitting their 'blind spots', or making provision for them. The key actors in this part of the production process are those of the Art Director and the Deputy, or Associate, Editor. The closeness or otherwise of the editor's relationships with them – and their cooperative or conflicting nature – are indicative of the professional and emotional dependencies involved.

The Art Director   Every women's magazine editor valued 'having a good art man' – and more than one has been guilty of 'pinching' a good one away from a competitor. The importance of good graphics in getting the cult's messages across to the faithful is universally recognised: overall visual impact and coherence, together with compelling – and readable – cover design are the criteria applied. The ideal is one of a complementary relationship with 'art'. Content analysis and interview data suggest that the extent to which this goal has been achieved on 'Her Weekly' has varied between editors and within regimes over time. There have been times when the editor was 'not speaking' to the art director, and deputised lay-out and artwork negotiations to assistant, or chief sub-editors – whilst retaining the right of veto on the results. There have been other times when a new editor has insisted on bringing her 'own art man' with her from another publication, and imposing him upon an existing graphics production line of suspicious or hostile artists. And there have been still other times when, like it or not, the editor of 'Her Weekly' had a new art director imposed upon *her* by management.

Whatever the art status quo, an editor knows she is expected to combine creative thinking with 'word wizardry' and 'visual sense' (gut feel in pictures), whilst acknowledging a degree of dependence or deference towards the chief holder of visual expertise, the art director. Production pressures intensify this dialectical relationship, especially on a weekly magazine, where repeated last-minute or 'whim' changes can produce instant log jams of undone lay-outs and illustrations.

The three relationships which typically develop between editors and art directors are those of: delegation, dependency, or dictatorship. An editor uncertain of her visual sense has no option but to lean on her 'art man'. Whereas an editor who places graphics firmly beneath words makes a point of establishing who's 'boss' when it comes to decisions about the relative space given to text, illustrations or 'air'. On 'Her Weekly' confrontations with art directors are most likely on grounds of policy – 'too much pretty picture, too few words' – or taste – 'no nipples in that fiction illustration, please'.

The Deputy Editor   The other key acolyte at the top of the editorial tree is the 'no. 2'. This is the assistant or associate editor who minds the diocese when the high priestess is away, and generally helps to keep production moving. Within several of the women's magazines covered by this study, including 'Her Weekly', the position of deputy was found to be akin to that of the Vice-President of the United States of America, in that the model preferred by both presidents and editors appears to be one that combines a selfless devotion to service accompanied by a taste for modest anonymity. Occasionally an editor confronted by a potential Johnson or Truman welcomes such talent close to the top, or tolerates it if it looks like moving on before it becomes a threat. More generally, serious rivals are not encouraged to stand, or stay, too close to the priestessly throne.

Yet a strong bond often exists between editor and deputy. Cemented by ties of clientship, comradeship or some sense of common purpose, this relationship is one which can allow the deputy to exert considerable formal and informal influence on the selection and shaping of the message, as well as the appointment and promotion of staff. This influence is more informal than formal where the 'no. 2' functions as a personal and professional analyst *manqué*, a 'talking wall', or a 'sounding board' who weighs up the extent of under-or over-confidence, euphoria, panic, hysteria or despair in what the editor tells her – and makes recommendations accordingly. Often deputies perform the same role of confidante to the staff: 'I tell them I'm their Jewish mother', one said. On 'Her Weekly', throughout the period of this study, the creative and administrative tasks of the various deputies have been constructed to serve the needs and predilections of particular editors. The job specification has varied over the years but has tended towards 'covering the weaknesses, rather than reinforcing the strengths', one recalled.

An editor who favours remote control – for example by memo issued from behind closed inner office door – will deputise much face-to-face briefing and criticism. Another, who likes to 'get stuck in' to editing and leaves her office door open so that she can be observed up to her elbows in page proofs and lay-outs, may be impatient of 'admin' and will delegate the paper work to her no. 2. Editors also use deputies to exact extra work from journalists and artists – to catch up with issues, or get a last-minute scoop into print. Whatever psychological ploys or pressures, bribes or threats are employed to achieve these ends, the authority to command is explicit in the deputy title. Here as elsewhere, the ability to get people to do what they do not want to do – work harder – rests with the office rather than the holder (Weber, 1968b). Hierarchy, not charisma, is what gets the cult's message to the printers on time.

The editorial conference system 1950–80
While the structural features of the creative division of labour and the hierarchy of authority have remained remarkably constant on 'Her

Weekly' over three decades, the production process and its centre-piece, the conference system, have changed dramatically during this period. This change has produced a growth in the extent of formality within the editorial process, which parallels the increased bureau-cracy found within larger-scale publishing organisations.

Editor definitions of what constitutes a conference vary between an ad hoc consciousness-raising session and a status-minded gathering of the editorial elite. Either way, the practice of small group decision-making has become institutionalised on 'Her Weekly'. These meet-ings take place in a variety of atmospheres: the overtly sychophantic, the friendly family get-together and the viciously critical. Their pro-ceedings have responded to changes within the editorial process – and the increased frequency of senior editors' conferences are compared below. This shows how editors' personality, style, work approach, management relations and perceptions of changes outside their offices have had an effect on what magazines such as this one have been saying to their readers since the Second World War.

The structure of the editorial process has changed over time, moving from one of apparent departmental autonomy, to one of more centralised, formal control. This transformation has never seriously threatened the universal acceptance by all the participants of how the message actually gets into print – by the divine right of editors, that is to say the editor should have the last word.

In the 1950s, departmental heads and assistant or associate editors met with the editor and art editor approximately once every three months to discuss forward planning. Sometimes such a meeting was preceded by a more intimate one between the editor and the pro-motions manager who would evolve a plan for subsequent conference 'consideration'. There the main ideas for building a 'strong' (worthy of sales promotion) issue were chosen, and scarce-resource colour pages allocated for major features, leaving departmental heads free to choose monochrome page subjects themselves.

The 1950s were a time of optimism and economic growth, a time of apparently ever-rising circulation and advertisement revenues for magazines such as 'Her Weekly'. Confidence, status and positive reinforcement were accorded the editor and staff of the day on a regular, semi-annual basis when the circulation figures were released which showed they had 'done it again'. Two views of those heady days are given by a former editor and a former department head:

I regarded it as a triumph of team work, of individual teams very conscious of what they were doing. Each department had a department loyalty which one wouldn't have interfered with or asked questions about. They would come in together at staff conferences and, without apparently any hard feelings, see another department getting all the colour spreads.

Sometimes people from over the road came, from Research or from Promotion. If there was anything they wanted particularly emphasised they would come and say 'we are going to spend a quarter of a million and for God's sake put something worth reading in'!

(Women's weekly editor)

Advertisements were booked so far in advance, people were queuing up and being turned away, so that the actual number of pages, and the amount of colour you had was fixed in advance. Planning meetings at that time meant one would sit down and discuss maybe a three month span of issues. In fact, the editor was only concerned with whether she was going to give you some of her valuable colour.

She did most of her briefings by asking 'what will the readers want?' She would never say 'what's going to sell the magazine?', ever. It was always 'what will they be doing at this time of the year, what will they want?', turning to each section editor in turn. Sometimes she would gently steer people away from ideas she thought were too outrageous or didn't appeal to a mass market. I remember having it drummed into me that if you made a mistake you make it eight million times!

(Women's monthly editor)

The arrival in the early 1960s of a new editor with an entirely different style, approach and philosophy sharply upset this smooth-running, orderly system. 'Her Weekly's tried and tested editorial formula was still working, sales were still high, and whenever they looked like faltering, the promotional and editorial 'pluses' which had been employed occasionally during her predecessor's reign were pressed into service again. 'Free gifts' – of food or beauty samples, for example – would be inset by hand into every copy (lengthening the production schedule by two weeks, and creating storage problems for printers with nowhere to store millions of extra magazines). Or sometimes editorial 'pluses' would be added: knitting or beauty supplements – 'free, pull out and keep sixteen-page booklets' (the centre four pages, pulled out, folded and cut).

One way or another, sales remained satisfactory. Yet this new editor dared to question the received wisdom of the editorial formula – though not the importance of knitting and fiction; for example, she asked questions about what was to be covered on the health and problem pages. Worse, she arrived at answers to her own questions, and made *changes* in the form and content of this journal's messages, hitherto regarded as holy writ.

Added to this, her preferred style of editing was to gather around her a few key associates, and to hold only infrequent, full-scale conferences. To implement her changes, she chose to originate and edit much of the content herself, in sharp contrast to the previous delegatory system. The staff hostility aroused by this dramatically new approach, style and production procedure was considerable, and underground resistance groups formed within some departments. 'Old hands' long acquainted with the company's editorial director could, and did, telephone and complain directly to 'the top' that their authority was being undermined, or the sacred tenets of the oracle violated. In the event, the reign of this editor was innovatory, conflict-laden and brief.

Some measure of that period's tensions and drama were recalled by a participant:

Well, if her predecessor's way was having instilled the philosophy into you then delegate, for her it was 'the staff are your suppliers and the editor is the person who takes the material and processes it'. So immediately the staff were sort of denigrated, demoted to people who simply supplied the raw material for the editor to process. I don't think she realised that for a magazine of that size and structure no one person can process the lot. Consequently she gathered around her a few people that she felt she could mould to her way. We too were processors.

(Women's weekly associate editor)

An interregnum editor followed this tempestuous epoch. Previously assistant editor in charge of production, she reinstated the first editor's methods of delegation and occasional planning meetings. Hers was a caretaker government which concentrated on day-to-day personnel and production problems. Hers was a time of getting back to 'normal'. It was a time of returning to an earlier status quo both within the organisation of the editorial process, and to the earlier editorial precepts which had guided 'Her Weekly's fortunes. The messages of this era were based upon not upsetting the readers' assumptions about herself or the magazine, and the assumptions that the magazine was making about her. Nothing new was tried.

Sales were still holding up, but whenever they looked like falling the audience – and 'the trade' (wholesalers and newsagents) – could always be persuaded to buy or to stock with more 'free' pull-outs or inset plastic 'gifts'. A former member of the editorial team recalled those days:

It definitely was a sort of 'limbo', nothing really happened. I can remember her saying that she had never realised how much paperwork was involved. She was staggered by the behind-the-scenes administration she had to cope with. The sad thing was that the world was moving on and nobody was giving any thought to trends at that point at all.

(Women's monthly editor)

The next editor brought with her her own method of working. She used a combination of the first two editors' organisational methods. She preferred ideas to be submitted in writing for prior evaluation by herself, or in consultation with senior editors, before final decision-making with department heads:

She was more inclined to edit by committee but she could never bring herself to call the committee meeting. She would do it by individual conversations then try to amalgamate what she'd learned from the individual contacts. She was very much an absorber of other people's thoughts and when she'd got them she would come out with her policy. A good sponge sounds bad, but a good sponge can be a good thing. It's much better than something that's non-absorbent.

(Women's weekly editor)

This editor's reign coincided with the most difficult years in 'Her Weekly's history – towards the end of the critical 1960s. This was a time when things were going badly wrong for this journal. Sales were falling – and falling again. Previous assumptions about profitability based on a stable audience of millions to justify high advertisement rates went out of the window as readers and buyers disappeared faster than any editor – or publisher's – worst nightmare. There was a marked trend to increased management intervention in the editorial process, and directly and indirectly on the extent to which the cult's messages should – or should not – be responsive to perceptions of social change.

The impact on the editorial process when things went wrong towards the end of the 1960s was manifested at three levels: in the communication and authority links with the wider organisation, in day-to-day working in the editorial offices, and in what actually got into print in the pages of 'Her Weekly' (cf. e.g. Burns, 1963; Burns and Stalker, 1966). This troublesome era was a time when the plant bedecked offices of 'Her Weekly's most senior editors sounded to typewriters turning out not new pronouncements for the cult, but elaborate public relations scenarios of forward editorial planning. These were written winningly to 'sell' the ideas that they contained to managers, and were submitted for approval – along with cover lines, photographs and key lay-outs during particularly critical periods. Decisions and feed-back were sometimes long in coming, journalistic judgements sometimes overridden, and editor autonomy manifestly undermined during this time of unrelenting pressure on this editor and her team to find a magic formula for turning back the tide of circulation decline.

The previous flurries of free gifts became a regular storm in an effort to halt falling sales. In the words of one Promotion Department veteran:

The variety of gifts was colossal. Lipsticks, eyeshadows, shampoos, plastic everything – combs, hair brushes, plant pot holders, knitting and crochet needles, omelette whisks, spatulas, icing pipes, measuring spoons, pastry wheels – and then recipe cards, flower seeds, food samples, curry mix, variety custard – you name it, we gave it!

What was the net effect of all this on the editorial process, and through it, on the messages of 'Her Weekly'? At the level of the editor's links with the wider organisation, conflicting signals of criticism and support tended to produce conformity to judgements which arose from outside the editorial process. At the level of day-to-day working within the production process, they tended towards more time being spent on political than journalistic activities, with senior editors 'tied up' with the editor pondering what the editor's response should be to the latest missive from on high. At the level of what 'Her Weekly' was saying to its diminishing band of followers, it meant that for long periods, consideration of what the message should or could say about any perceived changes in female attitudes and behaviour often went by the board. The editorial staff were so busy trying to please their masters that they had little time to see what women were doing in the world outside their walls.

During the 1970s – the decade when women's magazine editors the world over confronted the question of how to deal inside their pages with the changes that they perceived were happening with many of the members of the cult – this editor was succeeded by another who brought along a different editorial style, organisation and conference system learned in a different editorial tradition. This new editor introduced a more open communications system, and a more formalised production structure. Now the inner office door was ever open (and the main door onto the passage left unlocked), first names were used, and two set-piece weekly conferences, the 'pre-plan' and 'the conference' examined below, were established: all were stunning innovations to the staff of 'Her Weekly'.

By this time the worst circulation falls were over. All the participants had adjusted their spectacles to take in the new scaled-down audiences, and were busy producing reasons why 'smaller, more tightly targeted audiences' were a good thing – quite apart from the fact that printing fewer copies did make commercial sense because less copies meant lower 'run-on' paper and printing costs at a time when these were escalating. Management control lessened sharply. No longer were covers, lay-outs and selling scenarios of editorial content passed on up the line for 'OK'. Internally, the introduction of regular weekly conferences was accompanied by regular informal group meetings, in comparison with the previously preferred system of one-to-one consultations, and occasional larger group meetings.

The same conference system was followed by 'Her Weekly's next editor with only minor alterations. These included much tighter briefing at all stages, tighter personal control of copy, pictures and 'sells'. In addition there was increased reliance on assistant or associate editors responsible for each feature rather than with department heads. Sales began to steady, and appeared to stabilise. Management control lessened again and a very much more subjective form of editing reasserted itself; what one participant described as 'sometimes even editing by whim, or by bullying people to do what she wanted'.

Into the 1980s

How did the conference system operate on 'Her Weekly' towards the end of this study period? Which kinds of constraints operated within the group situation, and which different work approaches did senior editors demonstrate during their brain-storming sessions?

The expectations and wants which individuals bring to their work situation, the dynamics of group decision-making, and the formal and informal power structures of organisations have interested many social scientists (e.g. Becker, 1960; Lindblom, 1959; Kroger and Briedis, 1970). Their findings suggest several factors are critical in this context. Everyone at the editorial conference is concerned to make a good impression. Everyone is mindful of his or her self-image and future career prospects ('how will this affect me?'), as well as degree of personal responsibility for the subject under discussion. There are also the influences of an editor's known style of operation and the past history of the group on tension levels around the conference table ('is she going to bully poor old A again today?'). Finally, there are considerations of possible approval or disapproval within the wider organisation ('Old Gumboots won't like this'), or the economic environment ('are ad bookings up or down?'), which further impinge on editorial decisions.

After several years of operation, the present conference system on 'Her Weekly' has become part of the 'taken for granted' world of all the participants: department heads, journalists, artists, secretaries, picture researchers and merchandisers. Yet it is costly of time and temper, and opinions vary as to its usefulness. The two main conferences present interesting contrasts in terms of who goes, and what is discussed, and are explored below.

One of 'Her Weekly's senior editors explained that 'it is only at the pre-plan that the whole thing comes together'. It is there that all the department heads – whose ideas have been assessed, chosen, scheduled and briefed in prior and individual conclave with the editor and

'Her Weekly' – the pre-plan conference

Participants	Editor, associate (or deputy) editor, assistant editors (2), production editor, and department editors (8)
Setting	The conference room
Timing	Approximately three months in advance of publication, e.g. 25 April for 12 August
Editorial aim	To bring together for the first time on a particular issue all the key participants; to evaluate what has already been planned with and done by individual departments, and complete the contents planning for this single issue

her deputy – learn what one another are doing in the same issue.

The pre-plan conference goals are twofold: to reassess the 'mix' and make sure that it adds up to a 'strong' issue (two or three features worthy of cover line treatment or promotion to help sell the issue), and to resolve any clashes of contradictory editorial matter. The goal of maximising reader interest/sales potential had already been given priority at the time when the original content choices were made. It is the goal of overall editorial balance which takes precedence.

This means that if the issue concerned contains a story about a successful actress who happened to be fat, and whose story is seen as 'clashing' with a beauty feature on slimming, then one of these comes out. Such decisions are based upon the premise that the cult's messages must harmonise, lest any discordant notes tax or trouble the faithful with their dissonance. When decisions are made to scrap or hold over prepared material department editors reveal their degrees of selflessness or self-interest. 'You soon learn the professionals from the non-professionals and the selfish from the unselfish; who fights to hang onto their features and who is prepared to sacrifice something for a better issue,' a production editor shrugged.

Formal conferences such as the 'pre-plan' give the editor certain strategic advantages in moulding the message to her personal imprint. They provide the trappings of democracy for the exercise of autocracy, and put the top talent of the editorial team on its mettle on a regular, scheduled basis. Moreover, by actually or ostensibly sharing responsibility with senior editors as a group, decisions about changes and continuities in the message can become a collective rather than an individual affair – which is useful when inspiration flags or the going gets tough. Whatever degrees of egoism that individuals display within it, the conference group structure provides a committee system for decision-making. This masks the extent to which editors can operate set-piece conferences to control personalities as well as content. In the conference context the editor can and does manipulate. Individuals can be cajoled or humiliated, lavishly praised or verbally lashed – or the whole group can be jollied along with the serving of an 'impromptu' bottle of champagne, mid-slog.

There is a second, formal weekly conference called 'The Conference' which was also introduced by the editor who started the 'pre-plan'. This meeting occurs on 'conference day' in the 'conference room' and is attended by only the most senior editors. This conclave is the last round-up of editorial inspiration on a given issue, where the fine points of balance, look, selling titles and cover lines of a given issue are raked over and finalised.

'Her Weekly' – the 'conference day' conference

Participants	Editor, associate editor, assistant editors (2), art editor, features editor (department editors, singly)
Setting	The conference room
Timing	Approximately two-and-a-half months prior to publication, e.g. 20 April for 8 July
Editorial aim	Dissection and refinement of one issue at a more advanced stage of deciding the form, content, and final positioning

---

The conference room setting shows the stage is set for serious business. One wall is covered with 'mock-up' lay-outs for all the major features. These are produced after the appropriate fashion, beauty, home or knitting pictures are taken but before their choice is finalised. The relevant copy is 'up for discussion' and department heads summoned to discuss the total treatment may be told 'they don't think like that in Boundary Road, Port Slade'. Some features are approved, others changed. Anything can be 'shot down' – and subsequently rewritten or scrapped. The editor instructs the cookery editor, 'Tell them *why* they should do it. Have we invented this new way of eating?' Group discussion is also aimed at getting the visual emphasis right, while the words rated as the most important are written on the spot, as a team effort, by the editorial elite: major titles, 'sells', and the cover-lines.

This is the conference where the knives come out. Here, where production is much advanced and close to printing deadlines, interpersonal rivalries surface and the editor's skills (or lack of them) in group psychology emerge. Previous squabbles can re-surface, turning discussion into discord, and creative tension into blistering attack. Yet many survivors of these skirmishes believe that this competitive, pressured environment helps to produce a more lively message, and that the sparks of conflict produce 'better stuff' than the nods of consensus in putting the final touches to what gets printed on the pages of 'Her Weekly'.

Whatever the level of competition or cooperation within the group, 'conference day' begins at 11 am, allows an hour for lunch at 1.30 and continues until 9, 10 or 11 pm – pausing only momentarily for coffee, tea, and around 7 pm, drinks. Occasionally the editor is called out to deal with an urgent crisis. This happened during the observation research for this study. Upon her return, she announced: 'Stock cubes have dropped out of the £30,000 competition because we wouldn't agree to feature them in an editorial. Where have we got to?' The last task of the day, after all arguments, decisions, and changes are made, sees 'Her Weekly's senior editors add up the number of 'read' words in that issue. Only major features are counted, and in an eighty-page October issue, the 'read' totalled 22,000 words.

Two further meetings, which follow on from the 'pre-plan' and the 'conference day' ones, complete this picture of *Her Weekly*'s conference system. These are the 'post conference' conference and the 'dummy approval' meeting. The former involves all members of the art and production departments, representatives of all other departments, plus the associate and assistant (practicals) editors. 'Dummy, approval' follows on Thursday when those who attended the 'Conference Day' see a 'pasted up' version of the issue with all lay-outs, titles, 'sells' and advertisements in place and make any final changes.

What the development and institutionalisation of such a conference system shows is that although the *creative* processes of women's magazine journalism – the origination of ideas, words, lay-outs, illustrations – cannot be formalised and rule-bounded, this is not the case with their implementation. The weight of evidence, as typified by this account of 'Her Weekly's conference system, points to the growth of formal bureaucracy in the Weberian sense (Weber, 1968b). Where hierarchy, specialisation, rules, record-keeping and loyalty to the office rather than its holder have expanded most dramatically is within the editorial processes of the largest staffed weeklies. Here as elsewhere scale appears to be the critical variable influencing the trend to increased formalisation (cf. e.g. Hall, 1968; Pugh *et al.*, 1968): the larger the organisation, the larger the editorial staff, the greater the degree of rule-boundedness within the editorial process.

This chapter has explored how organisations, traditions, techniques and production processes all make their mark on what gets into print in women's magazines. It has shown – through the interview, observation, and documentary data gathered for this study – how the total publishing structure, both inside and outside an editorial process, can serve to protect, or bring pressure to bear, upon the key figure of the editor. This structure is one which both allows an editor a good deal of autonomy – by virtue of the focal position assigned to her and the professional qualities traditionally expected – and is also a vehicle which can convey pressures towards her. Through the editor these impinge upon the editorial process and its product.

In detecting and responding to social change, this production process is an imperfect one, dependent heavily on personal insights, chance, and the scope allowed when economic pressures have been satisfied. For in so far as women's magazines are responsive to the world outside – and in some cases this is not the aim – their response is heavily conditioned by the commercial imperative, and the search to find a message which will sell.

Moreover, these pressures and processes have implications for the cult of femininity. Women's magazines exist as a gender genre apart. Like 'women's things' and 'woman's place' they define themselves, and are defined, as separate and different from other media forms. The internal organisation of the production process attests to this. It assigns separate specialist departments to traditional areas of female concern and competence which help to reinforce the legitimacy of labelling categories of expertise and experience as 'female' only. Findings such as these raise wider questions as to whether the maintenance of such traditional boundaries and concepts within the manifestos of the cult are appropriate to the society and culture of today. And it is to these, and other questions, that the concluding chapter turns.

7

Plus Ça Change . . .

Earlier chapters have tackled specific questions about how women's magazines operate and about the impact upon them of social, economic and cultural change upon this medium. This final chapter brings together the answers to those questions and relates them to three particular issues: the role of women's magazines in society; the ways in which their messages have altered or stayed the same in the context of a changing society; and the declining audience of these periodicals in the face of competing sources of information.

The role of women's magazines in society

I have argued that women's magazines collectively comprise a social institution which serves to foster and maintain a cult of femininity. This cult is manifested both as a social group to which all those born female can belong, and as a set of practices and beliefs: rites and rituals, sacrifices and ceremonies, whose periodic performance reaffirms a common femininity and shared group membership. In promoting a cult of femininity these journals are not merely reflecting the female role in society; they are also supplying one source of definitions of, and socialisation into, that role.

Instruction, encouragement and entertainment to do with the business of being a woman are directed at specific client/target groups such as housewives, younger women, mothers, brides and slimmers. By fostering this learning process through the messages disseminated by their editors, or high priestesses, the cult's oracles help to sustain the faithful in their beliefs, and to attract new followers to worship its totem: Woman herself. In maintaining the desire of adherents new and old to perfect and display their femininity, these journals can be seen to fulfil another of their most enduring purposes – the creation of profits for their owners in a market where the few organisations own the many titles.

To state that women's magazines promote a cult of femininity is to state more than the economic truism that they do this to maximise profits. A larger and more circular process is at work. By identifying the female sex aged 15 and over as their main target group, women's magazines promote the market importance of that sex and thereby confer status on women as a group, and make womanly things a serious business. They provide a public platform and a symbolic social order which consistently offers a woman a cheap and accessible source of positive evaluation, alongside practical directions for fulfilling her potential as a cultist – and as a consumer. They consciously set out to foster a woman's sense of her own worth – at a fraction of the cost of alternative sources of therapy such as psycho-analysis or plastic surgery, available only to the privileged few.

They also preach the ideal of a woman's power of self-determination. They do this through their overwhelming emphasis on self-help. Putting Samual Smiles into petticoats, they proclaim self-help as the doctrine of salvation for all areas of a woman's life from the most public to the most private. This ethic is harnessed to the specific aspirations that they set concerning female achievement and fulfilment. These aspirations are to do with the whole range of tasks, goals, and obligations inherent in becoming a woman. 'True' feminine fulfilment and personal happiness are found through achieving these material and emotional ends.

The recipes of femininity
Women's magazines also provide the syllabus and step-by-step instructions which help to socialise their readers into the various ages and stages of the demanding – but rewarding – state of womanhood. Novices are led through the appropriate attitudes, rituals and purchases to achieve their chosen ends of *femme fatale*, super cook or office boss. In following their leaders, individual women help to produce and maintain a cult of femininity which has potent, if unintended, consequences for women as a group, apart from their quite specific intended, commercial aims and consequences.

What collective behaviour do women's magazines foster in this way? These journals attempted to promote a collective female social 'reality', the world of women. This is a world founded on conformity to a set of shared meanings where a consciously cultivated female bond acts as the social cement of female solidarity. This is pre-ordained. Through the selective perception and interpretation of the wider world from the viewpoint of the 'woman's angle', the editors of these sacred oracles sustain a social 'reality' that is 'forever feminine'.

This process invokes a shared and common culture, one which is bounded by the customary and expected categories of female interests and experience. Sharing in this culture constitutes the female bond, a bond from which derive the messages of female solidarity that these periodicals promote. These journals do more than reflect and reinforce traditional or emergent beliefs about the place of women in society. The cumulative and covert meaning of the cult's messages is not only that sex is the ultimate dividing line. Rather, biological determinism is the manifest and latent ideology of women's magazines: only females can qualify for membership. Thus is this cult made conscious of itself. Individual members are socialised into their personal and collective identities through shared rites, rituals, parables, maxims, catechisms, badges and totems, in the same way that they are habituated into making the monthly or weekly dues they contribute towards the maintenance of the edifice itself.

The existence of a cult conscious of itself raises a question which derives from marxist–feminist analysis. Whether women constitute a sex or a class, can a cult that is conscious *of* itself be transformed into a cult *for* itself? Does the content analysis of women's magazines suggest such a transformation: a new speaking *for* women, rather than *of* women? The findings from the mid-1970s do reveal a distinctly more open, articulate and aggressive tone of voice than formerly on issues related to women's 'rights', such as improved day nursery facilities or equal taxation. In putting such items on the agenda, women's magazine editors are sometimes leading, sometimes lagging behind, the attitudes and actions of their followers.

Differentiation has occurred within the cult, and the consistency of the message has been diluted to some extent in recent years. Recognition of the differences between life-situations of women of different income, ages and experience is reflected in the trend of those who 'know', to launch (and re-launch) magazines for the 'new' audience constituencies that they identify or seek to create. Whatever the degree of specialisation of content towards more narrowly focused target/audience groups, women's magazines are still culture and category-bound. They still select and shape their messages to fit the parameters and precepts of the cult of femininity. In this, they resemble minority, religious or ethnic group publications and the purposes which they serve (cf. Park, 1955; Husband, 1977). All such media proffer their readers a distinctive self-view which is both an aid to individual identity formation, and a means whereby group members identify one another. This is their ultimate and distinctive role.

Sexual politics: the medium and the movement

The fact that it is possible to suggest answers concerning the wider role of women's magazines in society, points to the further parallels – hitherto unexplored – which exist between this medium and the women's movement.[1] Both the medium and the movement define their constituencies in the same terms: women are separate and different. Both promulgate the same message: women must band together for reasons of social support and female solidarity. On the one hand this binds them to the cult of femininity whose ritual observances must be reaffirmed on a periodical (weekly or monthly) basis; on the other hand it brings them together in small groups to raise their consciousness of a male-dominated power structure. The medium determinedly defines the female condition positively and, ultimately, around 'finding' a male. The movement, equally determinedly, defines women negatively in terms of their common oppression by men.

By rejecting the goal of male partnership which presupposes a commonality of condition, the women's movement posits a new basis for sisterhood, that of putting women in the same situation as men. But the problem of the women's movement is that its existence still depends on the definition of a common problem. It goes against the prior condition of common identity – pursuit of the male – but still promotes a commonality based on the separateness of women as defined in terms of relationship to men. Both the medium and the movement are directed towards raising the consciousness of women: the one towards getting, if not keeping, a man; the other towards getting the better, or at least the equal, of him. In one sense the women's movement offers a counter culture, but in another sense it is an extension of the cult.

There is one women's magazine that uniquely in the world mediates between the mainstream cult and the feminist counter-culture. This is *Ms.* magazine founded in the United States, in the 1970s. Its aim was to raise the level of understanding of women about their position in society in relation to the social and economic policies that influence that position. As its title suggests, it is a gender-specific publication like all the others, but it is not committed to the traditional messages of the cult of femininity. It is the oracle of a counter cult.

It is unique because it was founded as an act of political commitment to the American feminist movement. It is unique because it has survived as a successful commercial product, against considerable odds and in the face of considerable scepticism from the Jeremiahs of traditional women's magazines. After eight years of struggle for commercial survival, in 1979, the United States government acknowledged that it had become a journal of living history of the women's movement in America and its educational value, by granting it a tax exempt status.[2] (It is also unique because it has attempted the only truly democratic editorial process of any of the magazines whose editors were interviewed for this study in having no high priestess, 'dictator' or 'bossy chief' in the established editor sense.)[3]

Agenda-setters of the female world

The impact of social change on this medium is a complex issue. It concerns how, and in what ways, and by whom its message has changed over time.[4] As the high priestesses who serve the cult, the editors of women's magazines also act as gatekeepers of the female world. They decide what will be placed before their followers and what will not. They decide the when, if and how of any changes to the feminine agenda – what will be deleted from, or added to, the cere-monial litanies and rituals to be observed at regular, periodical intervals.

These decisions are predicated, accepted and acted upon in accor-dance with the belief shared by editors that they possess special powers or sacred knowledge concerning 'what women are' and 'what women want'. Such beliefs are central to the 'editor mystique'. They also accord with their decisions being based more upon intuitive, 'gut feel' judgements than 'objective', 'rational' ones. Ultimately, it is these arbitrary decisions, and the legitimating beliefs of others as to their validity, which produce the cult's images of women.

There are constraints on this process. Staff quality and quantity, editorial production budgets, printing deadlines and technology, advertisers' pressures, union pressures, or changing organisational structures – all of these impinge on the editorial process, but only rarely dictate it. Their influence is only partial or intermittent when compared with that of the power invested in editors to decide the what, when and *how* of what is said. The importance attached by women's magazine journalists to the particular tone of voice with which they communicate demonstrates that form is as significant as content in putting the message across. The supportive, reinforcing 'we women' approach of these journals is manifested through journalistic techniques such as write–speak, personalising, and the consciously classless social structure which they project. (There are exceptions: the consciously *classy* titles which segregate their elite followers from the common cultists, e.g. *Vogue, Harpers and Queen*.)

The changing and unchanging message

When we look at content rather than form, many aspects of the cult's messages give the impression of having changed during the post-war period, but closer examination shows that much of the message remains the same. Women's magazines still define norms for what their followers should think, say, do, wear, cook, read, explore, ignore or care about. Overtly and covertly the basic dogma remains. Its maxims still rest on the premise of biological predestination and gender determinism and the 'woman to woman' approach.

On the surface, the range of roles and expectations has widened beyond the earlier emphasis on romance, marriage and the 'waiting to wed' girl. The roles of 'Wife' and 'Mother' remain paramount even when they are joined by a newcomer to the repertoire – the 'Independent Woman' who emerged from the editorial closet in the mid 1970s. Overtly, the Independent Woman is urged to achieve her full potential outside the home as well as within it. Covertly, she carries within her the cultural clone of the wife and mother of yesteryear whom she still is expected to replicate. This is evinced by the diminished importance of the dominant theme of the 1949–74 period, 'Getting and Keeping Your Man', which was overtaken by the second most dominant theme of that period in the 1979 and 1980 analyses. This was 'Self-help' – either as 'Achieving Perfection' or as 'Overcoming Misfortune' – the paramount theme for women today.

These results demonstrate the extent to which women are simultaneously presented with messages on two wavelengths. 'Yes, get out there and show the world you are someone in your own right', but also 'Remember you must achieve as a wife and mother, too.' The psychosocial tension generated by these dualistic messages is largely ignored – outside the pages of these journals as well as inside them. Yet these conflicting messages are overlaid with a seductive wrapping: every woman can choose the 'kind' of woman she wishes to be. They imply her choice is constrained only by her preferences from amongst the range of images offered to her. This freedom to choose extends to all areas of her life. Appearance, home, work or partner all express the 'kind' of woman she is, or aspires to be: 'the *Cosmo* girl', 'the *Good Housekeeping* wife', or 'the *Woman* woman'.

The conflicting messages of the cult, and the choices made by its followers, cannot be considered in isolation from the wider context of social, cultural and economic change over the post-war period. Some of the strands of influence in this contextual backcloth, which were of particular significance for women and for women'as magazines, are readily indentified.

The economic backdrop   In the competitive female periodical market cover prices increased faster than the rate of inflation in the 1970s. Competition increased from newspapers and Sunday supplements intent upon converting the female faithful from one medium to the other, and television viewing rose among housewives, lower socio-economic groups and the elderly. The almost threefold increase between 1950 and 1980 in the number of working married women had implications which extended beyond household income and expenditure into the social and cultural fabric of everyday life. New roles, rules and relationships were being negotiated outside as well as inside the home.

The social context   Powerful new patterns emerged. The fact of more married women working, with more money and less time to spend, produced preferences for more social leisure pastimes such as eating out, and less for solitary ones such as reading periodicals. Technical aids to housekeeping, such as freezers, and the retail trend towards more and bigger supermarkets combined to 'rationalise' domestic chores and possibly render less imperative the 'tips' of women's magazines. Above all, women were controlling their own fertility and confronting the social facts of more living-together couples, more divorces and more one-parent families.

The cultural climate   Traditions, values, attitudes and priorities: this is the sphere of social change where the interplay between the forces of tradition and innovation is most tantalising and obscure. If women's magazines both anticipate and lag behind such processes, their mirroring of behavioural change towards the end of the 1970s may also reflect a new confidence on the part of women which is in some way connected to those changes. If females have developed a stronger sense of selfhood, competence and self-esteem through increased education, travel, paid work experience and sexual awareness, they may be less dependent than formerly on external direction; they may listen more to themselves – or to other women.

Yet the impact of changing social conditions on the cult's message is one of *plus ça change*. . . . Everything changes and nothing changes. The medium is still a message in itself and that message continues to be that women are uniquely different, they require separate treatment and instruction in ways that men do not. Within the cult of femininity – fostered by women's magazine editors in their role of high priest-esses – Woman remains the cult object, the totem of this belief system, and Man remains the goal, not the god. Paradoxically, this order of things does not devalue the importance of the male as goal. His status ranking remains consistently high across the decades and the centuries, whatever other social, cultural and economic changes have impinged on the cultists or their journals. In the 1980s as in the 1950s, and right back to the eighteenth and nineteenth centuries (as can be seen from the women's press of the time), possession of a male partner confers prestige within the female world. The possession of this clearly identifiable status symbol, a male partner (and better still, provider?), continues to confer the ultimate badge of female belonging and of femininity fulfilled.

The old/new doctrines and audiences

Whether they led or followed their female audience in promulgating an intensified doctrine of self-help (including helping herself to find a male partner) is not the question here. Whether this doctrine has taken on a life of its own and become a self-fulfilling prophecy is a question which is much more germane to the fact of audience decline. If the answer is 'yes', then it suggests this cult contains the seeds of its own destruction. For when women 'get the message' – that they are released, made independent, free to choose the kinds of female roles they want, and the arenas in which they will perform them – and if they heed that message and apply the method, is there any further 'need' for the helping hand of women's magazines?

The evidence of the market suggests that the answer to this question may be 'yes'. The scale of audience decline which reduced annual sales of women's magazines by some 149 million between the mid-1960s and the start of the 1980s suggests more than a turning away from print towards electronic media on the part of women as well as men. The 'out of fashion' explanation is incomplete ('They just went out of fashion like navy bloomers did', an editor stated). Such global figures of decline contain specific support for the central argument of this book that women's magazines exist and persist to foster and maintain a cult of femininity. Those that stuck to the more traditional messages thrived; and those that challenged – to lesser or greater extent – these mainstream beliefs, did not. The evidence provided by the commercial success of titles like *Good Housekeeping* and *Women's Weekly*, and the limited following attracted by *Nova* and *Spare Rib*, attests to this.

An interesting scenario thus presents itself as to where the cult and its oracles may be going in the next decade. The pendulum of change which swung women away from the home during the 1960s and 1970s may bring them back to the fireside in the 1980s through such economic forces and technological advances as increased female unemployment or the growth of privatised, computerised, home-based work, shopping and entertainment. Will this housebound woman of the future be as tightly imprisoned within her technological cage as her predecessors were within their biological one? In her confusion, joy, despair and eagerness to perform all her tasks well, will she return to the fold, and seek oracles that define this old/new role for herself?

The rituals and beliefs of this group, like those of others, are not immutable. Like other belief systems, the cult of femininity experiences recurrent attacks on its central tenets, and revises its dogmas from time to time. In responding to these challenges its specialist periodicals may attract new followers but run the risk of alienating old ones. There are also competing beliefs and authorities: the shared home, school and work experiences of other women offer alternative sources of reference and support; as do 'women's' pages and programmes elsewhere. That today's women's magazine audience is smaller in terms of absolute numbers should not obscure the extent of commitment amongst the dedicated followers, the regular worshippers, who remain. For those females who seek the original, undiluted gospel, women's magazines still offer the most comprehensive and authoritative voice on the mainstream practices and beliefs of the 'true' cult.

Whither the cult's oracles and its followers?

Looking further ahead, what implications does this conclusion have for women's magazines in the future? There are two possibilities. The first is that the supply of women's magazines will continue to be produced on the twin principles of 'a woman is a woman' and 'publishing for profit', while on the demand side, so long as women seek to acquire and perfect the skills of their gender trade, then women's magazines will exist to satisfy their forever feminine quest.

The second possibility is a less sanguine one for publishers, and a more intriguing one for social scientists. It is suggested by the evidence which shows that these specialist periodicals are no longer the sole oracle, nor the unitary voice of the cult: there are new voices in the temple and in the market-place. Does this development herald a transformation whereby their role is changing from an institutional or structural one to a more purely symbolic and cultural one? If this is so, then women's magazines may be in the process of becoming an emblem or badge of femininity rather than arbiters of what femininity consists of, or a singular means of socialisation into that state.

The cult of femininity, then, has become less sacred and more secularised, less unitary and more sectarian. Its doctrinal force has been diluted through the appearance of diverse sub-cults worshipping diverse versions of its totem, Woman. Durkheim (1976: 387) suggests that for a cult to become conscious of itself and reaffirm its existence, the *sharing* of beliefs and practices is more significant than their substance:

. . . [the cult] does not need to perform certain acts in preference to all others. The necessary thing is that it partakes of the same thought and the same action . . . before all, rites are means by which the group reaffirms itself periodically.

In societies characterised by different female cultists performing different shared rites – not necessarily prescribed on a printed periodical basis – we can predict new oracles will emerge to speak to women about the old/new doctrines of the faith. When they do, they will provide them with a variety of revisionist totems, rather than the singular image of Woman hitherto revered by traditional believers in the cult. These new oracles will reflect a new symbolic order of womanhood in the making: the new/old cult of femininity which is being fashioned by women themselves.

Notes

Chapter 1

1. Maisel (1973), for example, postulates a three-stage theory which relates media growth or contraction to social change. He sees the third stage as 'characterised by a declining growth rate for mass media and an increasing growth rate for specialised communications directed to smaller more homogenous audiences' (p. 160).

2. The potential social influence of women's magazines in terms of defining, or reinforcing, a particular socio–cultural–historical view of Woman and her femininity, has been under-explored and under-researched by social scientists. The work which has been done on media messages and 'audience effects' has tended to concentrate on, for example, radio and television output with reference to children and television violence (e.g. Murray and Kippax, 1979), or their support for dominant class interests (Glasgow University Media Group, 1976, 1980). Others stress the interactive nature of media processes of social influence: Himmelweit (1980) points to both the need for their further study and to the impact upon them of 'cultural milieu': 'It is expressed in the institutions and in the quality of life the society has developed and in the priorities it assigns to given values. It concerns the country's class system, its style of work and leisure, its openness to outside influences, its mode of resolving conflict and of welcoming or retarding change' (p. 143).

3. Apart from the valuable historical study of British women's magazines by White (1970), and a racy chronicle of the launches and mergers in the British market by Braithwaite and Barrell (1979), what writing there is on this subject falls into two categories: 'images of women' covered by the feminist literature (e.g. King and Stott, 1977; Tuchman, 1978a; and Winship, 1978, 1980; Hobson, 1980) and analyses of the market (e.g. Bird, 1977, 1979).

4. In suggesting this model I am aware that there are problems with Durkheim's concept of a cult and the existence of a critical literature on Durkheim's theory of religion as the *locus classicus* of functionalism. The teleological and other problems of functionalism are dealt with in Cohen (1968, Chapter 3) and a host of other references. In employing Durkheim's ideas in the context of women's magazines I am using them as sensitising

concepts rather than using them in any sense as a literal model of a cult. Recent debates within the sociology of religion concerning the definition, nature and role of the cult concept have been analysed by Richardson (1978, 1979) who cites 'oppositional nature' as a major criterion: 'a cult is a group that has beliefs and/or practices that are counter to those of the dominant culture' (1978: 33). Thus, in proposing a cult of femininity in relation to the women's magazine messages and audiences I am not taking the cult model absolutely literally. There may be oppositional elements within it. The cult of femininity stresses symbolic differentiation but is not necessarily differential. It is akin to the phenomenon dealt with by subcultural theory in the sociology of deviance (see Downes, 1966, Chapter 1) in that it represents a group which pursues to a particularly intense and articulated degree certain norms and values, with reference to an unusually developed system of articulating that set of values, i.e. women's magazines.

5. There are affinities between this journalistic approach and the theoretical approaches of the symbolic interactionists (e.g. Mead, 1934; Rose, 1962) and the phenomenologists (e.g. Berger and Luckmann, 1967). The former are concerned with how we make sense of ourselves in terms of role-making and role-taking, the latter with how we construct the common-sense world of everyday life by social typifications: women's magazines in different ways are providing recipes for the practical accomplishment of femininity.

6. One area where this argument has been tellingly applied is with reference to girls' educational aspirations and post-adolescent educational performance (e.g. Blackstone, 1976; Deem, 1978). For a discussion of changing perspectives on processes of media socialisation in general, see McCron (1976).

7. There is a considerable literature on this subject which arises in part from Engels' (1902) model of the monogamous family wherein woman is assigned the proletarian and man the bourgeois role. For a discussion of the issues involved, see, for example, Mitchell (1971) or Gardiner (1976) in relation to the theoretical arguments, and the role of woman as unpaid domestic labour, respectively.

Chapter 2

1. White (1970) quotes the editor of *The Female Perceptor* (1813): 'that she had deliberately chosen this medium because "It is generally acknowledged that Periodical Works have a direct tendency to effect the grand object of all laudable exertions, viz. the expansion and illumination of the mind",(p. 38):an editor clearly intent on carrying forward the traditions of her eighteenth-century predecessors in improving the female mind'.

2. The extent to which female readers were being urged to help themselves was present in these messages even before Samuel Smiles in 1859 published his best-selling book on the theme. The women's journals of the day were filled with things for idle hands to do: patterns for feminine perfectability as well as patterns for needlework and dress fashions.

3. The expansion of the British popular press towards the end of the nineteenth century parallels the period of expansion described by White (1970) for women's magazines: both burgeoned on the basis of rising

advertisement revenues during the 1880 to 1900 period. For a critical review of the part played by those responsible for developing this new form of sales communication see Curran (1977, 1980).

4. Advances in photogravure technology were quickly absorbed by the British printing industry. Odham's Press, Watford, for example, had invested in the thirties in the Goss presses and Dulchen process which made it possible to print both more colour pages and maintain consistent production on cheap paper on the long press runs of the fifties. They printed over three million copies of *Woman* alone each week.

5. Neither White (1970) nor Braithwaite and Barrell (1979) fully discuss the importance of the role of the women's press during World War II. Quite apart from the potential social influence of these journals in rallying their readers round the flag, this was the period when audience trust was built up, and their appeal was enhanced by scarcity – two factors which contributed to post-war expansion, particularly of the mass weeklies. As Wilson (1980: 37) comments: 'Women's magazines had been used to help the wartime housewife "make do and mend" and use her rations wisely, and to explain the reforms that would come once fighting was over'.

6. I am indebted to a personal communication from Mary Grieve, editor of *Woman*, 1940–62, for various copy documents relating to this period including one on how paper rationing affected the production of *Woman* during the war.

7. Text of Mary Grieve's speech, 1941, copy document.

8. There have been few subsequent occasions when the combined efforts of the women's press have been enlisted to aid the government in 'the national interest'. One such was during the life of the Metrication Board in the 1970s when for example Cookery Editors of women's magazines were instrumental in co-ordinating recipe measurements with the conversion to metric food packaging.

9. Smith (1975) vividly describes this period in terms of the war between the *Daily Mirror* and the *Daily Express* (quite apart from war elsewhere) and stresses the distinctiveness of the *Mirror* as a paper which 'situates itself solidly among the people, a tribune loyal to its readers and owing no obligation of respectfulness to the government it criticises. The *Express* seems to speak from a position above debate or society: its first person plurals are normally used only by the sovereign' (p. 73).

10. The political, social and economic ends served by traditional female role ascription and its enshrinement in welfare policy and implementation, is, made clear in the Beveridge Report (1942), Cmd 6406: Sections 107–17. This gender role ascription was also evident in the educational policies for girls laid down in, for example, the Newsom Report (Ministry of Education, 1963).

11. Personal communication, Mary Grieve, notes of meeting, 5 July 1948.

12. For a recent statement of the competition between print and electronic media, see Tunstall (1980) who examines the role of British newspapers in a television age, and points to the fallacies attributing a direct causal connection between the decline of the former and the increased viewing hours devoted to the latter.

13. Copy document, former member *Woman* staff, personal communication.

14. I am indebted to Patricia Lamburn, Editorial Director, IPC Magazines Ltd, for a copy of 'History of the Development of IPC Magazines Ltd since 1958', from which this information is taken.

15. D.C. Thomson was the only major publisher of women's magazines in Britain to refuse to cooperate with this study. This gap was especially regretted because of this company's post-war market success in catering for the two age extremes of the young girls' market with *Jackie* (1964) and the older, poorer women's market with *My Weekly* and *The People's Friend*. Equally, the organisational and production aspects of a family-owned, non-unionised editorial process would have provided an interesting and useful comparison with the two organisations studied in Chapter 6.

16. *Over 21* was started by Audrey Slaughter; she and a small group of journalists pooled their resources (total: £25,000), and provided their own typewriters to do so. Their hard work paid off: *Over 21* prospered and was taken over by the Morgan Grampian Group in 1974. Similarly, two entrepreneurial journalists, Audrey and Tom Eyton, started *Slimming* magazine with £2,000 capital and themselves as staff, and sold it for £3.8 million ten years later.

17. The NRS classification of survey respondents by social class is by far the most commonly used way of providing some indication of 'life style' and spending capacity for publishers, editors and advertisers. It is normally based on the occupation of the head of the household. For many years this approach has been criticised – for example, on grounds of possible interviewer bias or subjective coding – by those who argue that occupation is a poor way of grouping people (see Monk, 1978). Other approaches have been suggested, but none has yet gained any widespread use. Inadequate though it may be on some grounds, grouping by social class is still one of the most effective and practical ways of classifying people; this was the conclusion, in 1980, of a special committee led by the Market Research Society and set up jointly with all other industry bodies concerned with the conduct of market research studies.

18. Source of all comparative data: IPC Ltd. The later period of rapid cover price increase coincided with the enforcement of the Price Commission Act 1977. For an interesting insight into how publishers went about fighting their case for higher cover prices see IPC's submission (IPC, 1978) and the analysis of it by Wemban-Smith (1978).

19. Some measure of the size of the advertisement revenue of women's magazines as compared with that for newspapers or television is given by comparative data for 1981, when gross advertisement revenue for television was £751,010 millions, for national newspapers £499,230 millions, and for women's magazines £113,861 millions. The three leading advertisement product categories in *Woman's Own*, for example, during 1981 were: 'food' 22.4 per cent; 'toiletries and cosmetics' 17.2 per cent; 'household goods' (equipment, stores, appliances) 16.9 per cent. Source: MEAL, IPC.

20. The circulations of comparable women's magazines abroad include the two monthlies with the largest sale in the United States (1981): *Family Circle*, 7,437,863 and *Woman's Day*, 6,896,819. In Europe, comparable

weeklies' circulations are (1980): *Elle* (France) 305,251; *Margriet* (Holland) 710,000; *Grazia* (Italy) 361,130; *Tina* (Germany) 1,656,000; *Frau im Spiegel* (Germany) 1,145,000. (Source: IPC, *Stern*, 1981.)

21. The retail revolution in the distribution of all print media including women's magazines represents a shift in purchase location from station bookstalls and independent, corner-shop newsagents to one of self-service in shopping centre multiples. This is illustrated by the declining number of CTNs (Confectioners, Tobacconists and Newsagents). Between 1950 and 1975, the number of independent outlets declined from 69,241 to 42,000; while W.H. Smith bookstalls alone were reduced from 176 to 65 between 1971 and 1976. (Source: IPC.)

22. The original advantages of web-offset printing technology over photogravure were those of lower origination costs and shorter deadlines on smaller press runs – advantages well suited to publishers of monthly magazines whose paper quality exceeded that of the weeklies. Further technical advances have eliminated the problems associated with good reproduction on long press runs using web-offset, and this process will increasingly be used for weeklies as well in the 1980s.

23. This journal is of social and cultural significance. Its messages are directed at changing rather than reflecting society's perceptions of women, and women's perceptions of themselves. These messages were not included in the detailed analysis of this study because *Spare Rib* does not satisfy its limiting criterion of magazines with circulations of 100,000 and over: its circulation stood at 32,000 in 1981.

24. Source: NRS, 1981. The demographic fact of fewer numbers in the category to whom these romantic fiction titles traditionally have been addressed – the 'bored, young, downmarket' housewives seeking an escapist read, cited by their publishers – is insufficient explanation for this scale of decline. There is scope for further research both into the initial hypothesis and into alternative sources of 'escapist' gratification in the 1980s for females classified by the NRS as under 25 and social grade C1, C2, D and E.

25. The part played by Dr Dichter in terms of influencing, or not influencing, the mainstream development of women's magazines in Britain during the 1960s is a matter of debate. White (1970: 223), for example, claimed that '*Nova* is the embodiment of the "intelligent" approach to women's publishing, and its launching was a direct outcome of Dichter's ("New Woman") findings'. Publishing veterans aver that Dichter's motivational research provided a useful *post-hoc* rationale for prior publishing decisions, on both *Nova* and *Woman's Own*.

26. Personal communication, Pat Miller, Director, *Cosmopolitan International*, text of speech to Fédération Internationale de la Publication Périodique (FIPP), Washington D.C., May 1981.

Chapter 3

1. The inferences made from this content analysis are exploratory. They are mindful of distinctions between the quantitative and qualitative approaches, and the use of 'non-frequency' indicators for purposes of

inferring meaning in the later, non-statistical approach (e.g. George, 1959: 9–10).

2. See, for example, Millum (1975) and Goffman (1979) in relation to advertisement images of women, Ferguson (1980) in relation to women's magazine cover photographs as smiling pleasers, McNeil (1975) on television serial images of femininity and Miller (1975) on news photograph images of male and female roles.

3. As Oakley (1982) comments on the narcissistic nature of such beauty rituals: 'the careful watching of one's body and its fabrication as a public viewing object, is one of the aspects of femininity Freud referred to when he identified women as narcissistic' (p. 82).

4. Source: IPC, BRAD, 1980. This compares with the lower revenues which *Woman's Weekly* attracts in the toiletries and cosmetics category – 10.1 per cent 1981 – which in part reflects its older readership profile compared with its sister weeklies.

5. Commentators and critics on the theme of romantic love in popular culture, and fiction in particular, point to 'escapism' and 'vicarious living' as gratifications assumed to derive from reading the latter (e.g. Hoggart, 1957; Hall and Whannel, 1964). Feminist writers who have analysed the pervasiveness of romantic love in the mythology of womanhood, or women's magazine fiction in particular, include Bailey (1969); Cornillon (1972); Dwayne-Smith and Matre (1975); Fowler (1979); and Winship (1978).

6. The two 'classical' sociological statements are those of Engels (1902) and Parsons and Bales (1955). The former assigns woman to an under-class within the family until she is freed of child minding and joins the labour force; the latter examine the evidence before permanently assigning her to the role of 'expressive' nurturer (a conclusion which was effectively challenged by the cross-cultural research of Crano and Aranoff, 1978). Both positions drew the wrath of feminists, for example Rowbotham (1972); Mitchell (1971).

7. For an enlightening account of the great popular impact which Samuel Smiles' *Self Help*, first published in 1859, made upon the Victorian public – male and female – see Asa Briggs' introduction to the centenary edition (Smiles, 1958).

8. International agencies have directed their attention to the question of stereotyping of female images in the media in general and advertisements in particular. UNESCO (1974) found in a survey of 28 countries that advertisement rather than editorial content was more culpable in this regard. Reporting to the European Social Development Programme, Marsden (1977) concluded that media sex–role stereotyping should be 'monitored and countered' (p. 82). More recently, the Equal Opportunities Commission (1982) has reported in *Adman and Eve* on some transformation of advertisement images of women which pointed to the sales success of products using non-traditional, 'modern' women in their sales approach.

9. Questions concerning the degree of female competitiveness in terms of achieving the high standards set for the rites, duties and obligations of female membership by primary and secondary sources of socialisation has

been under-researched and examined. Oakley (1979, 1981) has written about this in relation to child bearing: 'They [children] symbolise achievement in a world where under-achievement is the rule' (1982, p. 228). The findings of this study suggest that similar symbolic achievements are to be found in other areas definitional of femininity: principally those associated with the 'creative' rites of fashion, beauty and cookery.

10. For an examination of the oppositional categories assigned to males and females, including the emotion–reason dichotomy, from a feminist perspective, see Janeway (1972); see also Maccoby and Jacklin (1974) for the classic psychological evidence on this question.

11. Social psychology offers clarification on the notion of 'identification': individuals can be seen to respond to other individuals – or objects – by imitating their behaviour literally or symbolically (Kagan, 1958; Bandura, Ross and Ross, 1963); but principally this concept derives from Freud (1959, pp. 37–42).

12. Bettleheim (1968) commenting on the 'menstrual taboo' observes that 'if men had not envied menstruation *per se* they would have grown envious because it was tabooed' (p. 137). In July 1981, British *Cosmopolitan* initiated some taboo-breaking of its own when it exhorted on the front cover: 'Lift the curse, and make it *the most sensual time* of the month' (emphasis in original).

13. The classic account of the post-war discovery of teenage spending power is Abrams (1959); see also White (1977) and Braithwaite and Barrell (1979) for a discussion of the growth of young women's magazines.

14. The notion of industrial societies being 'achievement orientated' belongs to an earlier era of economic growth, full employment, and rising expectations (e.g. McClelland, 1961; Bell, 1974). It no longer seems so plausible for theorists to make such assertions in a period of falling expectations, or what Inglehart (1982) terms 'post-materialism'.

15. The literature which covers traditional, and emergent female roles ranges over a variety of theoretical perspectives including those of culturalists, structuralists, neo-marxists, psychoanalysts and male chauvinists. They include: Mead (1935, 1950); Lipman-Blumen and Tickameyer (1975); Epstein (1970); Barker and Allen (1976); Mitchell (1975); Goldberg (1977).

16. There is little empirical literature to suggest any extensive de-differentiation of male and female roles within the family. Symmetrical or shared roles are not nearly as well documented as has been suggested by some writers (e.g. Young and Willmott, 1973). Social change is slower than Young and Willmott suggest; attitude change is even slower and is also subject to reverse. An EEC comparative study of socio-political attitudes of men and women in the Community in 1978 found 'men everywhere have a less positive attitude to housework than women' (Commission of the European Communities, 1979, p. 105). Cross-cultural, time-budget research also shows that the majority of working women still do the bulk of domestic and child care chores (Szalai, 1975), a view shared by Rapoport (1978) in relation to sex–role stereotyping within the family.

17. Two early examples of response to the challenges posed by media content analysis of cultural values are those of Johns-Heine and Gerth (1949)

which looked at them in the context of American mass periodical fiction, and Lowenthal (1944) which explored popular magazine biographies. More recently in Britain, Golding and Middleton (1982) have explored the contribution of cultural values to media images of poverty and welfare claimants.

18. The most recent example of the large-scale omission of the feminine dimension of stratification was the Oxford Mobility Study, which used a 10,000 all-male sample (Goldthorpe *et al.*, 1980).

Chapter 4

1. Source: *Social Trends*, 11, pp. 32–3; see also Rimmer (1981) for further comment on changing marriage, re-marriage and family patterns, and the emergent model of a 'bi-nuclear' family (p. 4)

2. Source: Central Policy Review Staff/Central Statistical Office (1980, p. 89). More recent data show an almost threefold increase (from 7 to 20 per cent) amongst women marrying in the late, compared with the early, 1970s, where both parties were marrying for the first time; and that the total number of women under the age of 50 who are 'cohabiting' is estimated to be one third of a million (*Social Trends*, 12, p. 34).

3. Source: *Social Trends*, 11, p. 30; compare with Gittins (1982) on changing family size and structure between 1900 and 1939. As Lewis (1982) comments: 'The typical life experience of adult women in the recent past has included marriage and motherhood. Between 1871 and 1951, the percentage of women aged 35–44 who were married never fell below 74.6 per cent (a low reached after World War I) and in 1951 reached a high of 82.1 per cent. In 1871 the average woman married at age 24 and subsequently gave birth to six children. . . . By 1901, a woman at marriage would, on average, have been a year older, would have given birth to three or four children. . . while the woman marrying in 1931 would have been roughly the same age, the number of her children would have dropped to two' (p. 29).

4. This was the number of one-parent families caring for some one and a half million children in Britain in 1980, as estimated by the National Council for One-Parent Families. See Pierce (1980) for a discussion of the concept of female dependency in relation to the role of single mothers and the development of the welfare state in Britain.

5. Sources: *Social Trends*, 11, pp. 62–3, and Equal Opportunities Commission *Fifth Annual Report*, 1981, pp. 49–59; see also Deem (1978).

6. Sources: *Department of Employment Gazette*, 86 (4), April 1978, Table 1; Equal Opportunities Commission *Fifth Annual Report*, 1981, pp. 60–69; *Social Trends*, 11, p. 71. See also Department of Employment, *New Earnings Survey*, 1980. There are problems in comparing this female labour force with earlier census data on female economic activity. These problems have been summarised by Lewis (1982, pp. 29–30): the census data before 1911 did not break down the female labour force by marital status; only after the 1881 census was unpaid household work excluded from the economically active, nor was the extent of part-time working taken into account.

7. It was during this period that British *Cosmopolitan*, began to expand the magazine's involvement with its readers in pioneering a new form of 'reader service'. In May 1980 the first of what has become an annual series of *Cosmo* careers seminars was held in conjunction with the Industrial Society – as a practical extension of the 'Working Women' section the magazine started in September, 1979.

8. In May 1974, *Woman's Own* launched 'Mary Grant's Problem Page for Men' where, to no-one's great astonishment, the problems turned out to be the familiar ones of personal and sexual relationships. For some time it had its own separate identity in this way, but then, having established the fact that men have problems, and *Woman's Own* was willing and able to help, it was felt that the letters should form part of the regular page as they do to this day.

9. One Production Editor recalled of this time 'They were still using the Rule Book of 1870 in the Fiction Department when the rest of the magazine was using the Rule Book of 1970'.

10. The increased emphasis on individual choice, effort and self-direction in women's magazine messages suggests a reversal of the thesis advanced by Riesman *et al*. (1950): they explained what they detected as a basic shift in the American 'national character' in terms of the increased influence of peers (as a source of 'outer directedness') and the declining influence of parents (as a source of 'inner directedness').

11. For comparison of female journalist viewpoints on the changing and unchanging nature of the women's magazine message, see Puddefoot (1970) and Shearer (1980), and compare Guenin (1975) on the responsiveness to change of women's pages in American newspapers.

12. As Secretary of State for Education 1970–74, Mrs Thatcher – a former working mother herself – had promised improved nursery school facilities, which were spelled out in the 1972 White Paper, *Education: A Framework for Expansion* (HMSO, 1972). This promise was never fulfilled.

13. *Redbook* (January, 1980) published 'The strongest challenge to women since *The Feminine Mystique*', wherein Betty Friedan sounded the first trumpet call for a shift in the aims and philosophy of the American feminist movement. She said: 'Coming into the '80s, I sense once again new questions need to be asked . . . the new problems and questions seem to have been hidden, or been unanticipated by feminist assumptions over the past decade . . . Here are some of the new questions I have been hearing: "How can I have the kind of marriage I want and the kind of career I want, and be a good mother?" . . . "Can I really make it in a man's world, doing it a man's way? What other way is there? What is it doing to me? Do I really want to be like men?" ' (p. 46). The 'second stage' had begun.

Chapter 5

1. This raises the question of whether or not male editors of women's magazines are accorded 'honorary female' status by their staff in performing their high-priestess tasks? Alternatively, do they surround them-

selves with predominantly female staff to draw upon their intuitions and empathy with the female audience?

2. The editorship of *Woman*, was so advertised, December 1974, *Woman's Realm*, December 1976, and *Woman's Own*, July 1979.

3. The 'Unknown Outsider' group ranked third. Although no generalisation can be made from such a small sample to the women's media as a whole it is noteworthy that the 'Unknown' appointments typically were made during periods of editorial instability due to external pressures such as take-overs or amalgamations, or internal ones related to falling sales.

4. IPC, for example, appointed a Manpower Development and Training executive in February 1979, to coordinate and expand editorial training. A compulsory editorial training scheme was introduced in September 1979 for all journalists with less than three years' editorial experience which combined both 'on-the-job' training with a Company Training Centre course.

5. John Mack Carter, Editor-in-Chief of *Good Housekeeping*, told this story to a conference of magazine editors, academics and advertisers on the subject 'Women in the 80s' organised by Mondadori, publishers of *Grazia*, in Milan, September 1981. Before going to *Good Housekeeping* he had previously edited *McCalls* and *Ladies' Home Journal* where he was once besieged in his editor's office for eleven hours by angry feminists who demanded he do something about improving the magazine's attitude to women – he did (*Newsweek*, 17 February, 1975).

6. It is not easy to discover the truth about British women's magazine editors' salaries. Quite apart from it being considered in bad taste to ask, it appears to be considered in even worse taste to reply. Moreover, when the Company Secretary and the Editorial Director of the same company give differing figures for the salaries paid to editors some measure of the problem is gathered. The figures given here have been checked as far as it has proven possible to do so. The differentials which operate between editors of smaller and less commercially successful women's magazines, and with those who edit the most successful monthlies or the big weeklies, is on a par with the differentials which exist between magazine editors' salaries and those of national newspapers – which it is 'reliably reported' are 'roughly twice as much'. No hard data there either.

7. Stanislavsky was the professional name of Russian actor, producer and teacher Konstantin Alexeyev (1865–1938), founder of the so-called 'method' school of acting.

8. A senior editor of *Redbook* recalled that when Betty Friedan delivered her as-yet untitled revisionist thoughts on the feminist movement that it was the magazines editor-in-chief who gave her article the title which was subsequently used for the book, and which has now passed into the language as *The Second Stage* (Friedan, 1981).

9. Personal communication, Sey Chassler, Editor-in-Chief, *Redbook*, notes of address to 'Conference on Women in Public Life', Austin, Texas, 10 November 1975.

10. An informal international network exists based on ties of friendship and mutual exchange. More recently, the Fédération Internationale des Publications Périodiques (FIPP) has served to bring together editors – princi-

pally from Europe and North America – more regularly and more formally at annual international conferences.

11. Sociological arguments about the use or abuse of this term are not relevant here, aside from the question as to whether those who are members of a particular interest group can adhere to a particular ideology and act collectively for the interests of the group (see MacRae, 1961; Giddens, 1971). Women's magazine editors may share certain beliefs but they rarely act collectively to protect their group interests. An exception was in 1976 when the Trade Union and Labour Relations Bill was being discussed, when editors perceived the closed shop as a threat to their autonomy and met to consider its implications for production.

12. The extent to which editors are responding to readers in giving them what they 'know they want', or in shaping those wants to fit the particular identity of a given magazine can also be explored from the perspective of Enzensberger (1974). He argues that the media are not so much guilty of the commercial exploitation of the audience as they are of retailing the status quo social order. This editor belief also accords with what Cohen and Young (1973) term the 'commercial laissez-faire' explanatory model of media influence favoured by journalists. Both their model and the findings of this study suggest that the conclusion reached by the RCOP Working Paper is naïve in this regard: 'It remains true in 1977, as in the previous decade that the women's magazines – most of which are produced by IPC – provide an irreplaceable and vital network of social welfare services of incalculable value to women and to society' (White 1977, p. 70).

13. While empirical evidence suggests 'intuitive rationality' as the predominant approach to the editor task, as such it is sociologically complex and suggestive of links with studies of primitive thought. For example, the extent to which intuitive editing is equated with the possession of special powers or magical qualities which defy rational or logical analysis, compares with writings about the 'function' of magic in primitive societies (e.g. Frazer, 1959) or the extent to which concepts can carry social power and are socially derived (Gellner, 1970).

14. There is one other source of regular information on readership, apart from the National Readership Survey, available to editors, publishers and advertisers. This is the Target Group Index (TGI), a continuing research operation primarily designed to provide information on product purchasing, but also including readership and television viewing data. In addition publishers undertake special research studies for their own purposes. The techniques available include group discussions, insert questionnaires, telephone, mail, personal interviews and observations, the choice depending on the research requirements, circumstances and funds available.

Chapter 6

1. Significantly, perhaps, the IPC staff journal also changed its title and format three times during this ten-year period: from *em* (1969) to *Inform* (1971) to *IPC News* (1971). In 1971, *Inform* (1 April 1971, p. 1) quoted a Board statement: 'What is being done is to make the management structure more flexible, and get rid of a number of too-watertight compart-

ments. We need our best talent and creative skill to be available for problems throughout the Division and not to be deployed on narrow fronts'.

2. The Chairman explained (*IPC News*, April 1976): '. . . it is appropriate – with an eye for the future – to make management changes that broaden the experience of managers, and at the same time enable old problems to be looked at in new ways'.

3. With the further re-organisation of the Advertisement Department in 1979 the 'Group Sell' operation was radically reduced, with more autonomy given back to the three current women's magazine sub-groups: weeklies, women's home interest and monthly titles, young women's titles. By Spring 1981 the group sell principle was all but abandoned with the exception of a central Sales Development Unit.

4. With reference to the manipulation of message content, as opposed to its choice, the 'conspiracy' view of media production has both proponents and critics. For example, Miliband (1977) attacks media output as 'intended to help prevent the development of class-consciousness in the working class' (p. 50), while Richard Hoggart in his introduction to *Bad News* (Glasgow University Media Group, 1976, pp. ix–xiii) distinguishes between 'high' and 'low' conspiracy theory, and suggests that both approaches overlook the complexity of media agenda-setting and production. Similarly, Cohen and Young (1973) identify the 'Mass Manipulative' model as one where 'the public is seen as an atomised mass, passive receptacles of messages originating from a monolithic and powerful source' (p. 10). As such criticisms suggest, such uni-directional models of media influence fail to account for the active processes of audience choice (cf. Katz *et al.*, 1974), or for the interactive processes of journalists' audience perceptions.

5. Gertrude Stein (1874–1946) was an American writer, famous for her repetitive phrase: 'a rose is a rose is a rose'.

6. Editors also cited cases of mis-timing in discussing this critical aspect of their role: 'A few years ago I did six pages on what I thought would be the biggest problems of the world kind of thing. One was loneliness, another was pollution. I wrote four pages on pollution which I thought was cleverly done because it's no good going on about all the terrible things that are happening unless you give the housewife something she can actually do. We were one of the first people to talk about less washing-up liquid, that sort of thing. Total no, no. Total disinterest from everybody. A couple of years later we did something similar, only this time we called it 'War on Waste'. Totally different reaction, a lot of readers' letters. They just weren't ready for it before' (Women's weekly editor).

7. The sociology of communications has produced several useful analyses and empirical studies of the newsmaking process, for example Golding and Elliott (1979); Tuchman (1978b); Schlesinger (1978); Elliott (1980); Glasgow University Media Group (1976, 1980); Smythe (1975).

8. David Ogilvie (1964) has given the classic 'inside the industry' account of this approach and technique.

Chapter 7

1. I am indebted to Professor J.D.Y. Peel for drawing my attention to the significance of this parallel.

2. This represents *de jure* recognition of a *de facto* practice. *Ms.* is required reading for many hundreds of the women's studies courses in American colleges and universities, and to this end has an advisory panel of distinguished academics which advises on editorial matters. Whilst maintaining its position as the 'official' voice of feminists within the women's magazine world, *Ms.* also has included some of the topic areas associated with more traditional cult messages. For example, its January 1981 cover lines included: 'Sex: You Know What You Want But How Do You Say It' and 'Secretary as Hero'.

3. Alone amongst the editorial processes explored by this study, *Ms.* operated a democratic editorial procedure – one person, one vote, from advertisement sales persons to managing editors – on the selection of particular *Ms.* messages on which no earlier consensus could be reached. Didn't this procedure make it a little difficult to get to press on time? 'Yes, democracy takes a little longer' was the patient reply from the publisher. Moreover, democracy is demonstrated in the editing credits, where names are listed in strict alphabetical order including those of the publisher, and managing editor.

4. The processes by which editors of women's magazines perceive social change in relation to their female audiences, and the degree of responsiveness their messages reflect, has been explored in chapter 4. These processes of interaction exist between any medium and the wider society: see Golding (1980), for example, for newspaper responsiveness to change. For a socio–psychological analysis of these processes which themselves contribute to change, see Moscovici (1976). Concerning the more specific nature and impact of social change – including economic change – upon women in differing societies around the world, Cordell *et al.* (1975) suggest that the outcome of these changes has produced what amounts to three sexes, rather than two. They differentiate between men, economically active women, and women who are still located mainly in the home, stating: 'Gender role fixation is central to our discussion. It forms attitudes at the earliest stages and lasts throughout the life cycle. It is most resistant to change in almost all cultures' (p. 379). The historically and culturally specific recipes of the cult of feminity promulgated by women's magazines in differing societies is one source of such gender role definitions.

Appendix I. Comparative Sales, Readership and Demographic Data

Table 1   Britain, 1965–81: adult and young women's magazines circulation compared with the total periodical market (measured in terms of copies sold)

Year	Adult women '000	Young women '000	Total consumer periodicals '000
1965	555,346	51,516	2,144,922
1966	558,796	67,954	2,206,815
1967	547,399	67,855	2,200,708
1968	523,228	67,200	2,123,108
1969	529,081	68,307	2,125,720
1970	491,269	79,990	2,092,833
1971	475,183	80,198	2,019,324
1972	481,182	84,549	2,061,780
1973	479,934	81,252	2,139,069
1974	479,737	75,960	1,941,448
1975	449,872	73,259	1,782,137
1976	442,825	65,251	1,728,241
1977	441,497	65,664	1,717,690
1978	449,817	61,843	1,739,153
1979	450,404	59,008	1,739,402
1980	440,494	56,036	1,666,361
1981	407,428	50,732	1,538,054

Sources: ABC, Publishers' statements, BRAD, IPC, 1965–81. All figures represent total home and overseas sales.

Table 2 Net sale and woman readership trends, selected women's weekly and monthly magazines, 1956–81

Publication	1956 ABC sale '000	1956 Women r'ship '000	1959 ABC sale '000	1959 Women r'ship '000	1964 ABC sale '000	1964 Women r'ship '000	1969 ABC sale '000	1969 Women r'ship '000	1974 ABC sale '000	1974 Women r'ship '000	1978 ABC sale '000	1978 Women r'ship '000	1981 ABC sale '000	1981 Women r'ship '000
Weeklies														
Woman	3,366	8.616	3,188	7.676	3,103	8.789	2,533	7.524	1,771	6.223	1,542	5.603	1,335	5.206
Woman's Own	2,468	6.958	2,403	6.904	2,316	7.263	2,006	6.483	1,687	6.250	1,598	5.878	1,412	5.492
Woman's Realm	1st issue Feb. 1958		1,227	3.237	1,345	4.811	1,185	4.212	923	4.000	781	3.263	660	2.827
Woman's Weekly	1,737	3.303	1,509	2.782	1,515	3.281	1,777	3.777	1,780	4.639	1,463	4.443	1,380	4.155
My Weekly	—	—	—	316	243	763	732	2.127	921	2.913	867	2.708	786	2.279
People's Friend	—	—	—	867	—	785	499	1.112	741	2.170	596	2.282	670	2.194
Monthlies														
Woman and Home	825	2.536	693	2.399	723	2.396	682	2.805	765	3.205	644	3.455	603	3.023
Family Circle			1st issue Oct. 1964				1,156	3.150	933	3.613	717	2.978	635	2.501
Good Housekeeping	216	2.412	188	2.272	169	2.189	199	2.067	279	3.201	332	2.513	349	2.458
Cosmopolitan			1st issue May 1972						397	1.390	439	1.547	435	1.771

Sources: *Sales*: Audit Bureau of Circulation (ABC): Jan.–Dec. Audited Net Sales: The People's Friend, My Weekly
Prior to 1975 ABC sales figures were total 'Home' and 'Overseas'; thereafter UK and Eire sales listed separately, as here
Readership: Institute of Practitioners of Advertising (IPA)/National Readership Surveys (NRS): Jan.–Dec. each year (except 1956, April– Dec.)
NRS age base dropped from 16 to 15 in 1970

Table 3   Woman, Woman's Own and Women's Weekly: women readership (percentage of each demographic sub-group who read each title)

	WOMAN							WOMAN'S OWN							WOMAN'S WEEKLY						
	1956	1959	1964	1969	1974	1978	1981	1956	1959	1964	1969	1974	1978	1981	1956	1959	1964	1969	1974	1978	1981
All women	43	38	42	36	29	25	23	35	24	35	31	29	27	24	16	14	16	18	21	20	19
Age																					
16–24a	56	53	55	51	36	35	33	48	49	48	45	36	35	32	18	15	14	16	18	16	14
25–34	47	43	46	39	31	31	26	37	35	37	33	33	31	29	18	14	15	16	19	18	16
35–44	47	37	42	35	28	24	23	36	34	42	30	27	27	25	18	14	15	19	23	21	18
45–54b	39	36	43	36	29	26	22	33	33	35	30	30	26	22	16	14	16	20	23	23	22
55–64			38	31	27	22	21			32	27	27	24	22	16	14	18	18	24	24	23
65+	29	26	31	24	21	16	15	24	24	27	20	22	18	18	13	12	17	18	23	21	20
Social class																					
A/Bc	43	43	43	37	21/29	25/25	22/23	33	38	34	29	19/30	24/25	25/25	12	12	13	14	15/19	16/18	14/19
C1	49	45	47	39	33	29	26	40	38	39	34	31	30	28	18	16	12	20	24	22	19
C2	46	40	45	38	32	27	25	37	36	37	33	32	28	26	18	15	16	19	23	21	19
D/Ec	37	32	36	30	26/21	24/17	23/15	31	30	31	27	28/21	27/18	24/17	16	13	16	17	19/21	19/18	18/17

Source: NRS Jan.–Dec. (except April–Dec., 1956)
a Data base lowered to age 15 in 1970. b Age 45–54, 55–64 first split, 1972. c Classes A/B and D/E first split, 1972

Age-class maps, British women's magazines, 1960–80

The concept of 'age-class maps' was devised by Bird (1977). These maps group magazines into four sectors on the basis of their NRS audience profiles by age and social class (see Figure 1). They provide a useful means of historical comparison, as Figures 2 and 3 show: between 1960 and 1980 the women's magazine audience became more 'up-market', producing a greater number of titles in the 'younger richer', 'older richer' sectors than twenty years ago.

These maps are reproduced by kind permission of Michael Bird, National Magazine Company, IPC.

Figure 1   The four 'age–class' market sectors

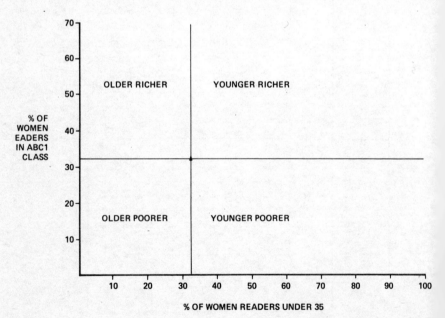

Figure 2   Age-class distribution

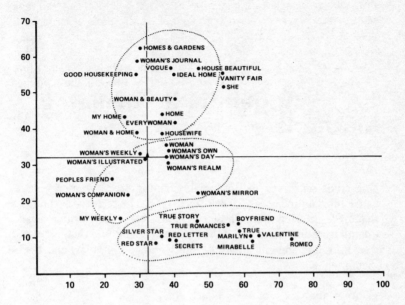

Figure 3   Age-class distribution

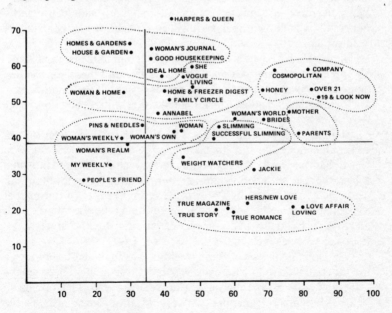

Appendix II. Research Methods

This study set out to identify, analyse and interpret women's magazine editorial processes and their messages. The research techniques that were selected were chosen to assist both the qualitative and quantitative dimensions, and the principal techniques that were used were those of content analysis, interviews, observation and documentation.

Content analysis

Content analysis is the accepted method of analysing communication content within the social sciences. What form it should take in a particular investigation, what units of analysis it should use and – above all – what level of analysis it will aim to achieve may not be easily determined.

These broader issues are discussed in relation to the content analysis applied to *Woman, Woman's Own* and *Woman's Weekly* in the first stage of research, 1949–74. Then details of sample selection, framework formulation and categories, analysis techniques and checks are described more fully.

'Content' refers to meaning, to what is 'said' in a given unit of communication. As such its analysis implies three general assumptions: that valid inferences can be made between content and intended effect; that the study of manifest content is meaningful to communicator, audience and analyst – or in Berelson's (1952: 19) terms that 'there is a common universe of discourse among the relevant parties'; and that the frequency of occurrence of various content characteristics is in and of itself meaningful (cf. George, 1959).

The content analysis of these weeklies was intended to produce a quantitative base for qualitative analysis. The distinction between the two forms and levels of analysis requires clarification. The former can be crude 'number crunching', a simple count of key words, or the length or prominence of words or text and thus operates at the surface level, whereas the latter qualitative approach attempts to probe for deeper levels of meaning. Berelson (1952), for example, sees no strict dichotomy between the two – much qualitative analysis is quasi-quantitative (as this study is), making use of terms such as 'tends', 'usually', 'often', 'rarely'. He states:

Qualitative analysis focuses on the intentions of a communicator or the effects upon the audience and uses the content as a spring-board to them. Quantitative analysis is more likely to focus first upon the straight description of the content itself, if for no other reasons because of the energy devoted to the counting procedure. (p. 122)

Further, qualitative analysis is concerned less with content *per se* than with content as a mediator or reflector of less manifest, more latent cultural phenomena. Thus, qualitative analysis allows the investigator to investigate more complex themes – such as goals or values – which are not easily categorised or readily quantified: the aim was to work with emergent categories of analysis.

Others have argued for quantitative analysis as a technique (cf. e.g. De Sola Pool, 1959; Gerbner *et al.*, 1969) but there have been criticisms that concentration on frequency counts can bias problem selection in over-emphasising precision of measurement at the risk of losing sight of the problem to be studied (cf. Beardsworth, 1980).

Holsti defines qualitative analysis as 'the drawing of inference on the basis of appearance or non-appearance of attributes in messages' (1969: 599), and goes on to point out that this dimension illuminates even the most rigorous quantitative study. Both George (1959) and De Sola Pool (1959) support this view. Thus

It should not be assumed that qualitative methods are insightful, and quantitative ones merely mechanical methods for checking hypotheses. The relationship is a circular one; each provides new insights on which the other can feed. (De Sola Pool, 1959: 192)

The approach of this study has followed this kind of circular relationship: the categories for quantitative analysis emerged from a preliminary qualitative probe. The approach used here is thus inclusive rather than exclusive, and conforms with the broad definition of Holsti (1969: 601):

Content analysis is any technique for making inferences by systematically and objectively identifying specified characteristics of messages.

The sample design
The three British women's magazines with the largest circulations, *Woman*, *Woman's Own* and *Woman's Weekly*, were chosen for content

analysis. Seven purposively selected years beginning with 1949 – to allow for a backwards look at the wartime role of these journals – and ending with 1974 – the last complete year of publication prior to beginning the analysis in 1975 – were sampled. Between these two benchmarks, the years 1952, 1957, 1962, 1967 and 1972, which are separated by five-year intervals, were chosen to allow a time interval sufficient to throw up any indices of social change.

Within each of these seven years, four issues each of the three weeklies were randomly sampled according to Blalock's (1960: 437) random numbers Table B, giving a total sample size of eighty-four issues.

Units of analysis
This aspect has already been discussed in Chapter 3 in relation to the selection of four a priori themes. To recapitulate briefly: four editorial areas were selected on the basis of preliminary analysis and previous participation as potentially illuminating of aspects of female social change: beauty, problem pages, fiction and general features. Choice within these units was as follows (see Chapter 3 for further details):
1. *Beauty* – this was self-selecting given that each issue (with some exceptions) carried only one beauty article.
2. *Problem page* – the 'lead' or most prominently displayed letter.
3. *Fiction* – the 'lead' short story in *Woman* and *Woman's Own*, the 'lead' serial episode in *Woman's Weekly*.
4. *General features* – the one most relevant to women's roles or female social change.

The content analysis framework
On the basis of previous participation and preliminary analysis two content analysis frameworks were piloted prior to devising the one used on the basis of these preliminary studies. A total of 196 variables were included under the following headings:

1. *Cover image*: the photograph only was analysed, e.g. 'Chocolate Box', 'Super Smiler', 'Invitational' (see Ferguson, 1980).
2. *Broad content trends*: e.g. this was extended to measure fluctuations in fiction and feature volume, as an indication of their relative importance to the editorial 'mix' and balance.
3. *Subject and emphasis*: e.g. the full title and displayed introduction were recorded together with placement and prominence, such as coverlining, colour or mono, pagination (spread, page, half page).
4. *Category classification*: e.g. was the fiction a serial or short story?

Was the feature about a celebrity, royalty, real reader? Was it a 'service' feature relating to work issues, sex relationships, child care, education? Was it a beauty 'how to' or a 'cinderella make-over'?

5. *Typical female roles*: e.g. the 'warm wise mum', the 'dutiful wife', the 'jealous wife', the 'teenage rebel', the 'good daughter', the 'selfish egoist', the 'calculating schemer' (both female and male roles were subsequently sorted into the labels used in Chapters 3 and 4).

6. *Typical male roles*: e.g. the 'rich charmer', the 'handsome baddie', the 'attractive boss', the 'aggressor', the 'protector', the 'mystery man', the 'professional batchelor', 'man as object' (of effort), etc.

7. *Socio-economic background*: e.g. explicit or implicit; occupational roles and material symbols of social class membership – working, middle, upper or 'consciously classless'.

8. *Time location*: e.g. at time of publication did the article refer to the 'topical present' (immediacy), 'dateless present' (unidentified contemporary), 'past', or was it 'anytime/timeless' content?

9. *Dominant values*: limited to four per item. Initially one item was to be 'reality or escapist orientation', a category so broad as to be meaningless in the event and subsequently discarded. Therefore four other values per item were chosen, e.g. conformity, duty, honesty, self-control, individuality, romance, work, leisure, etc.

10. *Dominant goal*: three per item, e.g. economic, security, emotional security, marital harmony, getting/keeping a man, personal happiness etc.

11. *'Norm senders'*: e.g. 'self', 'mother', 'father', 'generalised other' (a woman like you), 'mother figure' (friend of family, other kin) or 'generalised editorial' (non-identified editorial speak), 'personalised editorial' (named staff contributor), 'confidant editorial' (we and you and shared knowing).

12. *Normative tone*: posed in terms of binary opposites, e.g. factual/fictional, descriptive/prescriptive, tolerant/authoritarian – these turned out to be highly problematic with the fact/fiction boundary too rigid and the descriptive/prescriptive distinction too complex for analysis on this basis.

13. *Dominant theme category*: the four hypothesised a priori were 'getting and keeping your man', 'be more beautiful', 'heart versus head', and 'the working wife is a bad wife', plus 'other'.

14. *Sub-theme*: e.g. 'the happy family', 'the natural order', 'success equals happiness', 'self-help: achieving perfection', 'self-help: overcoming misfortune'.

The only categories of analysis that were not open-ended as to their numbers were those of 'values' and 'goals', limited to four and three respectively. However they too had an 'other' category which produced emergent data. In addition all goals, roles and values were evaluated as to their positive, negative or neutral evaluations within their content context.

After the content analysis framework was finalised, its application to the sample of eighty-four issues was divided between a research assistant and myself. Funds for this assistance were provided by the Central Research Fund of the University of London and the Sociology Department of the London School of Economics, to whom my most sincere appreciation is expressed as it is to Charlotte Lewis who assisted with this first stage of analysis.

Close attention was paid to the question of inter-analyst reliability throughout the piloting and analysis stages. At the framework drafting stage meetings took place to discuss and compare definitions and characteristics of the categories selected by me for piloting on the basis of preliminary content analysis and prior participation. During the piloting and early analysis period these meetings occurred at weekly intervals. Subsequently during the analysis and tabulation period, which extended over two years, regular consultations continued.

Some thirty issues were analysed by my research assistant and fifty-four issues by myself. In addition, to check for inter-analyst reliability, ten issues, or 12 per cent of the sample, were analysed by us both, and recorded a high comparability of results.

Post-analysis The findings concerning this wide range of hypothesised and emergent themes, values, roles and goals were counted and categorised according to the labels given to them in the tables shown in Chapters 3 and 4. None of the themes or sub-themes were combined for this purpose. However, with the findings on male and female roles some 'cruding up' or amalgamation proved possible, and in the case of values and goals this process proved imperative given the range of variation on a single theme found within the content analysis as a whole. For example, the goal labelled 'societal achievement' included within its boundaries aspects of 'job success', 'economic security', 'material acquisition', 'higher education' and 'status acquisition'. Similarly, a value such as 'self-control' included within it the individually identified strands of 'self-discipline', 'calmness', 'duty', 'sacrifice', 'responsibility', 'identity' and 'submissiveness'.

The second stage of content analysis, applied the same framework to a same-sized sample of these three weeklies for the years 1979 and 1980. The same four subject categories were analysed in eight randomly sampled issues of each title – twenty-four issues in all, or a 13 per cent sample over the two-year period. The results of this second stage of analysis are given in Chapter 4.

Interviews
This was the primary method used to explore the editor's role, the editorial processes and organisational structures of women's magazines.

Here my previous participation in their production – during the period 1960–8 as a writer, assistant editor and associate editor on one of the weeklies analysed here – conferred advantages as well as applied restraints. It facilitated access to informants at all levels of hierarchy, but especially to an elite group – the editors – while familiarity with women's magazine language, legend, and history added to understanding, analysis and interpretation of the interviews themselves. This prior involvement was also useful to me in maintaining both formal and informal lines of communication with these magazines and their organisations.

Inasmuch as my previous participation was always known – or made known – to all informants, questions of interviewer 'neutrality' and the interview situation role relationships were especially relevant (see e.g. Dexter, 1956). Self-examination for potential value bias was applied throughout, in the framing and asking of questions, and in the interpretation of answers. The problem of role relationships within the interview context revolved around the question of role definition in this case. For example, what value did informants attach to my current status as researcher in comparison with my previous one as journalist? Here the former was often legitimated by the latter. Residual status deriving from my previous occupational role was influential, in that informants both expected and attributed a greater degree of insight and understanding.

Reference to the literature bears out several of these points (see e.g. Bulmer, 1977; Denney and Hughes, 1956; Dexter, 1956; Deutscher, 1977; Platt, 1981; Dexter, 1970), for example, in discussing problems of elite interviewing, urges self-examination of the interviewer's input in terms of determining outcomes. For example, the use of provocative or deferential tactics, and the necessity for interviewer flexibility – in having specific objectives in mind, and not being 'led' by the data. The ability to 'manage' an interview, to allow fruitful, relevant topics to develop, are part of this, for 'to reduce interviewing to a set of techniques . . . is like reducing courtship to a formula' (Dexter, 1970: 110).

These considerations also relate to the interview situation and its setting. There is the problem of the nature of the evidence which is presented: the partial picture of processes or events an individual may or can present given the influence of factors such as selective perception, or the positive presentation of self. Such factors also relate to the reliability and validity of informants' accounts, for while individual attitudes and perceptions may not require cross-checking, 'facts' do. Here the wide range of the total interview sample, see below, was useful (and challenging). Not only did it demand frequent interviewer role redefinition, but also eternal vigalence in assessing the motives, perceptions and 'facts' presented at various hierarchial levels, and within various formal or informal settings. Moreover, the majority of interviews were conducted on a one-to-one basis. This situational factor influenced the kind and quality of information obtained – with some informants responding by a loosening of internal constraints more usually associated with the confessional or the analyst's couch.

Here 'setting' was significant as an interviewing variable. 'Setting' in the context of this study covered a wide range of social and environmental locations ranging from semi-structured interviews in luxuriously furnished offices, to conversation over expense account (theirs) luncheon tables, to informal chats in pubs, cars and kitchens, as well as gossipy phone calls about the latest 'you'll never guess what'.

The above gives some measure of the extent to which guarantees of confidentiality were essential in obtaining, and maintaining, informants' cooperation. Close attention has been paid to this issue throughout. The contents of interviews were never divulged to other informants, nor were initial sources of information revealed in cross-checking. Anonymity of sources has been respected, and there have been research benefits in the frankness arising from interviewer guarantees of confidentiality in this regard.

Whatever their situation or setting, whatever the quality or quantity of information imparted, all interviews were assessed for subjectivity and potential bias. Awareness of this, together with reference to other informants' accounts and my own previous work experience – as well as any potential value-judgements arising therefrom – helped to monitor this aspect.

The sample of editors

Women's magazine editors, like other occupational elite groups, are pressured by long working hours, continuous decision-making and considerations of staff control, internal politics and public relations.

Given that very few editors have either the facilities or the inclination to allow participant observation of their methods, investigation of their role involved extensive use of semi-structured interviews, using open-ended questions (cf. Powdermaker, 1950 and Cantor, 1971 with respect to Hollywood film and TV producers) as has been discussed in Chapter 5. Despite their personal and partial nature, the women's magazine editor interviews obtained here represent a unique collection of verbal evidence. The initial, first and main stage of interviews were conducted between 1975 and 1978. The second stage of re-interviews of seven British and five American editors was conducted in 1980 and 1981.

Two criteria governed the main sample collection:

1. Each was, or had been during the period 1949–1978, the editor of a British adult women's magazine with a circulation of over 100,000 per week or month;
2. Each was willing to be interviewed without questions being submitted in advance which would sensitise them a priori.

The editor interview topics
The use of open-ended questions within these semi-structured interviews assisted gathering of information relevant to attitudes, behaviour, personalities and events. Questions were framed around specific themes – such as an editor's self-concept or audience precepts – and designed to focus interviewee thoughts, but not so much as to exclude illuminating digressions. Questions were asked to discover not only how editors define their role and function, but also which economic, organisational, journalistic, technological and personality factors influence content selection and presentation.

Topic I – the editor role
1. How would you define your role as editor within the production process?
2. What are your main tasks?
3. Who helps you with them?
4. How is your time divided between creative and administrative jobs?
5. Any changes over time in all this?

Topic II – situational factors
1. What internal and external factors influence your decisions?
2. How much autonomy do you have – how free are you to make and implement decisions in the area of:
   a. Content; b. Staff; c. Advertisements; d. Promotion?
3. What do you think of your publishing organisation?

4. In what way, if any, and through whom, does 'management' intervene?

Topic III – *work orientation*
1. How do you know that what you think is 'right' for the magazine is right?
2. Where do 'right' ideas come from?
3. What sources do you use to 'keep in touch'?

Topic IV – *the role of women's magazines*
1. Why are women's magazines produced?
2. What do you think they 'do' for women?
3. Has this changed over time?

Topic V – *audience perceptions*
1. What have been the most significant social changes affecting women's lives during the past twenty-five years?
2. Have women's magazines responded to these? Your magazine?
3. What do you think of audience research? Do you use it?

Topic VI – *training*
1. When were you appointed editor?
2. What previous jobs in women's magazines?
3. And before that – any other training or jobs? Education?

Topic VII – *personal background*
1. Are you married or single?
2. Would you describe your origins as working, middle or upper class?
3. Where do you live?
4. What do you like to do when you are not editing?

The sample of other informants
A wide range of managers, journalists, artists were also interviewed. These were concentrated within the two organisations discussed in Chapter 6, and focused particularly on the three weeklies whose content is analysed in Chapters 3 and 4. These additional informants consisted of the following:
1. Editorial personnel – associate/assistant editors (8), art directors/editors (4), production editors (5), department editors (10), chief sub editors (3), artists (4), journalists (13), secretaries (4), others – including photographic editors and correspondence staff (9).
2. Management personnel – chairmen (3), managing directors (4),

directors (7), editorial directors (3), publishers (7), market research directors (2), others – including advertisement, promotion, circulation, printing specialists (11).

Interviews with other informants

Again the technique used was that of semi-structured interviews using open-ended questions. Unlike the editor interview topic schedule, where the same range of questions was put but not always in the same order, here the questions were designed to probe individual areas of expertise. In each case special questions were framed around the special knowledge of a circulation or promotion manager, or the 'inside' information held by a senior secretary.

The value of the former was primarily factual and informational, of the latter confirmational (or not) of events reported in other interviews.

Observation

This aspect of the research was often combined with, and integral to, interviewing. Thus the daily business of getting the magazine 'out' proceeded alongside, and interrupted, many such 'conversations'. Lay-outs and copy would be brought in for 'passing' by senior editors, while designers, sub-editors, artists, photographers, and freelance writers might pass through the offices of those being consulted both formally and informally. In this way the interviewer was often more observer than questioner and, on the magazine I formerly worked on, treated as part of the context – a familiar, not a foreign, presence there.

This form of observation was integral to the study as a whole, not only in an on-going investigative sense, but also in an historical, comparative sense. As Becker (1958) notes, in assessing the worth of participant data, it is necessary to consider the role assigned by the group to the observer–interviewer: such a definition will determine the extent of information that the group withholds or makes available. As noted above, the residual status attaching to my previous participation conferred more benefits than costs. It facilitated a frankness and immediacy of exchange and assisted the evaluation and interpretation of prior or conflicting accounts. Thus, however fragmented, the observational evidence contributed to the total picture, given the caveat that 'an individual's statement and descriptions of events are made from a perspective which is a function of his position in the group' (Becker, 1958: 655). This positional perspective was particularly evident amongst the participants in the 'set piece' observation situation: 'sitting in' on the editorial conferences described in Chapter 6.

Documentary evidence

There was little documentary evidence against which to test interviewee perceptions and recollections. Apart from a few 'personal communications', written sources were sparse.

For example, within IPC Women's Magazines Group the prior history of the three independent companies it amalgamated is largely non-existent. In some cases, individuals for reasons of their own destroyed confidential records when departments were absorbed or dissolved. More often, in an industry devoted to the production of future reading matter, the past is rarely seen as significant. For example, rationalisation processes within IPC's structure militated against accumulation of such evidence when in 1975, £1 was offered to staff members for each empty filing cabinet returned. Consequently the historical dimension here was often an oral one, with all the accompanying risks of randomness, selective perception, personal bias, vendetta, nostalgia, post hoc rationalisation, exaggeration or inaccuracy. These factors have been taken into account in the analysis, as has recognition of the degree to which such oral history has enriched this study as a whole.

References

ABRAMS, M. (1959) *The Teenage Consumer*, London: The London Press Exchange

ANDERSON, R. (1974), *The Purple Heart-Throbs*, London: Hodder and Stoughton

ARGYRIS, C. (1971) *The Applicability of Organisational Sociology*, Cambridge: Cambridge University Press

BAILEY, M. (1969), 'The women's magazine short-story heroine in 1957 and 1967', *Journalism Quarterly*, Vol. 46

BANDURA, A., ROSS, D. and ROSS, S. (1963), 'A comparative test of the status envy, social power and secondary reinforcement theories of identificatory learning', *Journal of Abnormal and Social Psychology*, Vol. 67, no. 6.

BANKS, O. (1981), *Faces of Freedom*, London: Martin Robertson

BARKER, D.L. and ALLEN, S. (1976), *Dependence and Exploitation in Work and Marriage*, London: Longman

BARTHES, R. (1967), *Système de la Mode*, Paris: Editions du Seuil

BASS, A.Z. (1969), 'Refining the "gatekeeper" concept: a UN radio case study', *Journalism Quarterly*, Vol. 46, no. 1, Spring

BEARDSWORTH, A. (1980), 'Analysing press content: some technical and methodological issues' in Christian, H. (ed) (1980)

BECKER, H.S. (1958), 'Problems of inference and proof in participant observation', *American Sociological Review*, December

BECKER, H.S. (1960), 'Notes on the concept of commitment', *The American Journal of Sociology*, Vol. 66, University of Chicago Press

BELL, D. (1974), *The Coming of Post-Industrial Society*, London: Heinemann

BERCOVITCH, S. (1975), *The Puritan Origins of the American Self*, New Haven, Conn.: Yale University Press

BERELSON, B. (1952), *Content Analysis in Communications Research*, Glencoe, Illinois: Free Press

BERGER, P.L. and LUCKMANN, T. (1967), *The Social Construction of Reality*, London: Allen Lane

BERNARD, J. (1975), *The Future of Motherhood*, New York: Penguin Books

BETTELHEIM, B. (1968), *Symbolic Wounds*, New York: Collier (first published 1954)

BEVERIDGE REPORT (1942), *Report on Social Insurance and Allied Services*, Cmd. 6404, Chairman, Sir William Beveridge, London: HMSO

BIRD, M. (1977), 'New opportunities in magazine marketing', ADMAP, March

BIRD, M. (1979) 'Innovation in women's magazines: the fourth dimension', ADMAP, January

BITTNER, E. (1965), 'The concept of organisation', *Social Research*, Vol. 32, no. 3, Autumn, pp. 239–55

BLACKSTONE, T. (1976), 'The education of girls today', in MITCHELL, J. and OAKLEY, A. (eds.) *The Rights and Wrongs of Women*, Harmondsworth: Penguin

BLALOCK, H.M. (1960), *Social Statistics*, London: McGraw Hill

BLAU, P.M. and SCHOENHERR, R.A. (1971), *The Structure of Organisations*, New York: Basic Books

BOORSTIN, D.J. (1961), *The Image*, London: Weidenfeld and Nicolson

BOWLBY, J. (1951), *Maternal Care and Mental Health*, Geneva: Bulletin of the World Health Organisation

BOYD-BARRETT, O. (1970), 'Journalism recruitment and training: problems in professionalisation', in TUNSTALL, J. (ed.) *Media Sociology*, London: Constable

BOYD-BARRETT, O. (1980), 'The politics of socialisation: recruitment and training for journalism' in Christian H. (ed) (1980)

BRAITHWAITE, B. and BARRELL, J. (1979), *The Business of Women's Magazines*, London: Associated Business Press

BREED, W. (1955), 'Social control in the newsroom: a functional analysis', *Social Forces*, Vol. 33

BROWN, R.L. (1969) 'Some aspects of mass media ideologies' in Halmos, P. (ed.), *The Sociological Review Monograph*, no. 13, University of Keele

BULMER, M. (ed.) (1977), *Sociological Research Methods*, London: Macmillan

BURNS, T. (1963), 'Industry in a new age', *New Society*, 31 January, pp. 17–20

BURNS, T. and STALKER, G.M. (1966), *The Management of Innovation*, London: Tavistock

CANTOR, M. (1971), *The Hollywood T.V. Producer*, New York: Basic Books

CECIL, M. (1974), *Heroines in Love*, London: Michael Joseph

Central Policy Review Staff/Central Statistical Office, (1980), *People and Their Families*, London: HMSO

CHIBNALL, S. (1975), 'The crime reporter: a study in the production of commercial knowledge', *Sociology*, Vol 9, no. 1, p. 273

CHRISTIAN, H. (1980), 'Journalists' occupational ideologies and press commercialisation', in Christian, H. (ed.), (1980)

CHRISTIAN, H. (ed) (1980) *The Sociology of Journalism and the Press*, Sociological Review Monograph 29, University of Keele

COHEN, P.S. (1968), *Modern Social Theory*, London: Heinemann Educational

COHEN, S. (1981), *Folk Devils and Moral Panics*, 2nd edn., Oxford: Martin Robertson (first published 1972)

COHEN, S. and YOUNG, J. (1973), *The Manufacture of News*, London: Constable

COMMISSION OF THE EUROPEAN COMMUNITIES (1979), *European Men and Women in 1978*, Brussels: EEC

COOTE, A. and CAMPBELL, B. (1982), *Sweet Freedom*, London: Picador

CORDELL, M., McHALE, J. and STREATFEILD, D. (1975), 'Women and World Change' *Futures*, Vol. 7, no. 5, October

CORNILLON KOPPELMAN, S. (ed.)(1972), *Images of Women in Fiction*, Bowling Green, Ohio: Bowling Green University Press

CRANFIELD, G. (1978), *The Press and Society: from Caxton to Northcliffe*, London: Longman

CRANO, W. and ARANOFF, J. (1978), 'A cross cultural study of expressive and instrumental role complementarity in the family', *American Sociological Review*, August, Vol. 43, no. 4., pp. 463–71

CURRAN, J. (1977), 'Capitalism and control of the press, 1800–1975', in CURRAN, J., GUREVITCH, M. and WOOLLACOTT, J. (eds.), *Mass Communications and Society*, London: Edward Arnold

CURRAN, J., (1980), 'Advertising as a patronage system' in Christian, H. (ed) (1980)

DECKARD, B. (1975), *The Women's Movement: Political, Socioeconomic and Psychological Issues*, New York: Harper and Row

DEEM, R. (1978), *Women and Schooling*, London: Tavistock

DELAMONT, S. and DUFFIN, L. (1978), *The Nineteenth Century Woman: Her Cultural and Physical World*, London: Croom Helm

DENNEY, M. and HUGHES, E.C. (1956), 'Of sociology and the interview: editorial preface', *American Journal of Sociology*, Vol. LXII, no. 2

DEPARTMENT OF EMPLOYMENT (1980), *'New Earnings Survey'*, London: HMSO

DEPARTMENT OF EMPLOYMENT (1978), *Department of Employment Gazette 86(4) April 1978*, London: HMSO

DEPARTMENT OF HEALTH AND SOCIAL SECURITY (1974), *Report of the Committee on One Parent Families* (Chairman: Sir Morris Finer), London: HMSO, Cmnd. 5629

DE SOLA POOL, I. (ed.)(1959) *Trends in Content Analysis*, Urbana: University of Illinois Press

DEUTSCHER, I. (1977), 'Asking questions (and listening to answers): a review of some sociological precedents and problems', in BULMER, M. (ed)(1977)

DEXTER, L.A. (1970), *Elite and Specialised Interviewing*, Evanston, Illinois: Chicago Press

DEXTER, L.A. (1956), 'Role relationships and conceptions of neutrality in interviewing', *American Journal of Sociology* LXII, no. 2

DONOHUE, G. (1972), 'Gatekeeper: mass media systems and information control', in KLINE, F.G. and TICHENOR, P.J. (eds.) *Current Perspectives in Mass Communication Research*, London: Sage

DOUGLAS, M. and GROSS, J. (1981), 'Food and culture: measuring the intricacy of rule systems', *Social Science Information*, London and Beverley Hills: Sage, pp. 1–35

DOWNES, D.M. (1966), *The Delinquent Solution*, London: Routledge and Kegan Paul

DURKHEIM, E. (1976), *The Elementary Forms of the Religious Life*, 2nd ed., London: George Allen and Unwin (first published 1915)

DWAYNE-SMITH, M. and MATRE, M. (1975), 'Social norms and sex roles in romance and adventure magazines', *Journalism Quarterly*, Vol. 52, no. 2, Summer

ELIADE, M. (1963), 'Survivals and camouflages of myths', *Diogenes*, Spring, no. 41, pp. 6–25

ELLIOTT, P. (1977), 'Media organisations and occupations' in Curran, J., Gurevitch and Woollacott, J., (eds), *Mass Communications and Society*, London: Edward Arnold

ELLIOTT, P. (1980), 'Press performance as political ritual', in CHRISTIAN, H. (ed) (1980)

ENGELS, F. (1902), *The Origins of the Family, Private Property, and the State*, Chicago: Charles H. Kerr & Co.

ENZENSBERGER, H.M. (1974), *The Consciousness Industry*, New York: Seabury Press

EPSTEIN, C.F. (1970), *Woman's Place: options and limits in professional careers*, Berkeley: University of California Press

EQUAL OPPORTUNITIES COMMISSION (EOC) (1981), *Fifth Annual Report*, Manchester: EOC

EQUAL OPPORTUNITIES COMMISSION (EOC) (1982), *Adman and Eve, A Study of the Portrayal of Women in Advertising*, Manchester: EOC

ETZIONI, A. (1964), *Modern Organisations*, Englewood Cliffs: Prentice Hall

FERGUSON, M. (1980), 'The women's magazine cover photograph', in Christian, H. (ed) (1980)

FIRESTONE, S. (1971), *The Dialetic of Sex*, London: Cape

FOWLER, B. (1979), 'True to me always': an analysis of women's magazine fiction', in *British Journal of Sociology*, Vol. 30, no. 1, March

FRANSELLA, F. and FROST, K. (1977), *How Women See Themselves*, London: Tavistock

FRAZER, Sir J. (1959), *The Golden Bough*, London: Macmillan (first published 1922)

FREEMAN, J. (1975), *The Politics of Women's Liberation*, New York: David Mackay

FREUD, S. (1959), *Group Psychology and the Analysis of the Ego*, London: The Hogarth Press and the Institute of Psychoanalysis

FRIEDAN, B. (1963), *The Feminine Mystique*, London: Gollancz

FRIEDAN, B. (1981), *The Second Stage*, New York: Summit Books

GALBRAITH, J.K. (1958) *The Affluent Society*, London: Hamish Hamilton

GALBRAITH, J.K. (1969), *The New Industrial State*, London: Andre Deutsch

GARDINER, J. (1976), 'Political economy of domestic labour in capitalist society', in BARKER, D.L. and ALLEN, S.A. (eds) (1976)

GAVRON, H. (1968), *The Captive Wife*, Harmondsworth, Middlesex: Pelican

GELLNER, E. (1970), 'Concepts and society', in Wilson, B.R. (ed.), *Rationality*, Oxford: Basil Blackwell

GEORGE, A.L. (1959), 'Quantitative and qualitative approaches to content analysis', in DE SOLA POOL, I. (1959)

GERBNER, G. (1958), 'On content analysis and critical research in mass communication', *Audio-Visual Communication Review*, Vol. 6, no. 3, Spring

GERBNER, G., HOSTI, O., KRIPPENDORFF, K., PAISLEY, W. and STONE, P. (eds.) (1969), *The Analysis of Communication Content*, New York: John Wiley

GIDDENS, A. (1971), *Capitalism and Modern Social Theory*, London: Cambridge University Press

GITTINS, D. (1982), *Fair Sex – Family Size and Structures 1900–1939*, London: Hutchinson

GLASGOW UNIVERSITY MEDIA GROUP (1976), *Bad News*, Vol 1. London: Routledge and Kegan Paul

GLASGOW UNIVERSITY MEDIA GROUP (1980), *More Bad News*, Vol. 2, London: Routledge and Kegan Paul

GOFFMAN, E. (1959), *The Presentation of Self in Everyday Life*, New York: Doubleday

GOFFMAN, E. (1961), *Asylums*, New York: Doubleday

GOFFMAN, E. (1979), *Gender Advertisements*, Basingstoke: Macmillan

GOLDBERG, S. (1977), *The Inevitability of Patriarchy*, London: Temple Smith

GOLDING, P. (1981), 'The missing dimensions – news media and the management of social change', in Katz, E. and Szecsko, T. (eds.)

GOLDING, P. and ELLIOTT, P. (1979), *Making the News*, London: Longman

GOLDING, P. and MIDDLETON, S. (1982), *Images of Welfare, Press and Public Attitudes to Poverty*, Oxford: Martin Robertson

GOLDTHORPE, J.H., LOCKWOOD, D., BECHHOFER, J. and PLATT, J. (1969), *The Affluent Worker in The Class Structure*, Cambridge Studies in Sociology 3, London: Cambridge University Press

GOLDTHORPE, J.H., LLEWELLYN, C., PAYNE, C. (1980), *Social Mobility and Class Structure in Modern Britain*, Oxford: Clarendon.

GOODE, W.J. (1969), *The Theoretical Limits of Professionalisation* in ETZIONI, A. (ed.), *The Semi-Professions and Their Organisations*, New York: Free Press

GORER, G. (1955), *Exploring English Character*, London: The Cresset Press

GUENIN, Z.B. (1975), 'Women's pages in American newspapers: missing out on contemporary content', *Journalism Quarterly*, Vol. 52, no. 1, Spring

HALL, R.H. (1968), 'Professionalisation and bureaucratisation' in *American Sociological Review*, Vol. 33, no. 1, February

HALL, S. (1970), 'A world at one with itself', *New Society*, 18 June

HALL, S. and WHANNEL, P. (1964), *The Popular Arts*, London: Hutchinson Educational

HALMOS, P. (ed.) (1973), *Professionalisation and Social Change*, Sociological Review Monograph 20, Keele University

HALSEY, A.H., HEATH A.F. and RIDGE, J.M. (1980), *Origins and Destinations: Family, Class and Education in Modern Britain*, London: Clarendon Press

HARRIS, J. (1977), *William Beveridge: a biography*, London: Oxford University Press

HASKELL, M. (1974), *From Reverence to Rape*, New York: Holt, Rinehart and Winston

HATCH, M.G. and HATCH, D.L. (1968), 'Problems of married working women as presented by three popular women's magazines', in *Social Forces*, Vol. 37, December

HENRY, H. (1977), 'Advertising expenditure 1960–1976', *Advertising Quarterly*, no. 52, Summer

HILL, C. (1975), *The World Turned Upside Down*, Harmondsworth: Penguin Books

HIMMELWEIT, H. (1980), 'Social influence and television', in ABELES, R.B. and WITHEY, S.B. (eds.), *Television and Social Behaviour: Beyond Violence and Children*, Hillsdale, New Jersey: Lawrence Erlbaum Associates

HMSO (1972), *Education: A Framework for Expansion*, Cmnd. 5174, London

HOBSON, D. (1980), 'Housewives and the mass media', in HALL, S., HOBSON, D., LOWE, A. and WILLIS, P. (eds.), *Culture, Media, Language*, London: Hutchinson

HOGGART, R. (1957), *The Uses of Literacy*, London: Chatto and Windus

HOLSTI, O.R. (1969), 'Content analysis', in LINDZEY, G. and ARONSON, E. (eds.), *Handbook of Social Psychology*, Vol. 2

HUSBAND, C. (1977), 'News media, language and race relations', in GILES, H. (ed.), *Language, Ethnicity and Intergroup Relations*, European Monographs in Social Psychology, London: Academic Press

HYDE, M. (1951), *Mr and Mrs Beeton*, London: George Harrap

INGLEHART, R. (1982), 'Post-materialism in an environment of security', *American Political Science Review*, Vol. 75, no. 4, p. 880

IPC (1978), *IPC Magazines Limited, Increases in Cover Prices*, London: HMSO

JANEWAY, E. (1972), *Man's World, Woman's Place*, Harmondsworth: Penguin Books

JOHNS-HEINE, P. and GERTH, H. (1949), 'Values in mass periodical fiction 1921–1940', in *Public Opinion Quarterly*, Vol. 13

JOHNSON, T.J. (1972), *Professions and Power*, London: Macmillan

KAGAN, J. (1958), 'The concept of identification', *Psychological Review*, Vol. 65, no. 5

KATZ, E., BLUMLER, J.G. and GUREVITCH, M. (1974), 'Uses and gratifications research', *Public Opinion Quarterly*, Vol. 37, pp. 509–23

KATZ, E. and SZECSKO, T. (eds) (1981) *Mass Media and Social Change*, London: Sage

KING, J. and STOTT, M. (1977), *Is This Your Life?* London: Virago

KOMAROVSKY, M. (1946), 'Cultural contradictions and sex roles', *American Journal of Sociology*, 52, pp. 184–9

KOMAROVSKY, M. (1973), 'Cultural contradictions and sex roles: the masculine case', in HUBER, J. (ed.) *Changing Women in a Changing Society*, Chicago: University of Chicago Press

KROGER, R. and BRIEDIS, I. (1970), 'Effects of risk and caution norms on group decision making', *Human Relations*, Vol. 23, no. 3, p. 283

KURTZ, I. (1981), *The Book of Crises*, London: Ebury Press

LANGHOLZ-LEYMORE, V. (1975), *Hidden Myth*, London: Heinemann

LAZARSFELD, P.F. and MERTON, R.K. (1948), 'Mass communication, popular taste and organised social action', in SCHRAMM, W. (ed.), *Mass Communications*, Chicago: University of Illinois Press

LEE A.J. (1976), *The Origins of the Popular Press*, London: Croom Helm

LEVINSON, D. (1957), 'Role, personality and social structure in the organisational setting', *Journal of Abnormal and Social Psychology*, Vol. 58, pp. 170–81

LEWIS, J. (1982), 'Dealing with dependency: state practices and social realities, 1870–1945', in LEWIS, J. (ed.), *Women's Welfare/Women's Rights*, London: Croom Helm

LINDBLOM, C.E. (1959), 'The science of "muddling through" ', *Public Administration Review*, Vol. 19

LIPMAN-BLUMEN, J. and TICKAMEYER, A.R. (1975), 'Sex roles in transition: a ten-year perspective', *Annual Review of Sociology*, Vol. 1

LOWENTHAL, L. (1944), 'Biographies in popular magazines', in LAZARSFELD, P. and STANTON, F. (eds.), *Radio Research 1942-43*, New York: Duell Sloan and Pearce

McCLELLAND, D.C. (1961), *The Achieving Society*, Princeton, New Jersey: Van Nostrand

McCLELLAND, W.D. (1964), 'The women's weeklies', *New Society*, 21 December

MACCOBY, E.E. and JACKLIN, C.N. (1974), *The Psychology of Sex Differences*, Stanford: University Press

McCRON, R. (1976), 'Changing perspectives in the study of mass media and socialisation', in HALLORAN, J. (ed.), *Mass Media and Socialisation*, International Assoc. for Mass Communication Research, Leeds: J.A. Kavanagh

McLUHAN, M. (1967), *Mechanical Bride*, Routledge and Kegan Paul

McNEIL, J.C. (1975), 'Femininism, femininity and the television series: a content analysis' *Journal of Broadcasting*, Vol 19

MacRAE, D.G. (1961), *Ideology and Society*, Heinemann, London

MAISEL, R. (1973) 'The decline of the mass media', *Public Opinion Quarterly*, Vol. XXXVII, no. 2, Summer

MAKINS, P. (1975), *The Evelyn Home Story*, London: Collins

MANN, P.H. (1974) *A New Survey - The Facts About Romantic Fiction*, London: Mills and Boon

MANSTEAD, A.S.R. and McCULLOCH, C. (1981), 'Sex role stereotyping in British television ads', *British Journal of Social Psychology*, Vol. 20, pp. 171-80

MARRIS, R. and WOOD, A. (1971) *The Corporate Economy*, London: Macmillan

MARSDEN, D. (1977), 'Background paper and summary of discussions, recommendations and guidelines for action' in *The Changing Roles of Men and Women in Modern Society: Functions, Rights and Responsibilities*, Groningen, Netherlands: European Social Development Programme

MAUSS, M. (1970), *The Gift*, London: Cohen and West (first printed 1954)

MEAD, G.H. (1934), *Mind, Self and Society*, Chicago: University of Chicago Press

MEAD, M. (1935), *Sex and Temperament in Three Primitive Societies*, London: Routledge and Kegan Paul

MEAD, M. (1950), *Male and Female*, London: Gollancz

MILIBAND, R. (1977) *Marxism and Politics*, London: Oxford University Press

MILLER, S.H. (1975), The content of news photos: women's and men's roles', *Journalism Quarterly*, Vol. 52, no. 1, Spring

MILLUM, T. (1975), *Images of Women*, London: Chatto and Windus

MINISTRY OF EDUCATION (1963), *Half Our Future: a Report of the Central Advisory Council for Education (England)* (Chairman, Sir John Newsom), London: HMSO

MITCHELL, J. (1971), *Women's Estate*, Harmondsworth: Penguin

MITCHELL, J. (1975), *Psychoanalysis and Feminism*, Harmondsworth: Pelican

MONK, D. (1978), *Social Grading on the National Readership Survey*, 5th ed., London: JICNARS

MOSCOVICI, S. (1976), *Influence and Social Change*, European Monograph in Social Psychology, London: European Association of Experimental Social Psychology

MURRAY, J.P. and KIPPAX, S. (1979), 'From the early window to the late night show: international trends in the study of television's impact on children and adults', in Berkowitz, L. (ed.)*Advances in Experimental Social Psychology*, Vol. 12, London: Academic Press

OAKLEY, A. (1974), *The Sociology of Housework*, London: Martin Robertson

OAKLEY, A. (1979), *Becoming a Mother*, Oxford: Martin Robertson

OAKLEY, A. (1981), *Subject Woman*, London: Fontana

O'BRIEN, E. (1976), 'Love and anti-love', *Vogue*, 15 October

OGILVIE, D. (1964), *Confessions of an Advertising Man*, London: Longman

PARK, R.E. (1955), *Society*, Glencoe, Illinois: Free Press

PARSONS, T. (1951), *The Social System*, London: Routledge and Kegan Paul

PARSONS, T. and BALES, R.F. (1955), *Family, Socialisation and Interaction Process*, Glencoe, Illinois: Free Press

PAVALKO, R.M. (1971), *Sociology of Occupations and Professions*, Illinois: F.E. Peacock

PERROW, C. (1972), *Complex Organisation: A Critical Essay*, Illinois: Scott Foresman

PIERCE, S. (1980), 'Single mothers and the concept of female dependency in the development of the welfare state in Britain', *Journal of Comparative Family Studies*, Vol. XI, no. 1, Winter

PLATT, J. (1981), 'On interviewing one's peers', *British Journal of Sociology*, Vol. XXXII, no. 1, March

POWDERMAKER, H. (1950), *Hollywood: The Dream Factory*, Boston: Little, Brown

PUDDEFOOT, S. (1970), 'The woman complex', in BOSTON, R. (ed.), *The Press We Deserve*, London: Allen and Unwin, pp. 73–87

PUGH, D.S., HICKSON, D., HININGS, C. and TURNER, C. (1968), 'Dimensions of organisation structure', *Administrative Science Quarterly*, June

RAPOPORT, R. (1978), 'Sex–role stereotyping in studies of marriage and the family', in CHETWYND, J. and HARTNETT, O., (eds.), *The Sex Role System*, London: Routledge and Kegan Paul

RIESMAN, D., GLAZER, N. and DENNEY, R. (1950), *The Lonely Crowd*, New York: Doubleday Anchor

RICHARDSON, J.T. (1978), 'An oppositional and general conceptualisation of cult', *Annual Review of Social Science and Religion*, The Hague: Mouton

RICHARDSON, J.T. (1979), 'Creative eclecticism in new religious movements', *Pacific Sociological Review*, Vol. 22, no. 2

RIMMER, L., (1981), 'Changing family patterns: some implications for policy', paper presented to the Symposium on Priority for the Family, Royal Society of Medicine, London, 3–5 November

ROSE, A.M. (ed.) (1962), *Human Behaviour and Social Processes: A Systematic Summary of Interaction Theory*, London: Routledge and Kegan Paul

ROWBOTHAM, S. (1972), *Women, Resistance and Revolution*, London: Allen Lane

ROYAL COMMISSION ON THE PRESS (RCOP) (1962), *Report, 1961–62* Cmnd. no. 1811, London: HMSO

ROYAL COMMISSION ON THE PRESS (RCOP) (1977), *Ownership, Control, Activities and Publications of the Largest Newspaper Undertakings*, Cmnd. 6810–1, Appendices, Appendix A, London: HMSO

ROYAL COMMISSION ON THE PRESS (RCOP) (1977), *Advertising and the Press*, Cmnd. 6810–1, Appendix E, London: HMSO

SAHLINS, M. (1976), *Culture and Practical Reason*, Chicago: University of Chicago Press

SALAMAN, G. (1981), *Class and the Corporations*, Glasgow: Fontana

SCHLESINGER, P. (1978), *Putting 'Reality' Together, BBC News*, London: Constable

SCHUMPETER, J.A. (1954), *Capitalism, Socialism and Democracy*, 4th ed., London: Allen and Unwin.

SHEARER, A. (1980), 'How *Woman's Own* learned to face reality', *The Guardian*, 17 December

SMILES, S. (1958), *Self-Help*, Centenary Edition, Introduction by BRIGGS, A., London: John Murray (Copyright 1859)

SMITH, A.C.H. (1975), *Paper Voices: The Popular Press and Social Change 1935–1965*, London: Chatto and Windus

SMITH, R. (1980), 'Images and equality: women and the national press' in Christian, H. (ed) (1980)

SMYTHE, D.W. (1975), 'Agenda setting. The role of the mass media and popular culture in defining development', *Journal of the Centre of Advanced Television Studies*

SOCIAL TRENDS, no. *11, 1980*, (1981), London: HMSO

SOCIAL TRENDS, no. *12, 1981*, (1982), London: HMSO

STERN (1981), *Consumer Magazines in Europe*, Hamburg: *Stern* Magazine

STINCHCOMBE, A.L. (1959), 'Bureaucratic and craft administration of production', in *Administrative Science Quarterly*, September

SZALAI, A. (1975), 'Women's Time, women in the light of contemporary time budget research', *Futures*, October, pp. 385–99

TUCHMAN, G. (1978a), 'The symbolic annihilation of women by the mass media' in TUCHMAN, G., KAPLAN DANIELS, A., and BENET, J. (eds), *Hearth and Home, Images of Women in the Mass Media*, New York: Oxford University Press

TUCHMAN, G. (1978b), *Making News*, New York: Oxford University Press

TUNSTALL, J. (1971), *Journalists at Work*, London: Constable

TUNSTALL, J. (1977), 'Editorial sovereignty in the British press', Studies on the Press, RCOP, Working Paper, no. 3 London: HMSO

TUNSTALL, J. (1980), 'The British press in an age of television', in Christian, H. (ed) (1980)

UDY, S.H. Jr., (1959), 'Bureaucracy and rationality in Weber's organisation theory: an empirical study', *American Sociological Review*, vol. 24

UNESCO (1974), 'Influence of mass communication media on the formation of a new attitude towards the role of women in present-day society', Commission on the Status of Women, 25th Session, Paris

VAN ZUILEN, A.J. (1977), *The Life Cycle of Magazines*, Vithorn, Holland: Graduate Press

VEBLEN, T. (1970), *The Theory of the Leisure Class*, London: Unwin Books

WEBBER, R.A. (1970), 'Perceptions of interactions between superiors and subordinates', *Human Relations*, Vol. 23

WEBER, M., (1958), *The Protestant Ethic and the Spirit of Capitalism* New York: Charles Scribner

WEBER, M. (1968a), *Economy and Society*, Vol. 1, pp. 24–5 New York: Bedminster Press

WEBER, M. (1968b), *Economy and Society*, Vol. 3. pp. 956–8 New York: Bedminster Press

WELTER, B. (1966), 'The cult of true womanood 1820–1860', *American Quarterly* Vol. 18, pp. 151–74

WEMBAN-SMITH, H. (1978), *Magazine Publishing: A Case of Joint Products*, Government Economic Service Working Paper No. 16, London: Price Commission

WESTERGAARD, J. (1972), 'Sociology: the myth of classlessness', in Blackburn, R. (ed.), *Ideology in Social Science*, London: Fontana

WHALE, J. (1980), *The Politics of the Media*, 2nd ed., London: Fontana

WHITE, D.M. (1950), 'The "gatekeeper": A case study in the selection of news', *Journalism Quarterly*, no. 27

WHITE, C. (1970), *Women's Magazines 1693–1968*, London: Michael Joseph

WHITE, C. (1977), 'The women's periodical press in Britain 1946–1976;, RCOP, Working Paper no. 4, London: HMSO

WILSON, E. (1977), *Women and the Welfare State*, London: Tavistock Publications

WILSON, E. (1980), *Only Halfway to Paradise*, London: Tavistock Publications

WINDLESHAM, LORD (1969), 'Some problems of creativity and control', in HALMOS, P. (ed.), *The Sociology of Mass-Media Communications*. Sociological Review Monograph 13, University of Keele

WINSHIP, J. (1978), 'A woman's world', in *Women Take Issue*, Women's Studies Group, Birmingham: Centre for Contemporary Cultural Studies

WINSHIP, J. (1980), 'Sexuality for sale' in Hall, S. *et al. Culture, Media, Language*, London: Hutchinson

YOUNG, M.D. and WILLMOTT, P. (1973), *The Symmetrical Family*, London: Routledge and Kegan Paul

ZWEIG, F., (1961), *The Worker in an Affluent Society*, London: Heinemann

Index